THAT'S FAST ENOUGH

Published in the UK in 2022 by Blue Agapanthus Publishing

Paperback ISBN 978-1-7391124-0-0
eBook ISBN 978-1-7391124-1-7

Cover design and typeset by SpiffingCovers.com

THAT'S FAST ENOUGH

Flying,
Family,
& Fleeing.

PETER HERZBERG

A career in aviation and unearthing family history

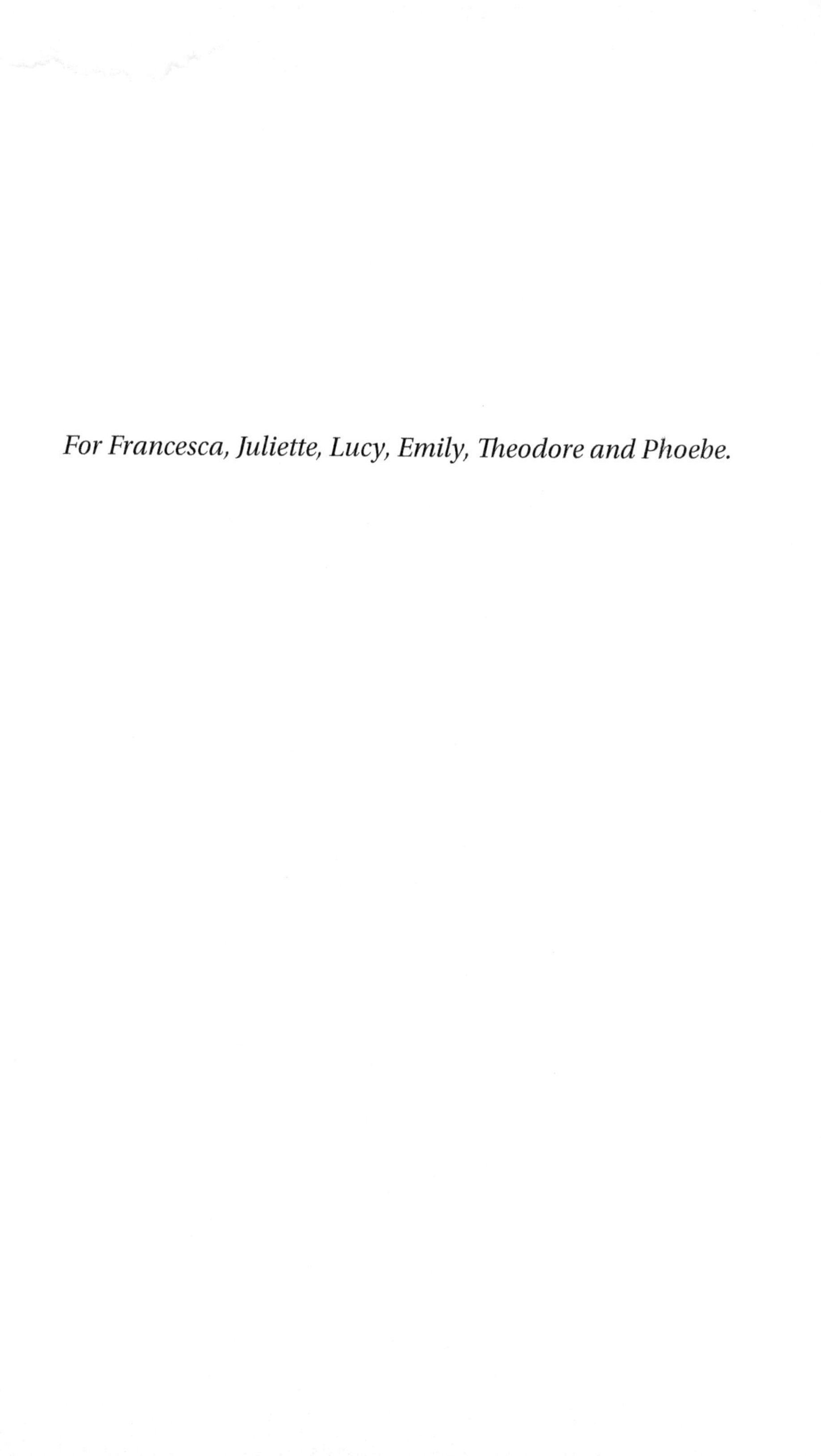

For Francesca, Juliette, Lucy, Emily, Theodore and Phoebe.

FOREWORD

I decided to write this book during the first lockdown period of the Covid pandemic. After the first few weeks of lockdown boredom set in, and I decided I needed another "big adventure" to keep my mind busy. My father had always spent hours telling us stories usually beginning with the words, "Did I ever tell you the story of ven I vas young and living in Vienna...?" (Despite living in the United Kingdom from when he was 9 years old he still had a slight accent.) Whenever he asked that question the answer was usually a resounding, "Yes you did, Dad!" To be fair, although he had a habit of repeating the same stories many times, we occasionally would hear something completely new. His stories were always interesting, and I tried to persuade him to put his own story down in writing. He never did, but he did leave a legacy on a DVD which, although my mother could never bring herself to watch, was quite a nice thing for the rest of the family to have.

It was only after his death that much more of the family history started to come to light.

I have always had a great interest in Second World War history. Just before the pandemic began, we went for a few days to Kraków, Poland. It was a city that we'd wanted to visit, and we went with our friends, Cliff and Sandra. Apart from the usual tourist areas, I particularly wanted to visit Auschwitz. Most people have read a lot about the atrocities carried out there, and I felt I would like to go. A good friend of Jan's had kindly given time to research my family tree for me, and I had never realised that several distant members of the family had lost their lives in Auschwitz at the hands of the Nazis. The morning of our organised visit to the camp, I was lying in bed, at the hotel in the centre of Kraków, looking at my family tree on my phone. As I looked at the members of the family who had lost their lives in that hellhole, it showed that it had happened seventy-five years ago to the day; quite eerie.

The same evening, we decided upon a small Polish restaurant for dinner. We met Cliff and Sandra, made our way through the backstreets and found the restaurant which we had booked. As Jan sat down on a bench seat at the table, she noticed there was a framed wine label on the wall above her head. On it was the name Oppenheimer. Not the same Oppenheimer as my family but, nevertheless, the same name. It was an Oppenheimer from the wine industry, again quite eerie.

The book was originally written about my life in aviation. I have been exceptionally lucky with my career, and I felt that one day, in the future, somebody in my family might be interested in my story. However, this has also been an opportunity to put down some of the family history for future generations to read about. I hope they don't forget the story of their ancestors and how they fled Nazi oppression.

I know it seems traditional to thank various people for their help in writing a book, but I wanted to mention a few people who I have crossed paths with during the course of my career and who it has been a great pleasure to know.

Bill and Edie Moore were great influences on my life. Bill called himself my "second dad", and his friendship and guidance when I started my career were invaluable. He encouraged me to follow my chosen path in aviation, and I think about him regularly.

My old friend Mike Hamilton has always been a source of inspiration. When we first flew together way back in 1979, he always (despite what he would say) had the patience and encouragement for new young first officers who were flying a jet aircraft for the first time. Not all captains were the same as him. We have become good mates over the last forty plus years, and he has always been a good source of advice on all matters including welding, car maintenance, laying tiles, electrics, whether or not I should have a tooth extracted, upbringing of children, electrics and more electrics. My knowledge of electrics has never been the best, and it has always been surprising to him that I would not know how to wire the Hadron Collider near Geneva. He would know how to do it.

My good friend Tony Foote provided me with some of the photos for this book. An enthusiastic photographer, he kept photographic records which I regret not doing. As he is such a perfectionist, his photos would always have been better than mine! I'm very glad I was usually (but not always) with Tony when things didn't go quite according to plan in an aeroplane.

Chris Wood has also provided me with some beautiful photos. We flew together in Dan-Air, and the last flight we both did for that company was with each other; another genius with a camera.

CHAPTER 1

We meandered slowly through the narrow country roads of the west coast of Cumberland in my father's Ford Popular. The car was a light shade of yellow and hesitated now and again as Dad accelerated through the gears. It was showing the age of its technology. Even the vacuum-powered windscreen wipers struggled with the odd spot of rain in the April showers. The faster the engine revved the slower the wipers and vice versa. This was the mid 1950s, and the old side valve engine was nothing like the modern car engine of the twenty-first century. We chugged along the quiet roads, the hedgerows preventing sight of anything of interest. I was bored and had been dragged out for a "run in the country". I had better things to do at home.

I have always referred to my home county as Cumberland and not Cumbria. Nobody consulted me about changes of name and boundaries. It always was and always will be Cumberland. I still have a very affectionate feeling for Cumberland and go back to see friends as often as possible.

I normally didn't enjoy going too far with my dad driving as he smoked and, as usual, I was starting to feel sick with the "fug" that he had created in the car. The windows were steaming up, and I wiped them occasionally with my hand for some reference to the outside world. Mum never said anything about the thick cloud that hung around us. In those days wives never complained much, as was the usual. In more modern times, one would be castigated severely for endangering a child's health. I had been dragged away from my plastic cowboys and Indians and did not relish being turned into a kipper in the back of our rather unreliable Ford "Pop". No doubt, we would be going to the hotel in Silloth for a cup of afternoon tea. There were much more interesting things to be done at home, with my friends, such as disappearing for hours on end into the fields and woods which surrounded our village of Tallentire.

This was a weekend run-out and, after an hour's drive from home, we came across an airfield. It was Silloth, a small wartime airfield, situated near the coast of the Solway Firth. It was still used as an RAF airfield in those days. Dad brought the car to a halt on the verge so that we could gaze across the runways and taxiways towards the hangars and other airfield buildings. My feeling of about to puke all over the floor in the back of the car, with associated huffs and sighs from the front, disappeared as, through the window, there were now things of great interest. There, in the distance, stood an aeroplane. It was an Avro Anson, a twin-engine, wartime aircraft that had various duties such as the training of navigators and also as a communications aircraft. A handful of people walked out to towards the aircraft and, after finishing their jovial banter, climbed on board. Dad wanted to get going, as he was ready for his cup of tea, but after much pleading, he agreed to wait whilst we watched this machine jump into life. The engines were started, and it slowly made its way out to the duty runway.

I watched, completely enthralled, as it accelerated down the runway and eventually got airborne. The wheels were retracted, and it eventually disappeared into the cloud. This was one of my earliest memories of seeing a real aeroplane, and I suppose it inspired me.

As we wandered home towards our small village of Tallentire, near Cockermouth, all feelings of nausea were forgotten, and my imagination ran wild. Where had this wonderful machine come from? Why was it visiting our sleepy hollow of West Cumberland? Who was on it? I was going to fly an aeroplane one day.

I was born in Maryport, West Cumberland, a few years after the end of the war. The county was still called Cumberland in those days, before the bureaucrats changed everything. It still is one of the most beautiful counties in England as is proven by the number of people who come to visit it every year.

Millions of years ago, the area was subject to radial glaciation (or so we are told) and, as a result, the lakes themselves radiate from more or less the centre of Cumbria (as it is now called) towards every point of the compass. The mountains and hills surround the lakes, waters and meres, and the whole area is a jewel to look at and enjoy. To the west, between the edge of the lakes, hills and the sea, lies a coastal plain running from Bowness-on-Solway in the north, which is the western end of Hadrian's Wall, to Barrow-in-Furness in the south where nuclear submarines are now built. The Isle of Man lies approximately 35 miles to the south-west of St. Bees Head which is the western most tip of the county. Local people say that if you can see the Isle of Man it's going to rain. If you can't see it then it's already raining. The coastal strip was quite industrious in the 1950s and '60s. There was a large iron and steelworks in Workington, and one of the specialities of that particular works were railway lines. They were made and exported throughout the world. They used to say that if you looked closely at a railway line in India you would probably see the name Workington marked in the steel. Coal mining was also big in the area as was the fishing industry. A lot of young people left school and ended up working in one of these industries. As the years progressed, as with many parts of the country, most of these industries were cut back and eventually shut down.

Before moving to Tallentire, Mum, Dad and I lived in a small, modest flat behind the main street in Maryport. My grandfather ran a factory on the edge of the town and lived near Cockermouth, a few miles away.

My paternal grandfather was a great man in my eyes. He could do no wrong. As a very young boy, I would get on a stool, in order to reach the phone, and ring him at his home just outside Cockermouth. It was a large company property, called Hundith Hill, which is now a hotel. I would usually ask him when he was coming round to take me to the beach. Within half an hour, he would arrive in his Humber Hawk and off we would go to Allonby. On the way, we would stop at the railway bridge at Gilcrux and wait to see if a steam train would appear. One usually did, eventually, as my grandfather was very patient. After the excitement of the steam devouring us as the train went under the bridge, we would set off again for the beach. Our journey would consist of thousands of questions of no real importance, but he would patiently answer all of them. There was a family-run ice cream shop in Allonby. It is still there today. Here we would eat masses of ice cream and run down to the edge of the sea. Divorced from my grandmother, my hero lived with a housekeeper in the grand company's house. He was affectionately known as "Papa".

He worked as managing director of a company which started to produce plastic buttons (instead of using animal horn) for uniforms for the armed forces. The company had been given a government grant to locate to either South Wales or West Cumberland. He travelled to both areas and decided on the latter. The company was called Hornflowa, and my main memory of it was a large factory and big, noisy machines but wonderfully friendly people who worked there. My grandfather was a very popular boss especially with my father and his brother Charlie who both worked under him. My mum worked there as a secretary, and it was here where she met my dad. The company did well, and Grandfather always managed to enjoy life to the full. He would sneak away early one or two days per week to go fishing. He had private fishing on the River Derwent which, in those days, was one of the best salmon rivers in England. The river flowed from the western end of Bassenthwaite Lake, through Cockermouth and ended its journey at Workington, on the coast. It is said to be the fastest flowing river in England and flows through some of the most beautiful countryside. I spent many happy days there watching Grandfather who was a master with a salmon fly rod.

Hundith Hill used to be owned by Hornflowa, and my grandfather lived in one of the halves of the house and another senior director in the other part. It was enormous to me, and I spent hours exploring the many rooms and running around the massive gardens. The whole property was surrounded by large trees and countryside which gave hours of exciting exploration opportunities to a small boy. We had a few Christmases there, and I learnt to ride my brand-new, blue, two-wheeler bike on the very long drive. If I went into Cockermouth with my grandfather, he would put me on his knee and I was allowed to steer his Humber Hawk down the drive to the main road. Life was so exciting with my grandfather.

My grandfather – "Papa"

My grandfather was born on Boxing Day, 26th December, 1886 at 11 Rüsterstraße in Frankfurt am Main. He was one of five brothers; himself, Max, Ernest, Paul and Kurt. His parents were Karl and Amalie. After schooling in Frankfurt, he went on to obtain a degree in mining and smelting as well as mine surveying and geology. A doctorate was then completed in Dresden in 1908. He completed his compulsory military service in the German horse artillery and achieved the rank of junior lieutenant. He was mentioned in dispatches for assisting in rescue work in a collapsed factory. Work in mining and geology took him initially to Norway and, eventually, he was assigned to the Spanish government where he assisted with the modernisation of old iron ore mines in the Spanish province of Tarragona. He was eventually asked to go to the Spanish Sahara (now Mauretania) where he helped open up the large iron ore mines which are still in operation. Looking for new areas for mining in that part of the world involved expeditions into the wild interior, up to 300 kilometres from the nearest civilised outpost, and one of these had to be abandoned due to the native Rif Kabyles shooting at him and his staff!

In 1914, he was asked to retrain and specialise in the petroleum industry. He was to go to Baku but, when war broke out, he was recalled to the German Army. During the first year of the war, he served as an artillery officer on the Western Front. Later, he was transferred to the Eastern Front in charge of supply columns. This was dangerous, because the Russian cavalry, who were usually Cossacks, operated regularly behind German lines. In the last few months of the war, he was posted to the military government in Brussels as the commissioner for mining and banking. He was eventually awarded several medals including the Iron Cross second class.

Grandfather (left) with his brother Ernest

After Germany collapsed in 1918, he returned to his homeland which was in a state of chaos. The country was awash with unemployed soldiers, and many released prisoners of war (mainly Russian), who were roaming the countryside. The political extreme left was setting up a party along the Bolshevik lines called the "Spartacus League". The industrialists, landowners and bankers got together and formed a militia unit called the "Freikorps" to restore law and order and put down the revolutionaries. These men were mainly ex-NCOs from the

German Army. Grandfather had always been popular with his men during the war and many were happy to work with him now. He had a connection, through his father, to a financial consortium, and he became paymaster to the "Freikorps". The whole operation was very successful and it became the German Weimar Republic.

Eventually, he decided on a career change, as he wanted to enter industry. This was where the future was following the war. To do this, he joined a bank in Vienna, Austria and moved into a small flat opposite the stage door of the Vienna opera house. During this time, he met a German girl, Marie Louise Oppenheimer, who was visiting an uncle. They were married in 1923. Their first son was Karl Franz (Charles Francis, my Uncle Charlie) and their second son was Hans Peter (John Peter), my father.

Eventually, Grandfather worked his way up in industry and became managing director of Burgenländische Kreide & Chemische Werke A.G. who had a lime quarry and factory producing pure lime products. The family moved into a larger flat in Vienna, and Grandfather then also joined the board of a chemical company called Josef Estermann A.G. This company produced margarine, soaps and other similar products. He soon became joint managing director of this company as well.

Great-grandfather, on my grandmother's side, was Dr Franz Oppenheimer and was born on 1st August 1871 in Hamburg. He was the son of a lawyer, Dr Ruben Leopold, and his wife, Rebecka Oppenheimer. He studied law in Berlin, Heidelberg and Leipzig where he completed his doctorates. In 1899, he took a post as an in-house lawyer with Emanuel Friedländer &

Co which was one of the leading companies in the coal mining industry at the time. In 1908, he became a shareholder in this company and joined the board of other companies in the coal mining business. He married Margarethe Knapp, who was born on 8th August 1878, and together they had two children. The children were Marie Louise (my grandmother) and a son, Franz Karl, who was known in the family as "Uncle Bobby".

All members of the Oppenheimer family were of Jewish descent. The family eventually settled in Berlin. Dr Franz Oppenheimer lived on Großadmiral-Prinz-Heinrich-Straße (today Hitzigalle 2), on the corner to Tiergartenstraße in Berlin-Tiergarten. Before WWII, this area was very affluent and a lot of embassies were situated there. The area was heavily bombed during the war, and most of the buildings (including the one where he lived) were destroyed. It had been designated by Albert Speer, the minister of armaments and war production and close ally of Adolph Hitler, as an area which was going to be acquired and redeveloped to build large, palatial houses for high-ranking Nazis. This district was to be part of a complete makeover of Berlin, which was also to be renamed, as the power of the Nazis grew throughout Europe. Unfortunately, the Allies bombed that area before the changes could be made by Speer.

Franz Oppenheimer had his office on the large boulevard in Berlin called Unter den Linden. He was a co-owner of Emanuel Friedländer & Co which, as mentioned before, was one of the leading companies in the coal mining industry at the time.

Due to Nazi persecution, they were forced to move initially to Vienna, where their daughter was living, in December 1936.

Top Row: Grandfather, Grandmother, Uncle Bobby
Second Row: Great-Grandmother Oppenheimer, Uncle Charlie, Great-Grandfather Oppenheimer, Dad

My Grandfather Herzberg's side of the family. Top Row: Max, Paul, my grandmother, Ernest, Franz Moritz (my grandfather) Middle Row: Paul's daughter Lili, Max's wife, Great-Grandmother (Amalie), Great-Grandfather (Karl), Paul's wife (Clare), Paul's daughter Edith Bottom Row: Uncle Charlie, Karl Leopold (one of Paul's three children), Dad

My mum's family came from Cockermouth and lived in or around the small market town. Mum had two brothers, Frank and Jack. The family all ran a mill and a farm supply business in Cockermouth which supplied fodder to local farmers. Very much a local family, they had lived in Cumbria and the Cockermouth area, but some members of the family had lived in the south-west of Scotland for several generations. My grandfather, David Harkness, died when I was very young and, as a consequence, I don't really remember much about him. He was a miller by trade. The mill, which he ran initially in Cockermouth, had a waterwheel (that is still there) which, in turn, ground the grain and was sold to local producers of bread. The family actually lived about a mile to the west of Cockermouth in a little village called Papcastle. There they had a large family house by the name of Glengarry. My grandfather's sisters, Auntie Isobel and Auntie Manie (Mary Agnes), lived next door. These two sisters never married but treated their niece and nephews as their own and are looked back upon with great affection.

Auntie Isobel suffered badly with rheumatic fever and was permanently confined to her bed, as happened in those days, until a new, young doctor came to Cockermouth and encouraged her to get up and get on with her life.

Auntie Manie (Mary Agnes)

Auntie Isobel

Auntie Manie spent many years, towards the end of her life, virtually deaf. In this day and age medicine would probably have been much kinder to her, but those around her said she benefitted from an extra sense which perhaps made up a little bit for her lack of hearing.

My grandfather was a very caring person who worked hard travelling around the county, in his later years, selling fodder and other such animal stuff to the local farmers. He used to leave early in the morning and return home late at night just trying to make a living like everybody else after the war. The roads were not particularly good in those days, and his small car did not have the modern-day reliability. I can only imagine that his life was similar to that of James Herriot. He was well liked by all the farmers and was always given "a little something" to take home for his family. They were never particularly short of sausages, fresh meat, cheese and butter, especially during the war years.

Grandmother (Mary Jane) was a large woman who had all the culinary gifts of that generation. As a young girl, she was "in service" in London with a pleasant family who treated her very well. She came back to the north and eventually married Grandfather. A brilliant cook, everything was home-made, and a visit to her was something to look forward to. Cakes, sandwiches and home-made ginger wine were always available as a light snack when we popped in. I just didn't like tongue in my sandwiches. She used to press tongue herself; awful stuff.

My Uncle Jack was always a firm favourite. He and Auntie Betty lived in Papcastle. He served with the Eighth Army, during the war, and fought in North Africa. He then moved on through Sicily, after the Allies landed, and made his way up through Italy. He was a real country person; a keen fisherman and able to turn his hand to anything mechanical. He was always ready and willing to give me help with machinery that needed repairing. This was particularly true when I started driving and was running old cars that needed regular attention.

Uncle Frank served in India during the last war and ended up with malaria. Another great practical person who also knew everything there was to know about anything mechanical. He had a little bit of a reputation for being moody, but his wife, my Auntie Irene, knew how to handle him. I never had any problems with him, and he was always very kind to me.

Mum's side of the family.
Grandmother, Mum, Uncle Frank, Uncle Jack and Grandfather

In 1954, we moved to Tallentire. We moved into a terraced house, in this tiny village, with a large back garden and wonderful views over the Solway Firth. The sunsets were stunning. Initially, Dad was away from Monday to Friday working as a commercial traveller. Mum and I stayed at home, and Mum supplemented her housekeeping by selling eggs from the hens which we kept in the back garden. I was always in trouble, as I had a habit of grabbing them by the tail, letting them walk forward a few steps and then pulling them back! Great fun! We also had a good crop of raspberries in the garden. I used to help myself and end up scolded for stuffing my face. I don't know how Mum knew. It was probably the debris left around my mouth.

Mum and I during the "early years"

Just off to check out the hens! Circa 1955

CHAPTER 2

Mum was a good cook. We always had simple, home-cooked meals, a warm coal fire and an early black-and-white television which provided me with a weekly dose of The Lone Ranger. I was either going to take his job when I grew up or fly aeroplanes. It very much depended on the day. I remember watching Spitfires, Shackletons, Avro Ansons and other old aircraft flying over the house on their way to who knows where. Dad used to buy me plastic kits of aeroplanes. He made them initially, and they took pride of place on my chest of drawers. As I got older, I started to build them with his help. There was more glue on me than anything else.

Mum and I used to get on the local bus and go shopping in Cockermouth, a pretty, little market town which sits on the River Derwent. Shops in those days were small, and I remember the local grocery shop which always smelt of coffee and smoked bacon. We didn't have such a thing as a freezer in the 1950s, so shopping was quite a regular expedition. Mum didn't drive in those days, and we would have to walk a good mile to visit Grandmother and then a mile back to the bus stop to get home.

I was usually rewarded for being good with a comic. The Beezer was the favourite.

It was a wonderful life living in the countryside on the edge of the Lake District. A group of us, as kids, would disappear for most of the day playing in the fields and streams but always getting home for tea. Nobody worried in those days. The area was rich in wild flowers and wildlife and, at the right time of year, covered in primroses, bluebells and cowslips. We were encouraged to pick rose hips. They were gathered together at the local village school, and we were supposed to get a penny for every colossal amount that we handed in. I never received a thing! It was something to do with the vitamin C content. I never did find out where they went. The village had about three or four farms around it and, if we were in the vicinity, my friends' mums, who were farmers' wives, always gave us home-cooked buns or cakes in passing. We spent hours exploring the local farms and haylofts. Life was simple living there, in those days, but full of fun and adventure.

One of the farmers in the village kept a fox in a cage in the farmyard. We would go and have a look at it occasionally. It wasn't really very pleasant to see this creature kept captive, but we were fascinated by it. I remember the stink to this day!

Bonfire Night was usually in our large back garden. The people from the village brought wood and anything else which would burn, and Mum spent the evening cooking chips and handing them out in greaseproof cones whilst Dad set off the fireworks.

Dad's Ford Popular lived in the garage next to our house. One particular day, for some reason unknown to anyone, the car caught fire, though Dad had been fiddling with it. He was never much good with any form of DIY. Mum and I were ushered out of the house, and some of the neighbours rallied round and tried to push it out of the garage.

One of the local farmers, who was watching, shouted, "Push the bugger back in, John, it isn't done enough!"

I don't know what sort of a nightmare it was for the insurance company.

Dad built a soapbox cart, and me and the other kids would spend hours pushing it up Tallentire hill and racing back down whilst sitting in it, usually terrified, as there was no form of steering! On dry days, we would do this for hours and hours; the simple things amused. We also had a game where we would race along the pavement on our tricycles before jumping off at high speed. Unfortunately, I did this one day, and my tricycle leapt off the pavement only to be flattened by Mr Bouch who was coming round the corner in his mobile shop. Mr Bouch was very apologetic, but no matter how hard I tried to wriggle out of the blame it was definitely my fault. Mum used to buy, amongst other things, a few packets of crisps for me when Mr Bouch arrived in the village every Wednesday. The crisps (the ones with the blue packets of salt in them) were a treat to be handed out when I was in favour. Unfortunately, the tricycle incident set back relations somewhat, and crisps were off the list for several weeks. My transport was back again when two new wheels were fitted.

A pot of green gloss paint had been left in the garage, as Dad had been painting the new garage doors. I discovered this pot of paint and decided to put it to good use and paint the neighbours' dog. It was a very friendly and placid old dog and stood there quite happily, as I applied its new colour. There was hell on! It took hours and hours to clean the dog using gallons of turpentine. Fortunately, the neighbour soon regained his sense of humour, and I wasn't "in the doghouse" for too long.

Eventually, the day arrived when I had to go to school. I was about five years old. Dad used to take me and loads of the other kids from the village to Dovenby School. Dovenby School was only a couple of miles away on the main road into Cockermouth. It stood on a crossroads and is still there to this day. By now, Dad had graduated to a Ford Consul. It had a big bench, front seat and, looking back, it seemed as if there were at least five of us on the front bench seat and five more on the rear bench seat. It wasn't far to school, and things such as seat belts hadn't been invented. Dad would drive us all mad by asking us if we wanted him to sing on the way to school. There were loud screams of, "Nooo!"

I hated school. There were only two classes at this tiny, little village school. The class for the new starters was run by a rather large spinster. She had a very Jewish surname, and I never understood why I was in trouble for things I hadn't done. It got so bad that my mother went "to have words" about why her darling son was being persecuted. It only occurred to me many, many years later that I had a very German surname, and it could have been something relating to that. If only she knew the truth about my family.

During day two at this new school, I decided that they couldn't teach me anything worthwhile so, during the morning break,

I jumped over the fence and started to walk home. I got about a couple of hundred yards before someone came after me. I had made the mistake of telling the other kids that I was going home, and they "grassed" on me. I had decided that this school thing was a waste of time.

I looked forward to school holidays immensely. It had been explained to me that we were off to Austria in the car, to a country with beautiful mountains and lakes. Off we set, in our Ford Consul, with me sitting on the centre armrest, in the front. After half an hour, we were passing Bassenthwaite Lake near Keswick. Skiddaw was off to the left. I enquired if this was Austria.

We spent weeks travelling to Austria and Germany in those days. It just so happened that we would drive as far as Lydd, in Kent, and then fly across the Channel to Calais. The car would be loaded on to an aeroplane at Lydd. We used a car transporter aircraft called a Bristol Freighter which was operated by a company called Silver City. I watched, fascinated, as the car was driven up a ramp, through massive doors, into the nose of the aircraft. Once we had been led out to the aircraft, I was allowed to sit next to the window. The smell of old aircraft is unique; it's a mixture of leather, petrol, oil, wet carpet, old farts and coffee. Eventually, the engines were started, billowing smoke out of the back, and the aircraft made its way out to the runway, brakes squealing all the time. With a roar from the big radial engines, we were on our way. I was beside myself with excitement. The Bristol Freighter was not renowned for its stunning climb performance. It used to be said that should an engine fail on take-off then the other engine would take you to the scene of the crash. It wasn't known as the "Bristol

Frightener" for nothing! We crossed the Channel at a fairly low level, and very quickly we were descending towards the runway at Calais. With a bump, and more squealing from the brakes, we had arrived. This was the best part of the holiday, and I lost interest in most of the rest of the journey. Bugger the mountains and lakes; I was looking forward to the flight home!

By 1960, Dad had changed his job and, because his daily commute was quite long, we moved to Workington. It was a rather sad time leaving this pretty, quiet, little village. I wasn't happy to leave all my friends behind, but the "silver lining" was that my grandfather, who had recently retired, was coming to live with us. This was terrific news.

Workington was an iron and steel town on the coast. Mum and Dad bought a large Victorian, semi-detached house with three floors. It needed completely gutting and, when it was put back together, we graduated from coal fires to oil-fired central heating. Luxury!

Depending on the wind direction, in those days, one could suffer from the smell of the iron and steelworks in Workington. It was either that or the brewery. I was sent to St. John's junior school. This was right next to the brewery and the smell was quite prevalent. Despite my dislike of my schooling to date, I was reasonably happy at St. John's. It was a typical school of the times with large, old Victorian classrooms and an enormous tarmac playground. Memories from here consist of mainly learning to read, tell the time and seeing who could pee the highest up the wall in the brick-built outside toilets which had no roof. Unfortunately, the other side of the urinal wall was the playground, and I remember screams coming from the kids in the playground when one of us managed to actually pee over the top of the wall. It was an education in fluid dynamics.

Eventually, a group of us went to the other end of the building and started a higher class.

Meals involved crossing a road and going into the basement of a church. Here we sat on long, wooden benches, and ladies brought plates of things such as "tatty ash" for us to devour. I have no idea to this day what "tatty ash" was. I was a shy child and, one particular day, one of the ladies forgot to bring me a plate of food. I didn't say anything... I just went hungry!

After a couple of years, it was decided that my education would continue in a public school. I didn't really know what was going on, but I went with Mum on the steam train to Carlisle to get kitted out for Rickerby House public school just outside Ecclefechan, north of the border. I was about eight years old at the time. A large, wooden box appeared at home with my name on it. I was told this would be my tuck box. My tuck box was filled with my toys and a tin with chocolate crispies which Mum had made. Eventually, the day came and off we set to this new school. I was not enthusiastic. I started as a weekly boarder. I was absolutely miserable. I was so miserable that I descended towards the point where I wouldn't listen to anybody or do anything. It was a time of strict discipline, learning French that the others had started a year previously and, of course, bullying. I kept getting shouted at, and things went from bad to worse. I was offered all kinds of bribes to placate me. Dad was running a small petrol station in Cockermouth at the time. He suggested that he would get Bill, one of his mechanics, to build a go-kart which we could have a bit of fun with when I was at home. I looked forward, every week, to seeing what progress had been made with this go-kart. The chassis was formed very slowly, and I eventually came home one weekend to find it had been made into a carrier for the welding bottles! Eventually, I was taken to see the GP, and he told my parents that if they didn't bring me home permanently I would suffer some form of breakdown.

I was, at last, brought home and sent as a day boy to another private school in Cockermouth. This was Wyndham House. This school was very different and life here was good, except for the fact we got homework. I didn't like homework. We also had to go to school every Saturday morning. Homework and Saturday-morning school interfered with my plans. This school sat at the edge of Cockermouth town and in the most beautiful grounds. We were living about 7 or 8 miles from the school, but a school bus picked up those of us who needed transport every morning and took us home every evening. The school transport was an old Bedford minibus which had wooden benches up either side in the back. The driver, who was a fairly miserable character, stopped at our house at 8.15 a.m. every morning. Eventually, despite my mother shouting upstairs to get me out of bed, I refined the morning departure to getting up between 8.05 and 8.10 and still being outside, waiting for the bus, by 8.15. Such were the priorities of a young boy when it came to getting out of bed. Breakfast was just "breathed in" as I rushed past. The bus was well past it's "sell-by date", and there was always the hope that it would break down on our way to school. It did occasionally, and it was always a great pleasure to miss some lessons. The problem was that it could also break down on the way home. Having clambered through the back door of the minibus, or "The Tank" as it was affectionately known, we would endure the uncomfortable seat for the forty-five-minute journey whilst one of the boys had his small transistor radio tuned to Radio Caroline. We listened intently, through the hissing, to the latest sounds from the pirate radio ship which was anchored just across the water off the Isle of Man. Those were the days of '60s music and the start of the careers of people such as Tony Blackburn, Johnnie Walker, Dave Lee Travis and Simon Dee.

As a country boy, I spent all the break times and most of the lunchtimes in the grounds usually getting up to no good. I remember there was a steep slope down to a stream, which we would spend ages sliding down on a sheet of corrugated iron. I was going down, this one particular day, when the sheet of iron stopped abruptly and I kept going. I spent the afternoon trying to hide my backside which was hanging out of my shorts. That was another pair of shorts for my mother to mend.

In the autumn, we would spend ages looking for conkers in the school grounds. Some were left on the ground but some fell into the stream, and we would follow it all the way towards Cockermouth looking for these precious nuts. There were regular reprimands, as we were late for lessons after the breaks. We got so engrossed with messing about in these large grounds that we didn't hear the school bell calling us back for lessons. I remember the punishment after a severe bollocking from the headmaster was a whack across the back of the legs with a ruler. The food at this school was awful. I could never drink milk by itself as a child, but the old metal crates of milk, containing one third of a pint bottles, were always left next to a radiator or, in the summer, in full sun. It had virtually curdled by the time it was made available to us. Thank God I didn't touch it.

Lunchtime involved sitting at a table with three of us at each side and a master at the top. He served up the grub! There were no "requests", and you got what you were given and had to eat it. The mashed potato was made from powder with water added. It was disgusting. The worst meal of all, which most of us dreaded, was liver. I think the liver must have been that of a dinosaur. It was large, full of all sorts of pipes and, if you caught it in the right light, it had a tinge of British racing green about it. For me, I'm afraid liver goes in the same column as tongue.

We played sport every day for an hour. I have never been particularly interested in sport but, in those days, it was compulsory; football in the winter and cricket in the summer. Although not a sports fan, I was tall and could run fast, so it was inevitable that I was picked for the school team. Which schools did we travel to for matches? Well, Rickerby House was one of them, and I remember living in fear of those days travelling to that school. I'm not sure to this day why, but that short time in my young life had a profound effect on me.

It was here that I was offered the opportunity to go to cycling proficiency lessons. My bicycle was taken to the school and left in the bike sheds. We went to lessons every week. We had to go down the road from the school to a big hall where a police sergeant gave us the required tuition. After a few weeks, we underwent a test, which I passed. We were then presented with our highly coveted cycling proficiency badge. Another big step in life!

I wasn't the sharpest tool in the box but did reasonably well, or so I thought. Despite being given extra tuition, I still managed to fail the eleven-plus exam the first time around. The extra tuition was once a week at the house of a schoolteacher in Maryport. I dreaded it, and it didn't do me any good preparing for this exam the first time round. I passed it a year later and ended up going to Workington Grammar School. Here I caught up with old friends that I had been with at St. John's junior school when we had originally moved to Workington.

I walked to school on the first day wearing my new long trousers. I was slightly apprehensive, due to stories I had heard, about first day initiations. Sure enough, there were loads of new boys getting their heads pushed down deep into the toilets and having the chain pulled. I managed to steer clear of this, as it appeared most of the "casualties" had already been earmarked by older boys who already knew them. I was a new face and of little interest, thank God!

Life at the grammar school was much better for me. I went home every day and had a good bunch of mates. Weekends were spent with friends racing into town on our bicycles to a shop called "Browns". I received two shillings of pocket money, and we always wanted to see if there was a new release in the Airfix model range. Saturday afternoons were spent sticking models together and, if we were really lucky, there was a film on TV that might have a couple of seconds of an aeroplane in it. As the years progressed, the plastic aeroplanes developed into balsa wood aeroplanes, and we would walk into town every Saturday, as biking into town was for "kids".

CHAPTER 3

My grandfather and I had a very close relationship. He had come to live with us in Workington, during his retirement years, and it was great fun having him around. Typically German, he sat at the head of the table for meals and enjoyed a bottle of beer every night in his silver tankard. As we lived in a rather large, semi-detached, Victorian house, he had his own sitting room and bedroom. He enjoyed his retirement years living with us, fishing and travelling. He booked many holidays and would disappear for several weeks, sometimes to the other side of the world and sometimes just to Germany to visit the graves of his parents.

As Grandfather got older and his hearing and his driving ability deteriorated, I always found it slightly embarrassing to go anywhere with him in his car. He had a Hillman Minx and, due to his age and deafness, he found it much easier to go everywhere in first gear. The engine would be revving wildly, virtually jumping through the bonnet, as it protested at this mechanical torture. The car was a regular visitor to the local garage, as Grandfather went through goodness knows how many clutches.

Grandfather had a permit to fish the River Derwent on some of the local beats. The area of the River Derwent where he fished was glorious. There were three fishing beats, and a day's fishing with him started with a drive of thirty minutes to park in a local farmyard. The journey was usually in first gear, with the car engine suffering the usual torture. I was always hoping that nobody who we passed along the route knew me. Once parked up, we would empty the car of rods, fishing bags and other tackle. Lunch bags, which my mother had packed carefully for us, were an obvious necessity. We then walked twenty minutes or so along the riverbank to the fishing hut, which we had permission to use on that particular day. Here we would assemble the fishing rod, and my grandfather would choose which fishing fly was right for the conditions of the day. I would always start with lunch even though I had only consumed my breakfast within the last hour. I spent many happy days watching him fishing and occasionally carrying a salmon home for him! There was a railway line near to where he fished. Whilst he made his way up and down the river, casting away with his fishing flies, I used to wander over to the railway line to watch the trains. I used to put old pennies on the line, and I still have one in my possession which was flattened by the local steam train. These days, we would be sent to prison if we did that sort of thing.

My grandfather and grandmother were divorced in the late 1940s. By this time, she was living in a rather posh apartment in London. Whenever she came to stay with us, the house seemed to descend into a state of panic. She always insisted on sleeping in my room. Apparently, she preferred my room, as the view was nice and it was much quieter than the guest room. Various pieces of furniture had to be moved around the house, as she particularly liked these pieces and what Grandmother wanted, Grandmother got. Breakfast was served to her in bed, and my room ended up stinking of cigarette smoke, as she would spend an hour or so after breakfast during the morning sitting in bed "holding court". My father and grandmother would chat away, usually speaking German, and I didn't have a clue what was being discussed. I remember on Sunday mornings, she would say we were all invited to a local hotel for lunch. My grandfather was not included in this invitation, so I usually stayed at home with him. A lunch out in a posh hotel was not my idea of fun anyway.

Occasionally, she would invite me to London to stay with her during school holidays. I always enjoyed the journey to London on the train. This was a taste of independence and an excuse to not only go to Heathrow for the day, to watch aeroplanes, but also to go to the big aero modelling shops in London and drool at the latest products in the modelling world. I used to make my way out to Heathrow and, in those days, one could sit by one of the large windows in the terminal in full view of aircraft touching down. I would spend a full day there just watching. The journey around London, using the Underground, was another sense of achievement. I was quite happy to go out and about for the day and explore. She would take me out for a meal in the evenings or, occasionally, cook a schnitzel herself. Unfortunately, she drank quite heavily by this time, and the effects of the vodka and tonic meant she never noticed the ash dropping off her cigarette into the schnitzel in the pan. It didn't seem to do me any harm.

At one point during my time at grammar school, we were all sent to see a careers officer. He had a look at how I was doing and asked me what I wanted to do. I told him that I wanted to fly.

He said, "Don't be ridiculous. Have you thought about a career in catering?"

I was still totally smitten with aviation and anything to do with it. Summer afternoons were spent lying about in the sunshine, looking up to the sky and wondering where all the various aircraft were going. Books were devoured, films were watched, and the closest I could get to flying was through aero modelling. I still go back to it to this day. Evenings were spent listening to an old VHF radio which I had been given. It was exciting hearing all the aircraft, within range, flying up and down the country. This was a whole new fascinating world for me. My imagination went wild! That old radio still sits (and works) at the back of my garage. It brought me a vast amount of pleasure all those years ago.

Summer holidays now tended to involve an early morning drive to Newcastle to get on a flight to London. This was of great interest to me, as we would drive over the moors on the A69 and sometimes, just sometimes, we would see massive plumes of smoke coming from what was the Intermediate Range Ballistic Missile Test Centre. Here, rocket engines were tested for the Blue Streak missile project. This was a British design but was eventually cancelled by the British government.

As the journey to Newcastle progressed, there was excitement about what kind of aeroplane would we have today. BKS airline flew the route between Newcastle and Heathrow, and I knew it would be either an Airspeed Ambassador or a Bristol

Britannia. BKS eventually became Northeast Airlines who operated Tridents on the route. Then, of course, we had a flight from Heathrow to wherever we were going. I had all this excitement to look forward to with the thought of a boring old holiday to put up with before the flight home. One had to get one's priorities right!

I had been told that if I joined the air cadets there was a good chance that I could get a flight in a Chipmunk or a glider. This seemed like too good an opportunity to miss, and so I joined the air cadets with a mate of mine. We were issued with a uniform and made our way down to a wooden shack at the bottom of town every Monday evening. There were pieces of aeroplane lying around the building along with interesting stuff to read. We were taken to the local Territorial Army buildings to go shooting. I managed to achieve my marksman's badge at the first attempt. We had to get three .22 bullets in the target that could be covered by an old penny.

We had to learn "drill". I hated that. Where were the aeroplanes, and when were we going flying? Eventually, we went over to RAF Ouston to fly in a Chipmunk on what they called an air experience flight. The one time I went it was bitterly cold, as it was in the middle of winter, but totally thrilling. I was strapped into the back of a Chipmunk and spent an exhilarating twenty minutes flying along the Roman wall dodging the snow showers. This flying thing was definitely for me!

At 16, I went to Biggin Hill for "tests in advance". This involved three days of aptitude and intelligence tests and, at the end, we were told what career we could expect to be offered in the Royal Air Force. I had noticed a deterioration in my eyesight at school and had, unfortunately, been informed I had to wear glasses. I was told that, despite a good performance with the aptitude tests, I would not be able to undertake any form of flying career. I wasn't interested in anything else, so I went home a day early!

Despite the close interest with aviation, I eventually left the air cadets. I found the drill boring, and the amount of times we did anything that satisfied my continued craving for flying was few and far between. I really wasn't "service" material. I was now at the age where it just wasn't "cool" to be in the air cadets. How could we expect to attract girls when we were air cadets? It just wouldn't happen. And of course, we were all Adonises.

We had now all discovered the joys of beer. I was invited to go with a friend to a Bonfire Night "do" at the local golf club with his parents. His father ended up buying us both a couple of pints of lager. We were completely "stupid" with the alcohol, much to his dad's amusement, but the next day we could boast about how much we could drink and how bad we felt. We had reached manhood.

I never seemed to do much with my dad. He always worked on Saturday mornings, and Mum always made our "Sunday" roast on Saturdays. He was running a carpet and furnishing shop at this time and, after lunch on Saturdays, just wanted to sit and watch sport on the telly. My interest in sport was, and still is, zero. Despite asking to go somewhere or other on Sundays, I was always told "Your dad is too tired". We had the Lake District next to us but never quite managed to get to it.

At 17, I started driving lessons and looked forward to the time when I passed my driving test and could take my grandfather out rather than have him drive. Sadly, it was not to be. He had a heart attack and was in his bed for a week before passing away quietly. All he wanted for that last week was a daily bottle of beer in his pewter tankard. The doctor told Mum just to let him have what he wanted. He died around the time of me passing my test.

I got the use of my mum's old Triumph Herald and took any opportunity to get out in it. Although mum had passed her test, her confidence had waned. She was frightened that she would cause an accident on the roads. Should she need to go anywhere, I automatically volunteered. Unfortunately, as soon as we got above 30 miles per hour, I could see her foot pressing down in the footwell on the imaginary brake pedal and her uttering the words "That's fast enough!", so we never got anywhere quickly.

Despite the loss of my grandfather, passing my driving test opened a new chapter in transportation for me and my mates! Rather than be stuck around my home area, friends would "chip in", and we would disappear at the weekends to pubs and clubs around new areas. There were, of course, visits to local airfields, such as Carlisle and also to the old RAF wartime airfields, to see if there was anything interesting to look at. The drink-driving laws had not been tightened up to the extent that they have become today, and many late-night drives home were probably undertaken when they shouldn't have been. On Sundays, I used to drive the 7 miles to Cockermouth where my cousin Frank and I would spend the morning tinkering with cars before adjourning to one of the local pubs in Cockermouth. There used to be a pub on the main street that was run by two elderly brothers. The pub still had spittoons and sawdust on the floor. On Sunday mornings, the smell of a roast of beef or lamb would drift through into the bar. In years gone by, the brothers used to own and operate steam-driven thresher machines which were used in farming. Now they were retired, they just ran the pub. The local beer was always good, and I used to make my way home (eventually) for lunch usually the worse for wear!

As I mentioned before, my Uncle Jack was also a keen fisherman, and I remember going with him and a friend of his to fish on Bassenthwaite Lake. We had the use of a rowing boat, and off we went to enjoy a day on the lake. My uncle managed to catch a pike and, just as we reached the middle of the lake, a squall blew up. We managed to get to the shore without the boat capsizing, but it was the opposite side of the lake from where we had started. It then involved a long walk back to the car. I knew that it would be river fishing only after that experience.

Mum and Dad would disappear for several weeks at a time on holiday. Dad always used to say "Your mother needs a rest" which actually meant he wanted to go away. I don't think Mum was always that enthusiastic, but she went mainly for his sake; or so she said. Whilst they were away, I had a free run of the house, and my friends would appear after the pubs closed with bottles of beer "acquired" from their parents. I was surviving on those curries which came in a plastic bag. The curry needed water added to it, and the rice needed to be boiled in the bag. One particular night, after one of these curries, I was led astray by friends and drank too much beer. I got up out of bed at some early hour and opened the window to be sick. My mother had arranged for a cleaner to come in whilst she was away (probably just to keep an eye on me), and the next morning I was woken by her asking me if I had heard a cat being sick on the yard below my window. I denied all knowledge and suggested it was probably a dog.

Unknown to me, my grandfather had left me a huge Cromwellian wardrobe in his will. This great big piece of furniture lived in his bedroom, and I used to hide in it as a child. It had to be dismantled to get it out of the house. It was sent to auction and the money eventually came to me. This was my opportunity! My father had started flying lessons when I was 16. I was so jealous, but he gave up after just a few hours of flying. He was never seriously interested. We had significant disagreements regarding my career, as all I wanted to do was fly, but he insisted on me doing something sensible such as banking or accounting. I had done quite well with my O levels but had been studying maths, further maths and physics in sixth form. I was not doing well, as I just wasn't interested and I wasn't paying the required amount of attention at the various lessons. My mind was elsewhere.

At 17, I went on a week's gliding course with a couple of mates. We had saved enough money and, with a bit of help from Mum and Dad, we had enough to pay for the week. We drove down to Sutton Bank in Yorkshire and stayed in the club accommodation. It was great fun and, as well as the flying, there was a lot to be learnt from the instructors. One of the part-time instructors, a guy by the name of Charles, was a very nice chap who flew Caravelles for some airline out in the Far East. Talking to him did nothing to quench my enthusiasm to go and fly aeroplanes for a living. The chief flying instructor was a Polish gentleman who flew Hurricanes with one of the Polish squadrons during the Battle of Britain. He had both legs in plaster from some car accident. It certainly didn't stop him from flying! He used to fly the light aircraft known as the "tug" which pulled the gliders into the air. Once at the required height and in the required geographical position, the glider pilot would pull a handle which released the towline and the tug was free to go back to the airfield for his next customer.

We underwent all the basic tuition and then spent lots of time undergoing winch launches, flying around the circuit and landing. The winch was one end of an old London bus with a cable attached to a drum. The cable was pulled out of the drum to the glider by a tractor. Once attached, when the "all out" signal was given, the bus drove the drum which pulled the cable and, in turn, the glider accelerated along the grass runway. There was enough cable to get the glider airborne, let it climb to an appropriate height and then the cable was released by the glider pilot.

Much of the time was spent moving gliders, retrieving the cable and being the general dogsbody. The weather was beautiful all week, and evenings were spent driving around the local area and enjoying the local pubs. We were close enough to 18! The week went by in a flash and then it was back to more confrontation at home about who decided what my career would be.

CHAPTER 4

Eventually, my dad and I seemed to reach a compromise, and I started my private pilot licence (PPL) course with the money my grandfather had left me. I think Dad hoped that I would develop a "sensible", secure career and fly for fun. I had absolutely no intention of following that path.

The PPL course was at Carlisle. I met my instructor who was a chap by the name of Bill Moore. Bill was to become a great friend and influence on me. As the years went by, he called himself my second father. Bill started his working life on a farm and then went on to become a milkman. Having worked hard, he completed his private pilot licence and went on to complete an instructor's course. He was a Cumbrian with a heart of gold and a wicked sense of humour. His wife, Edie, was a lovely lady, and I would quite often drive up to Carlisle and spend the evening with them and their enormous Labrador "Dookie". Dookie would slobber all over me whilst I listened to Bill's instructing stories completely enthralled. Bill always claimed that he didn't have the education to go on and obtain a commercial pilot licence (CPL). In later years, I tried to encourage him and offered to help in whatever way I could to get him through the written exams, but it was never to be.

On that first day, Bill supplied me with all the reading material that I needed and with a local area chart and a few other bits and pieces that I was going to need.

Bill looked at the weather and said, "It could be a bit bumpy today."

I didn't care. I just wanted to get airborne.

"That's alright; I'm just looking forward to starting the course. Can't we give it a go?"

Off we went towards the various aircraft sitting outside.

There, out in the distance, sat a smart-looking, single engine aeroplane painted blue and white. It was a Beagle Pup. Manufactured in the south of England, it had a 150-horsepower engine.

"That's the one booked for us today."

At last, I was going to learn to fly.

Having had a walk round the aircraft and been shown what I had to look for on the "external check", we were ready to climb aboard. Bill showed me where not to put my feet, and I carefully climbed into the left-hand seat. There was that wonderful aeroplane smell; leather, oil and a touch of petrol and paint.

This one was virtually new. The instruments in front of me looked vaguely familiar from all the pictures I had looked at, but Bill went on to explain them in detail. He started the engine, said something on the radio, which I didn't understand, and we made our way out to the runway. He showed me how to taxi the aircraft on the ground. No steering wheel here, the rudder pedals had to be pushed using one's feet – push left to turn left and push right to turn right. After completing the power checks to make sure the engine was performing well, we did the before take-off checklist with Bill explaining everything as we went. Eventually, with Bill muttering something else completely unintelligible over the radio, we taxied out to the runway and, after a short run with the engine revving away happily, we were airborne. Away we went, climbing steadily at the correct speed of 70 knots. He very quickly handed over control to me. This was wonderful. Bill pointed out the local landmarks. We passed over Carlisle heading west. Over to the left, the mountains of the Lake District were standing out proudly and on the nose was Workington. We went through some of the early exercises in the course, and my first hour of learning to fly passed in an instant.

There was absolutely no question over what I was going to do for a living. Sorry, Dad, but your idea of a career just isn't going to happen with me.

Bill did so much for me over the years, and we were to remain close until the day he died. Flying was brilliant and, under Bill's tuition, he taught me everything I needed to know to be on the way to achieving my coveted private pilot licence. Every day that I could, I would make my way up to Carlisle for another lesson. We went through the syllabus covering everything from the basics to what was needed to get me up to standard for my first solo flight. Bill nagged away at me to be precise with the aeroplane and not accept anything less than perfection. We went through all the requirements until he was totally satisfied with my standard. Stalling and spinning were covered. They were not particularly pleasant exercises but very necessary to prevent one getting into trouble and killing oneself. With his usual sense of humour, Bill said they would not appreciate losing an aircraft in an accident; I was of less value. Eventually, we started the circuit work. This consisted of a take-off, climbing to 1000 feet, flying around the circuit to position and carry out a landing. This was great fun, and Bill piled the pressure on me. I learnt how to carry out powered approaches, glide approaches and flapless approaches until I could fly them without prompting from the other seat. We also carried out practice engine failures after take-off, where Bill would close the throttle, at a very low level, to simulate the engine failing. The priority was to get the nose of the aircraft down, so that the wing didn't stall, and then quickly try and choose a suitable, clear area to land. All this was happening whilst I went through the drill to try and find the problem and get the engine going again, if at all possible. Having quickly told air traffic control that he was carrying out a practice engine failure, Bill let us glide down to very low altitudes so that I could see for myself whether or not I could have actually landed in the field I had chosen. Would I have made it, landed short or even overshot? If I would not have achieved a suitable landing, I was told in no uncertain terms before going around the circuit and practising another.

It was slightly sad that Bill was on a day off for one particular lesson, and I flew with another instructor. On this particular day, 20th November 1971, we did a few circuits in Cherokee G-AYMJ.

Eventually, the instructor said, "I think you can fly the next circuit by yourself. Are you happy with that?" And off I went. I remember the circuit was slightly up and down, with me climbing to 1200 feet instead of the usual 1000 feet, but I sorted it out and ended up with a very acceptable landing. It was just a shame that it hadn't been with Bill. First solo flight completed. I continued with the course, flying at every opportunity when the weather was good.

We started the navigation part of the course. Bill would choose a triangular route with two turning points. I planned the route and was shown how to map-read. I had to calculate my required headings and ground speeds and could therefore work out at what time I should be passing the next turning point. One of them involved a flight up into the Borders. In those days, we could see giant earth-moving vehicles constructing the Kielder reservoir which now supplies fresh water to places such as Manchester.

I devoured everything that Bill told me and eventually, in March 1972, I went on my solo qualifying, cross-country flight. This was from Carlisle to Teesside then on to Newcastle and back to Carlisle. This was part of the requirement to get my private pilot licence. It was a beautiful day. I had already flown the route with Bill, but this time I was by myself. I climbed up to 3000 feet and set course from above Carlisle to the east, aiming for my first turning point over the Derwent Reservoir. This was just to the south-west of Newcastle. I was told by air traffic control (ATC) at Carlisle to contact Newcastle, and they told me to report over the reservoir. I passed to the south of Haydon Bridge and Hexham checking that I was on my planned track.

I mustn't forget to change over fuel tanks. Keep checking the temperatures and pressures. Did I check the carburettor heat? I'll do it again. Keep the navigation log going. Bill will want to check it. Watch your height. Come on... get a grip! There's always something for me to do.

A small correction halfway along the route was keeping me in the right direction towards the reservoir. Eventually, I saw glinting in the distance which was the water of the reservoir. After reporting my position to Newcastle, I turned south-east and they transferred me to Teesside. I called them with my updated estimate. Bill had warned me that Teesside could be very difficult to see when approaching from the north and had told me to look out for some greenhouses just north of the airfield. He had drilled into me the importance of holding an accurate heading and not wandering off course. Sure enough, the greenhouses appeared on the nose and I could by then see the airfield. As instructed, I called "field in site" and flew over the top of the airfield before positioning to land on the south-westerly runway. I taxied in, shut down the engine and breathed the first sigh of relief. After climbing the stairs to the control tower, I got my paperwork signed, had a quick pee and was on my way to Newcastle. ATC at Newcastle asked me to call "crossing the river" which I duly did and, as I approached the airfield, the air traffic controller asked me if I could carry out a tight circuit, as he had other commercial traffic right behind. Rightly or wrongly, I said I could do that and managed to get around the circuit and land without any problems. I quickly cleared the runway to see the traffic, that ATC had mentioned, had obviously been right up my backside and was crossing the runway threshold. Again, I parked the aeroplane and made my way up to the tower. The air traffic controller complimented me for making my circuit so tight and, therefore, not delaying the aircraft behind. He signed my paperwork again and, after another nervous pee, I got airborne for my last sector back to Carlisle. Mustn't get complacent and cock up now. Bill will have plenty to say if I do. I made my way along Hadrian's Wall towards the west, passed just to the north of Hexham and close enough to Haltwhistle to see life going on in the streets below. Bill had warned me that arriving back at Carlisle at that time in the afternoon would mean the sun would be quite low.

"Pay close attention to finding the airfield when the sun is in your eyes! Don't fuck up at the last stage!" he said. If I did, there would be a bollocking!

Sure enough, there was Carlisle as planned! I joined the circuit downwind and landed back on the easterly runway.

Bill was waiting to meet me.

"Any problems?"

"No, it all went well."

"Yes, I know, I was keeping in touch with your progress," he said with a big grin.

What a great day.

After a couple more flights for a bit of revision, I was pronounced ready for my flight test.

On the 7th April 1972, I took the PPL flying test with one of the examiners at Carlisle. His name was Bob Barclay. He was a lovely chap who was a bomber pilot during the war and ended up as a POW.

He gave me a full brief with the usual comments such as, "If you see me writing anything down then don't worry… it's probably something I have to pick up at the shop on the way home for my wife." I took that comment with a pinch of salt.

I passed with only a few debrief points! I was 18 and this was the first step in my aviation career.

The small amount of concentration I had left at school was not going to improve, sadly, and unfortunately this left me with a slightly deteriorating relationship with my dad.

I had to try and earn sufficient money to keep adding hours in my logbook in order that I could increase my level of flying experience. I had thought of undergoing a flying instructor's course at some point, but it would be a long haul. I needed a hundred and fifty hours in command flying light aircraft before I could start the course.

My Uncle Charlie (Dad's brother) had always been an aviation enthusiast, and he used to send me his old copies of the magazine Flight International. When I used to visit him just before he died, he told me that he took credit for helping to get me into my chosen career. He was absolutely right, and I still think about him regularly with great affection.

I had seen an advert, in one of the magazines that he had sent to me, advertising for applicants to become an air traffic control assistant. I thought this might be worth investigating, as it may well be a stepping stone into what I really wanted to do and it meant I could leave school.

I applied and got an interview. I was told that the post would be at London Heathrow and after three years as an assistant, although I did not have any A levels, I could apply to become an ATC officer as I had a PPL. This seemed a good deal to me, and so I accepted the offer and got my parents to agree that I was to leave school. It was not going to matter particularly if they objected, as I was 18 and could decide my own destiny. There were more arguments at home and, at one point, my dad said he just wanted me to go and get on with things. I think he knew he was not going to win this one, and he gave me the impression he just wanted me to leave home and get on with it. It was a great shame really but, since that time, I became a great believer in letting people try to follow their own destiny. The same thoughts always applied to my own children.

November 1972. Still had hair in those days!

Off I went to London where arrangements had been made to stay, initially, in a hostel in Hounslow which was run for people joining the Air Traffic Control Service.

It was a grubby little hostel at Hounslow, and I was sent to work in the noise monitoring unit which was a small office next to the threshold of R/W 09R (one of the easterly runways). We had to sign the Official Secrets Act and pass a driving test to enable us to drive on the active side of the airport.

The first few days were spent getting to know what was involved in my new position and "shadowing" some of the more experienced students. We were told that one of the first tasks was to undergo the driving test with an examiner which would allow us to drive around the airport. The vehicles were loaded with equipment to go to various points on and around Heathrow and then, basically, to point a microphone on a stick at a departing aeroplane and record its noise levels. The driving test was undertaken in a Morris Minor Traveller, and the examiner was always the worse for wear with alcohol! However, we all took the test, and we all passed. Looking back, I don't think anybody ever failed.

One of my memories of working there was on a particular Sunday morning. The officer in charge of that particular watch was reading the paper, and the ATCA (air traffic control assistant) was giving noise readings to any aircraft which called. "London Noise", in those days, had its own VHF frequency which any aircraft could call up and ask for their decibel reading on departure. A particular flight from some remote part of the world, whose English was poor, had called the noise monitoring unit believing it to be the departure radar unit. As soon as he had become airborne, and he was given a frequency change, he had dialled up the incorrect frequency which just so happened to be "London Noise". When they called the noise unit, the young ATCA thought they were asking for their decibel reading and told them their reading was 105 decibels. The aircraft replied, in broken English, saying "Climb flight level 105", believing they were cleared to climb to 10500 feet. The officer suddenly realised what had happened, put his paper down, and frantically picked up the phone to the radar unit to try and avoid a mid-air collision. And no, it wasn't me!

I had been led to believe, when I joined the Air Traffic Control Services, that, as I had a PPL, after three years I could apply to become an officer. This was the man who actually talked to the aircraft. This, I thought, may be a good alternative to actually flying, as the pay was good and it would be interesting. However, shortly after joining, it all changed and anybody who wanted to apply to become an officer had to have A levels. I did not want to remain as an assistant and, therefore, it was time to move on. It hadn't lasted long and obviously was not meant to be. Plan A it was!

CHAPTER 5

I think the fact that I had been told that I needed to wear glasses had secretly pleased my father, as he now believed a career as a pilot was out of the question. I wrote to the Civil Aviation Authority over the subject of my eyesight. They suggested I should come down to London and undergo a full medical which would give me the answer as to whether or not I was fit enough for a professional flying licence. I was certainly not going to give up, and so I made an appointment and off I went on the due date. The medical was completed, and I was pronounced fit for a class 1 medical certificate!

I had spent a great deal of time writing to airlines all over the country and, indeed, all over the world asking for a sponsorship to a commercial pilot licence (CPL) in order to obtain a flying position with an airline. Many would not take anybody who required correction to their eyesight (glasses) and many required A levels and even a degree. The only way to get to a commercial pilot licence was for me to become a flying instructor, get even more hours in my logbook and pass the written exams for a CPL and the various flight tests. To start a flying instructor's course, I needed a certain number of flying hours and to get those hours I needed to earn more money.

My dad spoke to the manager of the local Clydesdale Bank about a job for me. I wasn't aware of this, and it came out of the blue. However, to keep the peace, I went for an interview and, surprise, surprise, was offered a job. I had to go up to Glasgow for a basic course. I was the lowest of the low, assistant of the assistant. God, it was boring, but I persevered with my dad telling me how wonderful life would be in high finance and having flying as a hobby. He did everything in his power to try and dissuade me from flying professionally.

I hated working at the bank. If it wasn't counting thousands of pounds of coins for the local bus company, it was sitting at a primitive computer called the "batch machine". Every transaction through the bank went through this machine and it had to balance at the end of every day. I eventually was put on this machine. Unfortunately for me, it sat facing a window which, in turn, faced north-west. There I could sit, and my attention was regularly taken by the trails of the aircraft following the major airway above. As I lost my concentration, I made errors with putting figures into the machine and, at the end of the day, it regularly would not balance for me. As you can imagine, this made me unpopular with the rest of the staff who were asked to stay behind and find the errors in the batch! I was forever in trouble with the chief accountant at the branch.

I was eventually sent on a "tellers" course to Glasgow. This enabled me to serve at the counter which, at least, made a change from the other boring jobs that I had to undertake. I also had to undergo various evening classes in accounting, general principles of Scots law and other such tedious subjects. Myself, and a young chap from the Clydesdale Bank in the next town along the coast, were enrolled in these classes. We went to the first couple of lessons, but eventually we ended up going to the pub instead, as neither of us had any intention of making banking our career. This eventually ended with another falling out with my father, but my mind was made up. There was no alternative. Despite the occasional veering off my chosen path, I would keep going. I was going to fly professionally.

The accountant kept asking me how the classes were going, and I kept telling him that I was doing well. I had taken a few weekend jobs to help my finances. I needed to achieve a certain number of flying hours to go on to the next stage of my flying career, so I worked during the week, filled in with part-time bits and pieces and went flying at every opportunity. Bill helped me out by letting me know if any aircraft from Carlisle needed to be taken to various parts of the country. Some had to go down to the main base near Oxford, and some had been sold. If the phone went and I was free, I got another free hour or two in my logbook. A couple of local guys let me fly an old French aircraft which they owned. It was a Rallye Club with a small, 100-horsepower engine and was the French equivalent of a tractor. Used by farmers and landed and taken off on rough fields, it had a short take-off and landing performance (STOL). This particular aircraft was very old, and it concerned me slightly that the oil pressure reduced gradually as the oil got warmer. It usually settled just above the red line. The engine was worn out. There was a badge under the propeller on the cowling saying "Made in Las Vegas from old slot machine parts". The flying was cheap, and it was more hours in the logbook. Every time I had money in my pocket, it was spent on flying.

I went everywhere and anywhere and, slowly but surely, the hours in my logbook grew. I did my night rating and completed my IMC (instrument meteorological conditions) rating which qualified me to fly in cloud should the need arise.

Flying from Carlisle around the Lake District was tremendous. I managed to persuade mates to "chip in" for the fuel, and I was airborne whenever possible. Four of us took off, one day, in a Cherokee from Carlisle. We were all fairly big blokes, and I had filled the aircraft full of fuel. By the time we passed the city of Carlisle (only a few miles from the airfield), we were still below 1000 feet. It was about then that I realised I should have paid more attention to the weight and balance of the aircraft. We were obviously way over maximum take-off weight. However, as the flight progressed, and we burnt more fuel, the aeroplane stopped flying like a semi-detached council house and slowly became livelier. We made our way down the coast to St. Bees Head and then further south, keeping well clear of the nuclear power station at Sellafield. We crossed Morecambe Bay and eventually landed at Blackpool. After a quick cuppa, we then took off for Teesside. I didn't need any more fuel! By this time, the aircraft was flying much better.

As we approached the Teesside airfield, I just couldn't see it, but Terry, in one of the back seats, said, "It's over there, to your right." He has never let me live that down.

Another cuppa and a pee, and we were off again back home; a great day out.

I found a flying club in the south of England, at Thruxton, which was renting light aircraft at quite a cheap price. I did the sums, and it was worth my while driving down there and staying with my godparents in Salisbury whilst trying to "cram in" some flying hours. This was advantageous from a flying point of view, but my godmother was an awful cook and, from that perspective, things were slightly risky. I drove down to Salisbury, having persuaded my mum to part with her car for a few days. My godparents were very kind and very pleased to see me. Tom, my godfather, had been an aircraft engineer during and just after the war, so he was always interesting to chat to. My godmother, Mary, had been a nurse and was, at this time, very religious, so I had to watch my Ps and Qs. The first night, Tom and I were given supper which consisted of some cheap cut of animal. I am not, and never was, a fussy eater, but the pipes hanging out of the lumps of whatever made me baulk slightly.

The next day, I drove up to Thruxton and got checked out on one of their Cessna 150s by one of the young flying instructors. I flew around the local area, trying to orient myself, and then it was back to Salisbury for tea. That evening we were dining on liver. It came in a delicious colour of British racing green if you got the light to reflect on it just at the right angle. It also seemed to have various hydraulic pipes hanging out of it. It was like being at school again! Tom and I managed to get through it without trauma or loss of life.

The following day, I flew up to Blackbushe airfield which was a new destination. Unfortunately, on the way into the airfield, my radio failed. I was given a green light from air traffic control and landed. Having rung Thruxton, they told me to return without a radio. This I duly did but, as they did not have a spare, the aircraft wouldn't be available for a couple of days. It wasn't worth staying in the south, so I drove home and my stomach gave a sigh of relief.

The school at Carlisle had two, 100-horsepower Beagle Pup aircraft. I got checked out on these and enjoyed flying them. They had been bought by the school to teach aerobatics (for which they were drastically underpowered), but they were great fun to fly. I was to go on and instruct on these lovely little aircraft in the future.

During the autumn of 1972, the flying club side of the school at Carlisle decided to run a competition for an award which was to be called "The Pilot of the Year Trophy". This was mainly to encourage people with a private pilot licence to fly with an examiner and undergo all the general handling which was required to obtain one's licence. It was really an opportunity for the flying school to keep an eye on us all and ensure no bad habits were creeping in. Bill Moore encouraged me to have a go at the competition and, lo and behold, after a flight test, it was announced that myself and another club member were to receive the trophy jointly. This resulted in a picture in the local paper.

Joint winner of "Pilot of the Year Trophy December 1972

Eventually, the day came when I had enough hours to go and do an assistant flying instructor's course. This was the first qualification in flying that I could have and get paid for.

The accountant at the bank kept asking me if I had received the results of the exams I had taken. These were from the evening classes. I had gone to Dumfries, with my mate from the other branch, to do these exams but had only filled in my name at the top of the exam paper and then walked out. I had to come clean with the bank and admitted to the accountant that I was resigning from the bank and that I had failed the exams. He wasn't too pleased, but I think he always had a suspicion that banking was not a long-term career for me.

At the time, there were several large, commercial flying schools around the United Kingdom. One of them, the Oxford Air Training School had their main base at Oxford and, because of the demand at the time, opened the smaller base at Carlisle. It ended up as a large and very busy airfield with nationalities from all over the world being trained to become commercial airline pilots. They were all sponsored by their national airline and spent up to eighteen months undergoing training.

I had the great fortune and privilege to mix with some very experienced flying instructors at Carlisle airport. All of them were very encouraging towards me, and they were an extremely interesting bunch with many stories to tell. Bob Barclay, who ran my assistant flying instructors course, was a Scot with a very interesting wartime history. Ernie White was a senior instructor/examiner at Carlisle. He had a club foot which was the result of an accident during the war in a Mosquito. Ernie didn't suffer fools gladly but, again, was an interesting and knowledgeable man to talk to. Eric Harrison did my final check on twin engine aircraft a few years later. He used to fly Sunderlands during the war and had many tales to tell of flying in the Far East. There were many of these characters, and I will always be grateful for the help and encouragement they gave over the years.

And so the flying of light aircraft changed from me sitting in the left seat to now sitting in the right seat. Traditionally, the pilot in command always sits in the left-hand seat but, as I would now be teaching people to fly, there had to be a change around. This took a little bit of getting used to, as it all seemed a little "arse about face". There were hours and hours of technical briefings from Bob, which I then had to give back to him. He was trying to instil in me an acceptable teaching style. Could I pass on the knowledge to other people in the best possible way? He would walk into his office in the morning and would say to me, "Tell me about the forces on a propeller", or "It's raining today... Why?", or "Why does an aeroplane fly?", or "Tell me about Fowler flaps", or "Brief me on forced landings", and so it went on. Bob just loved watching me digging a hole for myself and making matters worse. I made the mistake, one day, of referring to the control column as "the joystick". This brought hoots of laughter from Bob, and I never referred to it by that name again.

The whole course was, eventually, covered over the next few weeks, and Bob put me forward for the test with the chief flying instructor, Dave Davico. (Dave was one of life's gentlemen and was sadly killed, a few years later, in a wake turbulence episode. A large military aircraft had taken off from Carlisle, and Dave followed very soon afterwards. The turbulence, which was caused by the larger aircraft, caused Dave's aeroplane to invert quickly after take-off and very close to the runway. He didn't have the conditions to recover in the time available and that was it.)

The Oxford Air Training School had taken delivery of two new Japanese aircraft for aerobatic training, the Fuji FA-200, and Dave decided we would do the test in that. I had delivered one of these aircraft from Oxford to Carlisle, so this was only the second time I had been in it. However, all went well and after an hour and twenty minutes in the air, I passed the flying part successfully. Back to the classroom and a further grilling for an hour or so on the technical stuff, and I had passed the first milestone in my new career.

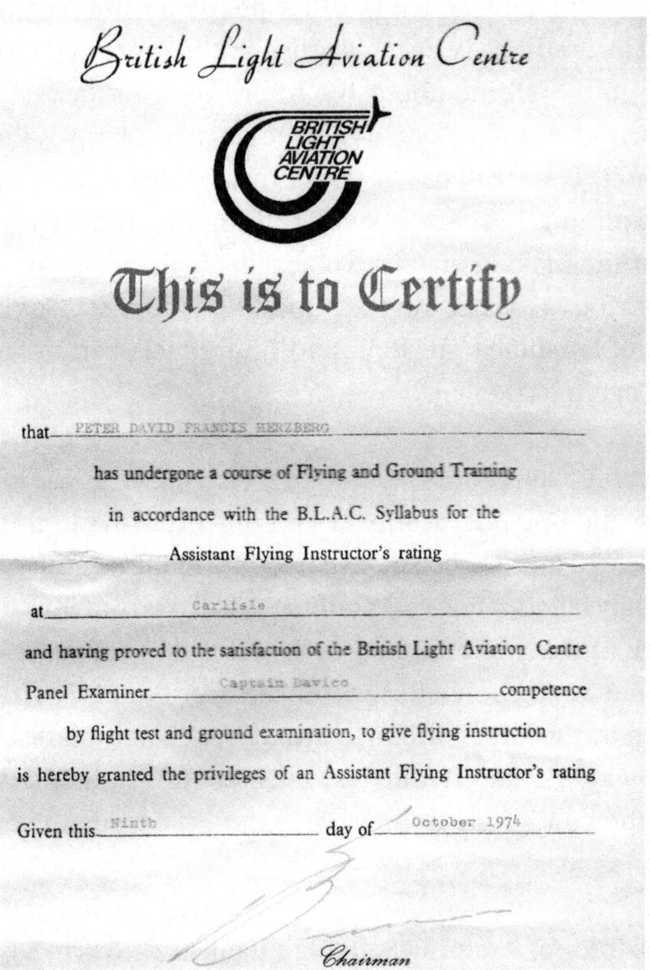

British Light Aviation Centre

This is to Certify

that PETER DAVID FRANCIS HERZBERG

has undergone a course of Flying and Ground Training

in accordance with the B.L.A.C. Syllabus for the

Assistant Flying Instructor's rating

at Carlisle

and having proved to the satisfaction of the British Light Aviation Centre

Panel Examiner Captain Davies competence

by flight test and ground examination, to give flying instruction

is hereby granted the privileges of an Assistant Flying Instructor's rating

Given this Ninth day of October 1974

Chairman

CHAPTER 6

I started to hunt for a position as an assistant flying instructor. The best place to look was usually the situations vacant columns in the back of Flight International magazine. A week or two after passing the instructors course, Bill rang me.

"We've just sold one of our Beagle Pup aircraft to a guy at a flying school in Kent," he said. "He's looking for an assistant flying instructor. Get your arse up here tomorrow, as he's coming to pick up the aircraft, and he would like to have a chat with you."

I quickly packed a bag, and the following day went up to Carlisle to meet the chief flying instructor of the Rye and Romney flying school. It was agreed that we would fly down to Lydd together, have a chat, and I could look at the school, and we would then see how things went. We flew the Pup down via East Midlands, where we stopped for fuel, and then on to Lydd. It was the 5th November 1974, and that evening I went with the chief flying instructor to a local bonfire and then a meal at his home. The next day, he had decided that he liked me enough. I got on well with him, and so I had my first flying job in aviation. I went home on the train to get the rest of my stuff together, and a week later I started my new job. I had found "digs" in Rye and had driven my old, but trusty, Mini Clubman down to Kent to act as my everyday transport. My agreed pay was £14 per week, and out of that I was paying £8 per week for accommodation.

We had three Beagle Pups at the school, and the building we were based in was on the western side of the main terminal of Lydd airfield or Ferryfield as it was called then. The clubhouse was an old wooden shack. Lydd was still quite a busy little airfield in those days. It used to be extremely busy with services operated by a company called Silver City. They had Bristol Superfreighters on which we used to travel when I was a child. I still have 8 mm cinefilm of our car being loaded into one of these aircraft when we were going on holiday. When I arrived, Lydd had a freight company called Skyways based there flying old DC-3s which were regularly flying in and out to various freelance destinations. Dan-Air had the odd flight to Paris Beauvais and there were two flying schools. Geographically, it was a nice part of the world but very flat.

Romney Marsh has a history of smuggling, and it was very easy to get lost on the small roads in the middle of the marsh particularly on foggy nights. We used to go to a pub in the middle of the marsh called the "Woolpack". A great pub but, occasionally, either difficult to find or more difficult to find the way home!

As an assistant instructor, life was busy for me. The school was popular and had a large number of members; people from various walks of life who wanted to enjoy the world of light aircraft flying. This meant people of various ages and also some of questionable ability. Some people needed more time to grasp the different challenges of flying a light aircraft and some people took to it like a duck to water. When the weather was bad, particularly during the winter, the days were long, as I was the only full-time instructor and the "boss" stayed at home, as he lived close to the airfield but I had to be there to answer the phone. I would spend all day in the shack, trying to keep warm, before returning back to my digs in Rye at night. Half an hour for lunch would be spent in the terminal eating a dry sandwich or scrounging a cup of tea from the rival flying school. We may have been in competition but the camaraderie was still there. They had two very pleasant instructors who worked for them, Nick and Colin, and they were always good company. Occasionally, we would adjourn to the local pub in the evenings before going "home". My accommodation was fairly soulless, and I had to watch the pennies. Apart from putting petrol in my car, I had to find the money for fags, beer and food; had to get the priorities right. The food usually came last on the list, and I remember the best meal of the week being fried rice from the local takeaway – just fried rice. Occasionally, when I had a few extra pennies in my pocket, I would go to the Woolpack and have a pint of Guinness and a plate of sausages and mash. That happened about once a month due to the lack of finances. I tried to remain healthy and always had a big lump of cheese and a bag of apples on the back seat of the car. This habit stayed with me for years and, when I first met my wife, she remembered that even then I had apples and cheese in the back of the car.

The days with better weather brought out all the enthusiasts, and I would spend up to five hours per day in the air. We had to be careful flying out of Lydd, as there was busy London airspace all around and above the airfield. Lydd itself was in its own "zone", and to exit the zone we had to fly towards Rye not above 1500 feet. Once past Rye, we were free to climb, but no higher than 3000 feet, as that was the base of controlled airspace around the London area which we had to keep clear of. This presented problems in itself as some of the exercises we taught required a good amount of height. At that time, a company called British Air Ferries existed based in Southend. One part of their operation consisted of an aircraft called a "Carvair" which was a four engine, converted, Douglas car transporter. There is a very good shot of several Carvairs in the James Bond film Goldfinger where both Auric Goldfinger and Bond are travelling to Geneva from Southend. British Air Ferries had a regular service between Southend and Le Touquet. These large, lumbering aircraft usually flew via the beacon at Rye and, as we passed that beacon at no higher than 1500 feet, it could be quite normal to see them lumbering past at the same time and not far above us. One of their Carvair crews was an all-female crew; captain, first officer and flight engineer. It was very rare in those days.

A picture taken from another club aircraft for the article in the local paper. The reporter was in the aircraft with me.

Most of the handling exercises we taught were either along the south coast, in the area north of Hastings and Bexhill, or around the Tenterden area. Should we ever see another club aircraft with an instructor on board, we would dive down towards that aircraft and, as we passed at high speed, make the required "dagga, dagga, dagga" machine-gun noise - all great fun. The chief instructor used to enjoy catching us out, but when I did it to him one day he lost his sense of humour!

Navigation training and qualifying cross-country flights, which had to be completed successfully for students to obtain their private pilot licence, were usually conducted along the south coast. The student was required to land away at two different airfields. We used various airfields along the south coast: Shoreham, Goodwood and Southampton being the main ones but also Headcorn, Southend and Rochester to the north. It was always interesting teaching navigation but, for the weaker candidates, it was better to use an airfield with the coastline to one side; less chance of getting lost! Shoreham had a busy light aeroplane scene, and Goodwood was always interesting to visit because of its history. The important thing was to not upset air traffic control by drifting into the wrong airspace.

TWELVE

Free as a bird above Romney Marsh

IT helps to know what does what when a plane is flying. Peter Herzberg uses a model to instruct

Local paper did an article about learning to fly.

The club had various part-time instructors who usually appeared over the weekends which were our busiest time. Jerry was a professional airline pilot who flew a four-engine, turboprop aircraft called a Merchantman. It was a freight version of the Vickers Vanguard which was used by British European Airways (BEA) who eventually merged with British Overseas Airways Corporation (BOAC) to become what we now know as British Airways. The Merchantman was quite a fast, modern machine in those days, and Jerry was always an interesting source of information and full of good "war stories". There was also a female instructor, called Ellie, who instructed at one of the London clubs during the week and came down to Lydd, where her family lived, at the weekends. Various other souls appeared as and when they could spare the time. There were enough students to go round.

On Saturday nights, we regularly went along the south coast to Hythe for a curry. The CFI, who was a car enthusiast, owned a couple of E-Type Jaguars. One of these was a convertible. I used to beg a ride in one of these beautiful cars with him, and all of us would set off in what could only be described as a race at breakneck speed along the road to Hythe. It was even more breakneck on the way home. One of the part-time instructors, Joe, had a permanent challenge with the chefs in the restaurant to make him a curry which was too hot to eat. They never beat him, and I remember him sitting there one night with his shirt off and the sweat rolling down him. Nobody ever wanted to sit too close to Joe.

We had some really funny characters who were members of the school. One of these people was a watch repairman from Ashford called Norman. He was a middle-aged, single guy who had his own shop. He slept under his own workbench. He always appeared at the airfield in a suit and tie and went flying dressed like that. He loved the girls, and one of the ground stewardesses at the airfield caught his attention. He managed to chat her up and went out with her a few times. She dumped Norman fairly quickly. We had professional people who were quite wealthy. One of these people was an Italian by birth called Aldo. He was an older chap and a delightful gentleman. He wasn't the quickest person to grasp the essentials of flying, but he got there eventually. I liked him very much and will always be grateful to him and his wife, as they used to invite me round regularly for a meal; good, home-made Italian cooking!

Howard was an older chap, an accountant by trade, and always liked to remind us that he did the accounts for one of the well-known, First Division footballers who played for Newcastle United. Roger was another businessman who lived in Hastings and there was also Tony, who was another character. He ran a business in Hastings in which he employed freelance photographers. He also had several small monkeys. The photographers would patrol the seafront and, when they came across holidaymakers, they would offer to take their photographs whilst they held the monkeys. It was obviously a lucrative business, as Tony and his wife appeared to do well, and he drove the most beautiful V12 E-Type. Tony went on to become a professional airline pilot.

Aldo, Roger, Howard and Tony decided to buy their own aircraft. They bought a Cherokee 140 from the Oxford Air Training School. I knew this aircraft well, as it had been based at Carlisle, and the maintenance there was first class, so I knew it would be in excellent condition. I flew with the new owners of this aircraft to familiarise them with the differences between the Beagle Pups, which they had flown to achieve their licences, and this aeroplane. Once they were checked out, they all decided to try their hand at flying into France. In those days, there used to be a low-level corridor across the Channel for light aircraft. It started somewhere near Folkestone and was a direct line across the Channel to Cap Gris-Nez. I can't remember the exact details, but it was something like southbound at 500 feet and northbound at 1500 feet. There was a little bit of paperwork involved for the crossing. Some of this was for customs and some of it was for air traffic control, so they knew exactly where you were and at what time you were expected to be at various points. This was in case you had problems and were forced to ditch, so they could raise the alarm quickly. Having arrived at the French coast at the compulsory point, you were then talking to French ATC and could continue towards usually Le Touquet or Calais to clear French customs. It was a great day out, and I was fortunate because I usually got my lunch bought for me. Once all the guys had been checked out on this procedure, they were free to fly the cross-Channel route without an instructor.

I do remember checking another club member out on the low-level corridor in a club aircraft. The bit across the water was only slightly over 20 miles. This particular day, the weather was not very good and visibility considerably reduced. The student had calculated all his headings to allow for the wind and the drift, and we set off from the UK coast. We couldn't see the French coast but, within a few minutes, looking at the white caps on the water, I had convinced myself that the wind blowing from south-west to north-east was way more than forecast. I told the student to turn another 15 degrees into the wind, as I was convinced we were drifting too far to the left. Of course, when we called the French, we were heading to intercept the French coast too far to the south-west of Cap Gris-Nez. It was a case of me being an idiot and not sticking to the calculations until they were proven to be wrong. There was a quick bollocking from the French! Don't do what I do...

The syllabus for a private pilot licence in those days included training for stalling and spinning. These are potentially "killers", and the students had to be taught how to recognise the causes, characteristics and recovery of both. Stalling was reasonably straightforward to teach, but spinning was a more advanced stage which could not only frighten students but kill them if the recovery was not flown correctly. They were not allowed to practise spinning solo, only with an instructor. A spin is classified as a stall resulting in autorotation of the aircraft about its vertical axis whilst taking a shallow, rotating, downward path. We won't get bogged down in aerodynamics in this book, suffice to say they are dangerous and can kill you. One particular student loved spinning. (Most hated it and were glad when they had demonstrated that they could recognise an incipient spin and recover from it.) The Pup is an aerobatic aircraft, and we could attach heavy weights to the ventral fin (under the tail) which affected the centre of gravity. For spinning, we had to be careful regarding the centre of gravity and the total weight of the aircraft. This particular day, the student turned up and asked me if we could do some spinning. He was a big chap. Although I was losing weight as an instructor, due to my low pay, I was still 6 foot 3 inches and not exactly small! I was far too blasé about the whole episode, as the aeroplane was also full of fuel, which was yet another reason for caution that I ignored. The last "hole in the cheese" to line up was the fact that we could not climb above 3000 feet in the local area to carry out the exercises because of the controlled airspace around London. Stalling and spinning should normally be carried out with enough height to recover by 3000 feet, not starting at 3000 feet. Spinning in the Pup consisted of closing the throttle, holding your height, by bringing the stick back slowly until it is all the way back, and as the wing stalls applying full rudder one way or the other to induce yaw. The Pup needed no encouragement to spin. The recovery, however, was a disciplined action. The rudder had to be applied fully in the opposite direction of the spin and, when the rotation had stopped, the stick slowly moved forward to pitch the nose down and decrease the angle of attack. As the airflow over the wing recovers and the speed starts to increase, then one is back into the recovery. This particular day, we started the spin at 3000 feet. The aircraft whizzed over keenly into the spin and after a couple of turns I said "recover". Suffice to say, the recovery technique was correct but nothing happened. I took control and tried everything I knew to recover. Eventually, by going through the correct technique for a longer period of time, the aircraft started to respond. When we came out of the spin, we were only 400 feet above the ground. I have never forgotten that day and learnt a valuable lesson.

After a few months of instructing, I had accumulated the necessary hours and experience to upgrade my instructor's rating from an assistance instructor to a full instructor. I had gone back to Carlisle and added a qualification to enable me to teach people to fly on instruments in poor visibility or cloud. I had also added the necessary qualification to enable me to teach people to fly at night. The full instructor rating would enable me to instruct as normal and also remove a restriction. This would allow me to send people on their first solo flight and also on a solo, qualifying cross-country flight.

To do this, I needed to arrange a flight and ground test with an approved examiner. The British Light Aviation Centre looked after all the administration for flying instructors on behalf of the Civil Aviation Authority, and I rang them up and booked an upgrade test with a gentleman called Peter Harrison, one of the approved guys. I asked the four owners of the Cherokee if I could borrow it, as I felt I would be more "at home" in that aircraft, having done my instructor course in the same type. This they agreed to without any problem. I was due to meet Peter at West Malling airfield, about twenty-five minutes flying up the road, just on the outskirts of Maidstone. West Malling was a famous airfield during the war and was home to many different types of aircraft. Unfortunately, it was dug up and turned into a housing estate quite some years ago. It was quite a hazy day and off I set. I landed at West Malling, parked the aircraft and found the office where Peter worked.

We introduced ourselves and, without further ado, Peter said, "Come and have a look at my office."

His "office" was an old Varsity. This was an old, twin-engine, piston aircraft which had come from the RAF. Peter did a lot of work for Sperry, the electronics company, and the aircraft was bristling with electronic equipment. I can't remember what it was for, or even if he told me what it was for, but it looked highly technical. Having had a good crawl around his aeroplane, we adjourned to his real office and got on with matters.

"What do you know about the medical side of the workings of the inner ear?"

Bugger all I thought.

"To be honest, it's not a subject I have put much study in to," I said.

"Ah well, it's not important. I just wondered if you would have had a look at something like this, as it's coming on to the instructor syllabus and anything medical which may affect performance whilst flying is of interest."

Fortunately, he changed the subject and asked me a few things that I did know about.

He then asked me to brief him about forced landings. In single engine aircraft, it is part of the syllabus to be able to deal with matters should the engine fail. Part of teaching is to brief a student, then "patter" or demonstrate a forced landing and then start to let the student practise one. This we duly did, and I was also asked to either "patter" various other exercises or just go through some general aircraft handling with him.

I was given quite a tough time, but eventually Peter said, "That's it, we're finished. You've passed."

All the paperwork was completed, and off I went back to Lydd a happy man.

The chief flying instructor said, "I suppose you want a pay rise?"

"Yes, that would be nice."

And so a small pay rise was agreed which would lift me off the poverty line.

The owners of the aircraft which I had borrowed were all very decent, and they wouldn't accept any money for the use of their aeroplane. Such was the camaraderie in small flying schools in those days. Everywhere that one flew to usually had a thriving community of private pilots who would make all newcomers welcome. Things seem to me to have changed these days. Private flying is a very expensive pastime and flying clubs do not seem to be as full as they were.

British Light Aviation Centre

B.L.A.C.

This is to Certify

that Peter David HERZBERG

has been examined for upgrading

from Assistant Flying Instructor to that of Full Flying Instructor

by Mr. P.Harrison

and having proved to the satisfaction of the British Light Aviation Centre

Panel Examiner his competence

by flight test and ground examination, to give flying instruction

is hereby upgraded and granted the privileges of a Full Flying Instructor rating

Given this Twenty-second day of May 1975

Chairman

Flying Instructor, Examining Panel

CHAPTER 7

As the weather slowly improved with summer approaching, we became really busy. I was now in a position to make more use of my full instructor qualification and particularly enjoyed sending people off on their first solo flight. This usually consisted of flying circuit after circuit until one felt that the student was proficient enough to be able to do it themselves. Engine failures just after take-off were practised time and time again until they were second nature. One of the first people who I sent off on his first solo was Terry. He had made a career in Africa in the copper mining business. He and his wife Sheila were regularly at the flying school. Unfortunately, Terry had lost a leg in a mining accident and had a prosthetic leg fitted. He managed to get a medical from the Civil Aviation Authority, and it was a great achievement for him to go on and get his private pilot licence. I was delighted to be the one to send him off on his first solo.

Claude was a club member. He was a builder and had lost an eye in an accident. He used to bring us fresh prawns bought from the fishermen at the coast. He owned his own aircraft and nearly came to a nasty end one summer's morning. He was doing a "walk around" on his own aeroplane and happened to turn the propeller over to check there were no obvious problems with the engine. Although this was not a requirement, a lot of people felt it was good airmanship. Unfortunately, there was a fault in the ignition system of the aircraft, and the engine fired despite the magnetos being switched off. Nobody was injured, but Claude was severely shocked.

Several of the aircraft at the school were owned by a gentleman by the name of Ronald Kellett. He was a well-known Hurricane pilot during the war and achieved the rank of wing commander. Wing Commander Kellett led one of the Polish Hurricane squadrons (303), and I was privileged to meet this gentleman during my time at Lydd. The wing commander had a small airstrip next to his home near Benenden. At the end of this airstrip was a small hangar where his son, Jonathon, and another engineer performed all the maintenance that was required on the Pups. The strip was short and on a distinct slope. We had to land uphill and take off downhill. We would fly whichever aircraft was needed for maintenance up to Benenden and then "buzz" the airstrip. At this point, Jonathon would usually come out and clear all the sheep so that we could land. It was quite tight, as there were trees at one end, so there was a low-level turn to line up at the last minute and a turn as soon as we were airborne when we were departing.

Another wonderful character who appeared at Lydd, one sunny day, was Wing Commander Ken Wallis. He not only had a distinguished wartime service record but was also a leading exponent of autogyros. He owned and flew the autogyro Little Nellie in the 1967 James Bond film You Only Live Twice. He was a fascinating man to talk to and had time to chat with everyone who showed an interest in his flying machine.

Although life was fun at Lydd, I was permanently short of money, and the next major step in my flying career had to be obtaining a commercial pilot licence (CPL). There was no other way to get a proper position in commercial flying without this licence. One of the requirements was to have over seven hundred and fifty flying hours in my logbook, and this was broken down into various categories such as navigation, night flying, flying as pilot in command and so on. I was conscious of these hours and my logbook was starting to slowly fill up.

I was, however, short of night navigation hours. A friend of mine, Neville, had an American licence and was flying a high-powered Robin aircraft around with its owner. He was also aiming to get a British commercial licence. He got the use of this aircraft for a few hours one night and said we could split the flying. The owner said we could have the aircraft for the cost of the fuel. We decided, on this particularly clear night, to fly up to Birmingham and fly a few approaches and go-rounds. The aircraft was fully equipped with all the latest navigational stuff and most of it we didn't know how to use. As we approached Birmingham, we were told to report "fully established on the ILS" (instrument landing system) for the north-westerly runway.

Neither of us had the correct qualification to fly an ILS and when we called "established" we were told, "Don't be ridiculous; no you're not."

So we went back to Lydd before anybody got really upset with us. It was another example of pushing the boundaries but not sure if we're doing it right.

Three of the owners of the Cherokee asked me to go with them on a long, cross-country flight. We decided that Lydd to Leeds Bradford to Carlisle and return to Lydd would be a good route. It gave them the opportunity to do a leg each and would be a good opportunity for me to say hello to Bill and catch up with other acquaintances at Carlisle. It was a great day and helped me by pushing up the hours in order that I could submit my logbook for inspection to the Civil Aviation Authority. If they were happy, I was in a position to continue towards my aim of getting a commercial licence. Shortly after this flight, I appeared to have all the hours required, and I submitted my logbooks to the CAA for confirmation.

Towards the end of that summer, things were starting to cause concern at the flying school. At times, the airport would only allow us fuel if we paid cash. It also appeared that the wing commander was reluctant to let aircraft go back to Lydd after maintenance. We kept getting other aircraft appearing at the school for short periods at a time, but they never seemed to stay for too long. The writing was on the wall.

After a few weeks, my logbooks were returned by the CAA with a letter stating all was in order and laying out the requirements to achieve a commercial licence. This involved passing all required written exams and four flight tests with a Civil Aviation Authority examiner.

I needed to organise a course to take the exams and pass various subjects to obtain the CPL and, to do this, I decided to go on an eight-week course at Oxford. This was the main base of the Oxford Air Training School (with the smaller base being at Carlisle where I had started my private licence). They had an excellent reputation for their pass rate. Although I was still instructing at Lydd, I needed to think ahead. This course was particularly for the likes of me and also for pilots coming out of the military who wanted to obtain a civilian licence. I booked a course for the coming winter.

One particular day, the airport authorities at Lydd told us we could not have any more fuel.

I rang the chief instructor who said, "Take all the cash out of the till and take the aircraft up to Headcorn. Ask Chris [who ran the airfield at Headcorn] to let you have a fill and give him what cash you have."

The chief instructor was spending a lot of time at home by now. It very much seemed as if he had resigned himself to the inevitable. I flew up to Headcorn and was politely told by Chris to "bugger off".

He said, "You can pay for the amount that you have money for [which was just over £4!], but I'm not giving credit."

We pushed the aircraft up to the pump and carefully put the amount that we had the money for in the tanks.

The school staggered on, but the weather was starting to get worse as we approached the end of the year. As I had a few days off, I decided to go home and see my parents. I hadn't been home for nearly twelve months, and they were shocked when they saw me. I had lost over two stone in weight due to my poor diet.

I went up to Carlisle and did a twin rating. My parents paid for it, and it meant I was qualified on twin-engine aircraft which would hold me in good stead for the future. It was about five hours' flying. I did this with an instructor called Mike Firth. He was a young chap from the Isle of Man who was following a similar path as myself but had already achieved his commercial pilot licence. We flew together and spent the few hours required on a Piper Twin Comanche aircraft mainly flying around on one engine which I had to master before taking the test. (Mike was sadly to lose his life several years later in the Dan-Air crash at Tenerife.) I did the test with Ernie White. As usual, Ernie was no nonsense, but as always I came away from the test with more knowledge than I started, and I was signed up for a twin rating.

I was booked in for my eight-week course at Oxford, and I went back to Lydd just before it started to do one or two hours instructing on the club aircraft. Sadly, due to the financial state of the club, there was only one aircraft left for us to use at this time. I had moved digs, as I had been offered a room on the seafront by one of the club members. The general atmosphere was fairly sombre by now, and members were starting to desert us. It was a good time to be starting a course which would hopefully lead to better flying qualifications.

CHAPTER 8

I started my course at Oxford just after the first week of December. I remember driving from Lydd to Cowley (near Oxford) in the thickest freezing fog I had ever come across. The M25 did not exist in those days, and I had to drive north up the A20, straight through the centre of London, and then up the M40 to Oxford itself. I had been recommended digs in Cowley, as they were cheap but warm. They were in the building which used to house British Leyland apprentices. It took me hours to drive up there, as I was literally driving at a walking pace at times. The windscreen kept freezing up, as the wipers smeared the water particles and they immediately froze. Eventually, after many wrong turnings in the foul weather and many stops to ask the way (no GPS in those days), I found the place. The room was reasonable, but it was noisy. I had to be able to study and pass these exams. I made my way to Kidlington the next morning and reported for the course. Once everybody had introduced themselves and we chatted, it was nice to find I was with a great bunch of guys. They included a couple of instructors like myself, a few military pilots trying to get the civilian licence and an American chap who was a helicopter pilot. There was also a Frenchman who had been flying dubious cargo in Africa.

One of the ex-instructors, Sant, was living in an old caravan for the duration of the course which he was to regret come the following month, as the temperatures plummeted. We were issued the necessary books and the eight weeks of lectures and study began.

It was a really tough few weeks, as the self-study requirement was unbelievable. Most of us spent several hours remaining in the classrooms after the lecturers had gone home. After that, it was a question of grabbing a bite to eat and then back to the digs for more self-study until the early hours. Next day was the same again. Every subject consisted of vast amounts of knowledge that had to be digested in order to spit it out again, word-perfect, for the exams. The lecturers insisted that it had to be word-perfect and seemed rather unmoveable about it all, but they were right. We had to learn Morse code and be able to receive it at a specific rate.

I fell foul of the law at this time. I had stopped at a service station, in the Oxford area, to buy myself a sandwich. Unfortunately, as I was in the main building, a random traffic police car was inspecting cars in the car park, and I eventually received a summons for having no car tax and a bald tyre. My fault entirely, so I had to plead guilty by letter to the local magistrates and was issued a fine of £25 for each offence. Under mitigating circumstances, I mentioned the fact that I was totally skint and trying to improve myself. This fell on deaf ears.

I had arranged to go back to the digs I had in Lydd for Christmas. This was a golden opportunity to study, and had I gone back to the north of England for Christmas the study time would, no doubt, have been spent with old friends in the pub.

I did not enjoy Christmas by myself. I had enough cash to buy myself a modest steak and a few potatoes for Christmas lunch. I cooked my feast and ate it by myself, it was all quite depressing. However, it was worth doing, as I did get a tremendous amount of revision done.

Once the second half of the course got started in January, I managed to get the flu. I had to continue to drag myself into the classroom, and there were comments from the others and the lecturers about not being there. This was partly because I appeared so ill and partly because they didn't want to catch it. There was a pub nearby with an open fire, and one evening, after some more study, I dragged myself over there and sat next to the warm fire. I must have looked dreadful, because the landlady took pity on me sitting there with a small drink.

She said, "You're not well are you? I've got just the thing for you." She disappeared into the kitchen and came back with a steaming bowl of chilli. "Get that down you... Kill or cure!" She wouldn't take a penny from me. There are still some good people in the world.

Eventually, we drifted into early February and the week of the exams arrived. Frantic study continued, and in the end all exams were finished.

By now, the school at Lydd had ceased trading. There was no alternative but to keep going and try and get a commercial pilot licence. I went back to Carlisle, and arrangements were made to undergo the four flight tests with a Civil Aviation Authority flight examiner. This was duly booked for March. I did a few revision flights with Bob Barclay who lent on me to achieve a good standard. The first test to be done was the night flying work. This had to be done in a twin engine aircraft, as the CAA examiners would not fly at night in an aircraft with one engine. We met the examiner at Prestwick, who was a very pleasant chap called Charles Walden. He immediately put me at ease, and we flew the necessary night exercises without any problems. I had been lucky, as there were several foreign students from Carlisle who'd had to fly with the examiner that evening. I had managed to relocate up to Prestwick, as a passenger in the back of the aircraft, and was able to fly back to Carlisle as a passenger which saved an awful lot of money.

The next day, I was due to fly with Captain Walden again in order to undergo General Flight Tests 1-3. This consisted of a navigation exercise, general handling and some instrument flying. I was given a route to plan which was from Carlisle down to a point on the western edge of the Lake District, across the Solway Firth towards the Scottish Lowlands and then east to Lochmaben. I remember that turning point well. The weather that day was not good; blustery winds and heavy showers. I had been told to plan the route but, in all honesty, I was concerned that should I get into the aircraft I may have been failed immediately, as the weather was borderline as to whether we should have even got airborne. I decided to come clean.

"Have you finished your planning?"

"Yes."

"Any problems?"

"Are you asking me to go ahead today on the basis of the

present weather being good enough for general handling, or are you asking me whether the conditions are good enough to complete the route as a commercial flight?"

"I'm asking you to fly the route on the basis of a commercial charter."

"In that case, the planning is complete, and I'm ready to go."

And off we went.

I made sure that everything I was doing was absolutely by the book. What worried me was that should we get into cloud then I would have to climb to a safe altitude in order not to hit any obstacles or high ground. This, in turn, would end up with us flying back to Carlisle at a safe altitude and then carrying out a procedure to descend safely and get back in sight of the ground. It was all perfectly doable, but any complications could just give an examiner more opportunity to fail a candidate, as there are more procedures, all of which are then judged.

We tracked south-west from Carlisle towards Cockermouth. It was turbulent, and the heavy rain showers kept blowing across my path. I had to keep changing course to keep clear of the worst of the weather. There was a large mast near Caldbeck which I was very conscious of, as it was over 1000 feet above ground level. I was lucky in that I knew the area reasonably well having done a lot of flying out of Carlisle. The mountains of the Lake District were off to our left, which was a good reason not to end up off track and drifting towards them. Eventually, Cockermouth appeared where it should have been, and we turned right towards the next turning point which was Castle

Douglas. Most of this leg was across the Solway Firth, and the visibility in the vicinity of the showers meant that all the flying had to be done with particular emphasis on the calculated heading which allowed for the wind. I couldn't see the south coast of Scotland when we left the Cumbrian coast. There was nothing to do but be disciplined. Eventually, the coast of Dumfriesshire came into sight. A quick look at the map showed the two estuaries off to my left along with the lighthouse just off the shore. All appeared good, and Castle Douglas should have be about 10 miles ahead.

At this point, the examiner turned towards me and said, "I want you to carry out a diversion from here direct to Lochmaben."

A quick look at the map, and a few mental calculations, and we turned right direct to Lochmaben. I could see that the track would take us over Criffel, a rather large hill to the south-west of Dumfries. Fortunately, the weather was a little clearer towards Criffel, and there shouldn't be any problems with being near high ground and straying in to cloud for the next few miles.

The first two of the navigation legs went well, but then came the leg towards Lochmaben. Lochmaben sits to the north-west of Lockerbie and is in the foothills of South West Scotland. We skirted the southern edge of Dumfries which showed that I was, more or less, on track. As we bounced along in the turbulence, the weather deteriorated, and I had to descend to stay in sight of the ground. I also had to deviate to the south of my track because of the rising ground. Just as I was thinking about climbing up to safe altitude, the River Annan appeared and there sat Lochmaben off to my left.

“There it is,” I said as coolly as I could.

“OK, take me back to Carlisle.”

On the way back to Carlisle, he put up blinds across the windscreen and asked me to carry out a few exercises just using the aircraft instruments, without being able to look outside. We then found a relatively clear patch and did some aircraft handling before returning to the circuit at Carlisle.

A few more different types of approach and eventually he said, “OK, you can land now. We’re finished.”

Two hours had passed, and I was knackered.

But what would be said about the navigation?

“OK, Peter, you’ve passed. I’ve only one comment to make. Next time you’re navigating in that sort of weather use a 1/4 mill chart instead of 1/2 mill chart. It has much more detail on it and, although you found all the turning points, I didn’t have a clue as to where we were!”

So, I had achieved my commercial pilot licence. This was not a good time in aviation. Clarksons Holidays had gone bust the previous year, and the associated airline, Court Line, had dumped about 400 highly experienced pilots on the market. There was I, very little experience in the commercial world and without an instrument rating. An instrument rating gives the pilot the necessary qualification to fly the “motorways of the air”, i.e. airways, and fly proficiently all the necessary instrument approaches in virtually all weathers.

I had a friend who was flying regularly in the aerial photography business. There was no instrument rating required for this work, as it was all low level and required good weather. There was initially some hope of a job here but, in the end, nothing came to fruition.

I persuaded my parents to give me the money for an instrument rating now that I had got this far. This was duly booked at Carlisle. There was an aid to instrument training called a "Link Trainer" at Carlisle. This was basically a box in which there was a cockpit with all the instruments that one would normally find in an aeroplane. A pilot could sit in it and fly it like an aeroplane but without any visual reference. When the flying exercise was complete, it gave a printout of your performance. It was basic but, in those days, a good training aid. Tony Cosimini ran this department. He had been a commercial pilot but had unfortunately lost his medical. As his name suggested, Tony was of Italian extraction and a very talented and patient instructor. I had been very fortunate in that Bill Moore had taken me up to Tony's training department whenever the weather was bad during my time at Carlisle over the last year. I had "unofficially" been given time in the Link Trainer by Tony already. I therefore had a little bit of a head start, but now came the time to start instrument rating training for real. I spent quite a few hours, under Tony's eye, flying the various procedures to get up to the required standard. I then went on to the flying training which had to be done in a twin-engine aircraft and, as I had already done a twin rating, this was, again, a great help.

I started the instrument rating course with one of the Carlisle instructors by the name of "Red" Skelton. Red was an ex-Fleet Air Arm pilot who had flown Fairey Gannets. He had the reputation of being not only a fine pilot but also a highly intelligent guy.

Red and I flew to all the larger airfields in the north of England and Scotland and "pounded" their instrument procedures. It was highly enjoyable but hard work, and Red kept up the pressure to ensure I had achieved a good standard for the instrument rating test. The day came, and I flew up to Edinburgh with Ernie White to meet the examiner. He was, again, a Civil Aviation Authority examiner by the name of Bernie Mitchell. We had a cuppa in the terminal at Edinburgh while he briefed me. The route was to be from Edinburgh, where we would fly the majority of the procedures, and then a quick hop over to Glasgow, where he would carry out a test on one of the Iraqi students who was with us, before catching his flight back to London.

Off we went from Edinburgh, where I flew the various bits and pieces, and then landed at Glasgow after nearly two hours. On the debrief, he pointed out that when I'd carried out a non-precision approach (as the name implies, using an aid which is not quite as accurate as some) I had correctly extended the holding pattern outbound from the beacon before turning back towards the airfield, but I had made a mental calculation for a headwind instead of a tailwind. I had allowed for the timing, which was about 10 seconds, and made the correction the wrong way. He therefore allowed me a partial pass which meant carrying out another test on this part of the instrument rating on another day. I was a bit deflated but, all in all, Ernie, who was sitting in the back watching, said it was generally well flown and I was a "fucking idiot" to make that basic mistake. Enough said.

Three weeks later, I flew back to Edinburgh with Sig Evans, another of the senior instructors at Carlisle. Sig was another ex-military man who spent hours telling stories of when he flew the Berlin Airlift in Hastings aircraft. He used to tell us that one of his main cargoes was coal and, having flown backwards and forwards into Berlin with the aircraft full of coal, he looked very much like a miner at the end of the day. I flew the required retake part of the test with Hector Skinner; another CAA examiner and an absolute gentleman. This time I made sure I had got the timing correct and was awarded the pass I needed to achieve my instrument rating.

CHAPTER 9

I now had my commercial pilot licence with instrument rating but no job. It was a lean time for pilots, especially those like me who had no commercial experience. I spent time ringing and writing to dozens of airlines around the world without any luck. Eventually, one particular day when I was at Carlisle, the group chief instructor came up to me and asked whether I had found a job.

"No, nothing yet," I replied.

"If you're interested, we need another instructor on the single engine side of the business, as we are taking on more students from the Middle East. If you put yourself through our standards department at Oxford and upgrade to a commercial flying instructors rating, we can give you a job here at Carlisle."

It wasn't exactly what I was looking for, as I really wanted to get into the airlines. However, it was very well paid and beggars can't be choosers, so I snatched his hand off.

So in the spring of 1976, I set off to Oxford again to start a "standards" course. I did this with a gentleman called Dave Stuart. I was to meet Dave again over twenty years later.

The course was very thorough, and the department was run by instructors who had been responsible for checking standards of military instructors in a previous life. When they decided I was ready, I was to be put forward for test, again with the Civil Aviation Authority flying unit examiners. For the next three weeks, life was purgatory! Everything had to be briefed, pattered and demonstrated before being pulled apart back in the briefing room. A little light relief was found when we had to do the aerobatic side of things. This was done in the Fuji FA-200, which I had already become familiar with, but the test was not done with the CAA. They were not keen on doing aerobatics and had delegated Colin Beckwith, who was the chief flying instructor at Oxford, as their representative for conducting aerobatic tests. I duly did the test with Colin, and the next day I did the single engine flight test with the CAA man, Bob Whitehead. Bob was a white-haired gentleman with a phenomenal experience in training pilots. I had been warned that he was bound to ask me about errors in the turn of an artificial horizon. This was a gyro-driven instrument which shows the pilot the attitude of the aircraft when he has no external reference e.g. in cloud.

Sure enough, one of the questions Bob asked me was exactly that. I had made sure that I knew every last thing there was to know about the errors to be found in an artificial horizon. We did the briefing, flew the test and then when we landed for the last time. Bob spent five minutes on the apron of the airfield, going round in circles in the aircraft, showing me the errors in a turn!

Oxford Air Training School PA28 at Carlisle

Having passed the singles instructor test to commercial standard, it was now back to Carlisle to start work. I was given a handful of students who consisted of a few Iraqis and a few Sudanese. The Sudanese guys were at Carlisle in order to achieve a commercial pilot licence. This would not have an instrument rating qualification and would not be a UK commercial pilot licence. The reason for this was Sudan would send over their own examiners at the end of the course and, if successful, they would be awarded a Sudanese licence. They did not need an instrument rating for flying all the complex procedures, as they were to become crop dusters. If they only held a Sudanese licence, they could not fly for anybody else. The Sudanese government were then sure that they would not move on to better things having had all their training paid for.

On the other hand, the Iraqis were trained to the full British standard and, for their course, no expense was spared. A large amount of their course was on twin engine aircraft and hence very expensive.

This was the very hot summer of 1976. I plugged away with my students, some of which were very good. The Iraqis could not fail the full course. If they were failed on a progress check, they were just given more flying to try and get them up to standard. A few were sent back to Iraq but sometimes not for failing their flying tests. There were the other occasional indiscretions which meant being sent home rather than face any consequences which could cause problems in our country i.e. the law.

I was trying to get as much experience as possible, and if there was something such as an air test due on one of the twins, I would go along for the experience. As always, Bill and the instructors at Carlisle were extremely helpful in getting me the odd trip here and there which would add to my experience.

Sig Evans rang me at home on one particular day.

"Peter, a mate of mine is looking for someone like you to sit in the right-hand seat of an HS125 executive jet for a quick trip to Jersey and back the following day. You don't have to be qualified on the type, as it's a private flight. Are you interested?"

I had my bag packed before Sig had put the phone down.

I was fairly useless apart from operating the radio, but it was a fascinating opportunity for me, and I remember sitting in this "rocket" watching the altimeter after take-off. I thought we were passing 1000 feet but, on closer inspection, we were passing 10000 feet. Such was the difference in performance compared to what I was used to. We shot down to Jersey, had a very pleasant night stop, which was paid for, and shot back to Newcastle.

That was it. I had to fly something like that aeroplane.

I still managed to beg, borrow or steal the odd trip in a twin. The chief instructor asked me, one day, if I would like to fly a twin down to Oxford.

I jumped at the opportunity, and he said, "There is one small point. I want you to take an Iraqi student with you. He has been thrown off the course for misbehaving and is on his way home to Iraq. They are expecting him. Don't do him any favours such as allowing him to fly the aircraft." There was no chance of that.

Off we set after lunch one day. As we approached Oxford, we were told to hold, as there were delays landing at Oxford due to the density of the traffic.

He said, "I need to pee."

"Well, what do you expect me to do?"

"I need to pee."

"There's nothing I can do about it. We just have to wait our turn in the sequence of the traffic."

"I will pee in my trousers."

"If you do that you will get the aircraft to clean from top to bottom."

Eventually, we landed at Oxford. As soon as I had shut down the engines, he opened the door and ran off towards the offices. I never saw him again.

By now, I had to complete my check out as an instructor with the CAA on twin engine aircraft. There was a time limit between doing both singles and twins, and I was therefore sent back to Oxford to complete the twin stuff. I was back with Dave Stuart who again "put me through the wringer" and got me up to speed. A test was booked, and who should the examiner be but Bob Whitehead! He decided upon which subjects he wanted me to brief him and, when that was complete, off we went in a PA-39 to fly the required exercises, mainly on one engine.

We eventually landed back at Oxford and, as we taxied in, he said, "Did we discuss the errors in an artificial horizon in the turn last time I saw you?"

"Yes," I replied.

"Well, just as a refresher, let's have another quick look."

And off we went, taxiing around in circles again whilst we looked at the errors.

Bob was a very knowledgeable guy, and I learnt an awful lot from him on both occasions when we flew together. I shall never forget the errors with an artificial horizon in the turn.

It was back to Carlisle and the instructing world in singles. I never really got any opportunity to instruct on twin engine aircraft, as the senior instructors dominated that scene. I was starting to feel that I was not going to get much further with my career and any progression would be waiting for “dead men’s shoes”.

We had a problem with the different cultures of some of the students, particularly with those who observed Ramadan. The fasting during the month of Ramadan had to be monitored carefully, as the school did not want people to fly, particularly solo, with large gaps between their last meals.

An incident that I remember well was while coming back to the airfield at Carlisle with a relatively inexperienced student. For the first few flights with new students, they were encouraged to orientate themselves with respect to the airfield so, when they eventually flew solo, there were no problems with them getting lost in the local area. I let this particular student find his way back to the airfield. The easterly runway was in use i.e. we were going to land towards the east. It was a hazy day, and I suggested that he look for the River Eden. There was a particular stretch of the Eden that was parallel to, and very close to, the runway. With the sun glinting on the water, it should have put him into a good position for the final approach. He found the stretch of river and lined up with it descending at the same time. It became apparent to me that he was not going to make the required slight left turn towards the runway and continued the approach towards the river. I thought that by leaving him the penny would eventually drop and he would put matters right. Down and down we went, nicely lined up with the river, until at about 50 feet I took control of the aircraft, as air traffic control, who could see us and were asking if all was well, were obviously worried.

After we landed on the runway, as we taxied in to the apron, I said to the student, "Did you realise that you were lined up with and almost landed in the river?"

"Yes, sir, I did."

"Why didn't you do something to correct the situation?"

"By the time I realised my mistake, it was obvious to me that it was meant to be."

I didn't know what to say. We went to a briefing room and discussed the matter. I certainly didn't want to make a big issue of this incident, as culture obviously was different, but after a long and meaningful discussion, he realised the error of his ways. We had no more problems with him, and it could have been that he was using a higher authority to cover his mistake.

Life went on through that summer, and I still knew that I wanted to be flying in the airline world. I applied for two jobs that year; both seemed an exciting prospect for a young, single and newly qualified commercial pilot. Bearing in mind that there was still a glut of experienced pilots on the market, there was still hope that somebody might require someone of my experience level.

The first position was for a pilot with the British Antarctic Survey team. They were looking for somebody to fly a de Havilland Twin Otter. I was told that the aircraft would be in Canada for maintenance through the Antarctic winter and would then be flown all the way south through the Americas in time for the Antarctic summer. At the end of the summer, the aircraft would then be flown back north for its annual maintenance again. That sounded pretty good. The aircraft was a fairly simple type, but the type of flying that they carried out in Antarctica required a lot of experience. Everything was kept crossed in anticipation of a reply to my application which eventually appeared through the letter box with the inevitable rejection.

The other position that I had seen advertised was for a co-pilot on an Argosy flying freight in and out of Botswana. This seemed like an interesting job, and the aircraft was a four engine, turboprop which would certainly be a giant leap up the ladder for a young, enthusiastic chap such as me. Rejection soon followed. I couldn't complain, really, but I was getting slightly fed up by now with instructing on single engine aeroplanes even though I was being paid well. Teaching young people is a challenging side to aviation but probably more suited to pilots who had already had a long career and wanted a gentle descent towards retirement and to go home every night. I needed to move on. I needed to keep trying. As they say in the North East "shy bairns get nowt".

Mike Firth, who did my twin rating, had also been a commercial instructor at Carlisle and had left some months ago to join the world of airline flying. He had joined Dan-Air, based at Leeds, and I gave him a ring to see if he knew anything about potential recruitment in the company. At the time, Dan-Air had a fleet of turboprop aircraft (Hawker Siddeley 748) which was slowly growing and aircraft were being based in Aberdeen, as the oil industry was expanding and demanding seats on aircraft up to the Shetland Islands to get their rig crews out to the North Sea rigs. Mike gave me the name and telephone number of the HS 748 fleet manager who happened to be based in Newcastle. His name was John Ryder, and I found him to be very approachable.

"What kind of experience do you have?" he asked. I gave him the full details, and he said, "Just the kind of experience we are looking for, however, I really don't know when we will need more people. It all depends if and when we get more contracts in the oil industry. Ring me regularly, and I'll keep you posted."

I rang him every week. He was extremely affable and, fortunately, I never seemed to get on the wrong side of him by speaking to him so often.

When I was at work, one day, there was a telephone call from my mother telling me there had been a call from John Ryder at Dan-Air, and I was to ring him immediately. I disappeared into one of the instructor offices and used the phone to ring him.

"Can you be in Gatwick tomorrow for an interview?"

"Yes. What time do you want to see me and whereabouts shall we meet?"

John gave me the details, and I caught a grubby, old sleeper train from Carlisle down to London that night. The sleeper carriage was in a siding at Carlisle, and we were shunted to the main train in the middle of the night. The compartment was far too hot, and I didn't sleep at all, as I was too excited about the following day. I was desperate to be successful at the interview and join the airline world. When I got to Euston, I made my way across London and down to Gatwick. I was wearing a suit, shirt and tie and had my licence and logbook under my arm. I eventually found the room at Gatwick Airport where I was to meet my interviewers and waited patiently outside. Eventually, a gentleman came out of the office and introduced himself.

"Hello. I'm John Ryder. You must be Peter."

"Yes. Hello, sir. I'm Peter Herzberg."

"We meet at last," said John.

He took me into the office and introduced the other gentleman who was already sitting at the desk.

"This is Captain John Scotney who is the HS 748 chief training captain."

I think I spent at least half an hour with them. I was asked various questions, and they had a good look at my logbooks.

Eventually John said, "Thanks for coming, Peter. How did you get here?"

I told him that I had come by train. He offered me a free ticket with Dan-Air back to Newcastle, but I declined, as I had already spent money on a return train ticket.

"We'll be in touch," he said.

CHAPTER 10

On Christmas Eve 1976, I received a letter from Captain John Ryder thanking me for coming to Gatwick for interview and offering me a job as a first officer with Dan-Air Services. It was the best Christmas present ever!

I immediately rang Bill Moore, to give him the news, and wrote my letter of resignation to the Oxford Air Training School. My course was to commence in February. There was no word of where I was to be based but, to be honest, I didn't really care. Early in January, a letter arrived with full details from my new employer. I was to be employed by the Dan-Air training school on a salary of just over £2800 per annum whilst training and, upon successful completion of the course, I would be employed by Dan-Air Services and be notified of my base. My salary would start at £4200 per annum, which was about £300 per year less that I was getting as an instructor at Carlisle, but I now had the prospect of a proper career.

My resignation didn't go down too well at Carlisle. Although I had spent almost a year with them, they were a bit peeved that I was moving on. They pointed out that they had spent money on my training with them to achieve a commercial instructor rating, and I had to point out that I had paid for the training myself, albeit at staff rates for the aircraft. We owed each other nothing.

I finished flying at Carlisle at the end of December and, eventually, made my way down to Bournemouth towards the end of January where the Dan-Air training school conducted the course for the HS 748. Accommodation was provided in the Pavilion Hotel.

There were four of us on the course; two captains and two first officers. It was quite exciting sitting in that hotel in the evenings watching all the crews arriving and departing to operate the services that one day we hoped to be part of.

On the first day, we made our way out to Bournemouth Airport and found the building where the course was to take place. Not only did we have to pass a CAA exam on the HS 748, but we two first officers had to pass extra exams on AC electrics, DC electrics, air conditioning and pressurisation, and gas turbines. Neither of us had flown an aircraft quite as complex as this one up until this time, and the extra exams were a requirement of the CAA. We all got along well, and the guy who ran the course decided, after a week, that we would start revising the bits and pieces that we had covered in the airport social club. Not a good idea, as the alcohol consumption increased as we got nearer to the exams.

Eventually, all exams were passed, and the next step was to actually fly the aircraft. This was called base training; the exciting bit.

We now had to wait to find aircraft around the network where they were on the ground for an hour or two in order to get the base training done for all of us. As base training does not create any revenue, it is regarded as fairly low priority. We were called by the crewing department and told to report to Newcastle for the first of our details. I flew with two different base trainers on this fleet; John Scotney, who had been present when I was interviewed, and another training captain, Ray Liddiard. We spent the next three weeks chasing around the country following aircraft that were available and flew from Bristol and Bournemouth as well as Newcastle. This aeroplane was a completely different kettle of fish for me due to its size and different systems. It felt much bigger, and it had turboprop engines, which I had never come across before. We covered every handling aspect of the aircraft in the aeroplane; there were no simulators for this one. We took the aircraft up to above 10000 feet and practised stalls, steep turns, engine shutdowns and relights and all the various instrument approaches. Eventually we just "pounded" the circuit doing take-offs and landings. With the training captains' help and advice, we eventually all passed the base training. As this phase ended, we now had all the paperwork to take to the CAA head office in Gatwick and get the aircraft officially entered into our licences; a proud moment for us young folk.

We still weren't allowed to "fly the line" with any captain. We now had to undergo line training. This, again, involved flying with suitably qualified line trainers who would teach us how to operate the aircraft on normal routes with fare-paying passengers on board.

My line training was to be from my new base in Aberdeen. Just over a week after completing the base training and getting my licence stamped by the CAA, I found myself packing suitcases and setting off on the long drive north. From home in the Lake District, the route took me north up the M74, around Glasgow and then along the various A roads through Perth, Scone and Forfar towards Stonehaven and Aberdeen itself. The route these days is all motorway, or dual carriageway, but it was a longer journey back in the 1970s. I stopped in a lay-by, near Forfar, and ate my sandwiches whilst admiring the view of the distant mountains. I wondered what the future held in store.

We were given a few nights in the airport hotel by Dan-Air initially. We were expected to find our own accommodation after a couple of weeks. The hotel was on the eastern side of the airfield and was called the Skean Dhu. It was to a high standard and the bar was full every night with crews belonging to all the airlines and helicopter companies. I settled into my room and looked forward to my first flight in two days' time.

I had been told to make myself known to the senior pilot in Aberdeen before starting my line training. I thought it wise to put in an appearance in uniform, so the following day I made my way along to the Portakabins and found his office. His name was John Smith, known by everybody as "JGS" due to his initials. His wife, Anne, worked for Dan-Air on the ground in the terminal. I put my cap under my arm and knocked on the door. Having been invited in to his office, we introduced ourselves, and I found him very approachable. He asked me a few questions, gave me a rough picture of the operation and said he would look forward to flying with me over the next few days.

He also said, "We have a maximum effort, minimum bullshit regime here. We do everything in our power to get the job done because, if we don't, then somebody else will get the contract. Oh... and Pete, you don't have to call me sir. We're not in the military!"

In the mid 1970s, Aberdeen was expanding rapidly as the "oil city" of the UK. In the early '70s, the UK had been importing oil and paying the price of wars in the Middle East and the associated rollercoaster ride in the price of oil. Huge finds were made in the North Sea at the time, and oil fields with names such as Forties, Brent, Piper and many others became household names. The Americans, along with their technical ability to help get the oil ashore from under the North Sea, flooded into Aberdeen. As their influence grew, so did businesses, shops and house prices. It was an exciting place to be but, at the same time, older practices remained. When I arrived, the pubs were not allowed to open on Sundays. I was there to be part of the crewing requirements for the third Dan-Air aircraft. At its peak, Dan-Air had 20 aircraft based in Aberdeen. Room at the airport was in short supply, and the company headquarters consisted of three Portakabins on the eastern side of the airfield a stone's throw from the Skean Dhu Hotel.

It was a very early start for my first day of line training, and I walked across to the Portakabins nice and early to report for my duty. My training captain was a very jovial guy by the name of Tom Mullin. He had a wonderful sense of humour and had flown DC-3s in Burma during the war. The flying that he was involved with was taking freight across the Himalayas into China. The routes were well known for being highly dangerous due to the weather, particularly vicious thunderstorms, which could grow rapidly at the drop of a hat, and the terrain which was extremely high in places. If you ended up off track and weren't sure of your position then the high ground was a deadly trap. Many wartime pilots lost their lives "flying the hump" as it was known.

In those days, in Aberdeen, most of the cabin crew were loadmasters. Ron was with us today. He was the senior loadmaster at the base. There was a stewardess at the base, Heather, who was a lovely lady and married to one of the guys who I had been with at Oxford when I was doing my commercial pilot licence. He was an American helicopter pilot who wanted to work on the helicopters flying to and from the rigs in Aberdeen. Initially, the operation had loadmasters, as we carried either 48 or 52 passengers, depending on which aircraft we were flying, and it was felt that loadmasters could deal with these tough oil rig workers better than air stewardesses. This changed very quickly and more and more women came to the base and, generally speaking, coped with these guys, some of whom could be a bit rough at times, without too many problems.

The duty consisted of four sectors, which ranged from Aberdeen to Sumburgh, in the Shetland Islands, and then the return. The whole thing was then repeated. The first sector north usually consisted of a full load and, when we landed at Sumburgh, we would usually return empty in order to take another load of passengers north again from Aberdeen. By the time we arrived in Sumburgh the second time around, the helicopters had taken the first load of passengers out to the rig and they had brought a load back to Sumburgh who, in turn, would fly back to Aberdeen with us. This was generally the way the whole operation worked but, as the day went on, the flights may or may not be full of rig workers depending on how the helicopter rotations out of Sumburgh were going. We were very much at the beck and call of the oil companies, as they were the customers and they paid well!

It all seemed rather too much on my first trip. I was tasked to deal with the paperwork, read the checklists, operate the radio and so on. Fortunately, on early line training flights, there was always a safety pilot on the jump seat. They would sit on the spare seat between us and keep an eye on things in case anything was missed particularly by the "new boy". Not being used to this sort of operation, it all took a bit of time to settle in.

We took off from Aberdeen, and the first duty of the first officer was to close the "dump valve". This was a large lever near the right foot which had to be moved fully forward. This was the equivalent of putting the plug into the fuselage to stop the majority of the air escaping. It was, in effect, the start of the pressurisation procedure. As soon as the "dump valve" was closed, the first officer had then to start gently closing the "spill valves". These controlled the rate of air leaving the cabin and hence pressurised the aircraft. All this had to be done whilst talking to air traffic control and reading the checklist! We made our way out towards Peterhead with Tom flying the aircraft and making it look so easy. I was so behind matters on that first flight, I felt as if I was still in the car park. As we passed Peterhead, we turned north and, having climbed to 9000 feet, we levelled off in the cruise. Virtually all these HS 748s had no autopilot, so Tom was still hand flying the aircraft while keeping a very close eye on me. I slowly started to catch up with our progress. I filled out the flight log whilst Tom asked me questions about when we would get to such-and-such a point and how much fuel we would have when we got there. I quickly found there was lots of mental arithmetic to be done in this job. In the meantime, we were proceeding north at a rate of over 3 miles per minute which was unprecedented to me.

We soon were approaching an island just off to our left. This was Fair Isle. It was a fairly remote outpost, with only a few inhabitants at the time, but a popular place for birdwatchers and wildlife enthusiasts to visit. We had started our descent, and I was wrestling to get the aircraft pressurisation to slowly come down so that the aircraft cabin was the same as our altitude just before we landed. There were more checklists to read, and the weather conditions to be written down, as soon as we had changed radio frequencies from Scottish airways to Sumburgh. Steve, the extra first officer, who was "riding shotgun" today, kept me right and prompted me where necessary. Tom showed me the approach chart for the airfield. The conditions were fairly benign that day, and we were going to land on the north-westerly runway. I was quite shocked at this approach. Tom slowed the aircraft down, whilst I selected the flap as he asked for it. Sumburgh Head sticks out from the mainland to the south. At the southern most point there is a lighthouse. We passed to the west of the lighthouse with it almost level with us. Tom lowered the undercarriage, got the speed "nailed" and, with the runway off to our left, this was going to require a last-minute, low-level turn to line up with the centre line. I lowered the last stage of flap, as requested, and at about 100 feet, Tom turned the aircraft gently to the left and lined up beautifully with the runway. A silky smooth landing followed. We had arrived for my first time in Shetland.

We cleared the runway, taxied to the small terminal, and Tom shut down the engines. I felt as if my brain was still at the top of descent point. The customary paperwork was filled out, the aircraft paperwork was completed and the passengers got off.

"There you go," said Tom. "Piece of piss."

Well… not quite.

We spent a few hours in the crew room at Sumburgh waiting for a helicopter load to return from the rigs.

Eventually, as we got ready to return and walked out to the aircraft, Tom said, "OK, Pete, you fly the aircraft back to Aberdeen."

"Thanks, Tom, that would be great."

"Don't forget that we have a full load of passengers, so the aircraft will be a lot heavier than you're used to. The speeds will also be slightly faster than those you were flying the aircraft at when you were base training."

I passed the navigation log to Steve in the jump seat and watched Tom, as he started the engines.

With that out of the way, he said, "What would you like now?"

"Pardon?"

"Any particular checklist?"

"Oh... yes please, the after start checklist."

Tom's gentle, Irish humour gave confidence.

Off we taxied. We backtracked up the runway. All the aircraft handling on the ground was done by the captain, as he had the only tiller on his side.

We lined up on the runway, and Tom said, "Right... off you go, young man. You have control."

I pushed the throttles forward, at which point the captain took over control of them again, just in case we had to reject the take-off for any reason. That would be his decision, and he would action it as necessary. Tom called the speeds out and, on the call of "rotate", I pulled back on the control column. It was all a bit of a shock to me. We had to turn left immediately after take-off, and I was concentrating hard on letting the aircraft accelerate to 140 knots and maintaining that speed for the climb.

We turned left, and Tom said, "Can I help you with anything?"

"I don't think so."

My right foot had closed the dump valve, and I was gently closing the spill valves with my right hand; all appeared under control.

"How about retracting the undercarriage?"

Shit! I had forgotten to ask for the undercarriage to be retracted.

"Oh, I'm sorry... Gear up, please."

What an idiot. I was trying to impress and had cocked-up before we'd got up to a few hundred feet.

But Tom was smiling.

"We'll use a lot less fuel with the wheels retracted for the next hour!"

Point taken.

We climbed up to 10000 feet and settled into the cruise for the last time that day. I was hand flying the aircraft, due to the lack of autopilot, and started to settle down and enjoy things.

Tom suggested we started our descent about 35 miles from Aberdeen. Following his lead, I managed to fly the approach and performed an acceptable, but not particularly pretty, landing.

My first sector handling the aircraft was completed without any serious incidents. I was completely knackered but also elated.

No great debrief from Tom. He was happy with my performance for my first day.

The next day, I was rostered to fly with different trainer. We flew back to Sumburgh early in the morning with Don flying the aircraft and, again, we spent a few hours in the crew room before me being allowed to fly the aircraft south once more. All appeared to go well, and I made my way back to the hotel with plenty to think about.

On the third day, I was back with Tom, and we were flying a double return trip to Sumburgh. Tom decided to let me fly three of the four sectors to give me more exposure to actually handling the aircraft. It was a really busy day, with the pressure being applied, there wasn't even time for a pee on the first turnaround. As soon as the passengers were off, we were on our way back to Aberdeen empty. This was the first flight of the day into Sumburgh and, by the time we had got back to Aberdeen, picked up another load of passengers and come back to Shetland, the helicopters would have got to the rigs and come back with our first southbound load of the day. We would quite often have to wait in the crew room, in the terminal, for the helicopters if they were going to rigs further afield or if they were having problems with weather around the rigs. As the day went on, things started to get easier and, under Tom's guidance, I slowly started to add to my small amount of knowledge regarding this operation.

The training days continued to pass in a blur, but my knowledge increased, and I started to feel more and more at home in the aeroplane.

After about three weeks, I was rostered for my final line check. This was an assessment with a training captain who would judge whether or not I had achieved the standard required to be let loose with ordinary captains and fly the routes with fare-paying passengers. My line check was with John Smith, the base pilot who I had met when I first arrived in Aberdeen. John did not suffer fools gladly and was considered hard but fair. Fortunately for me, we got on well and, at the end of the four-sector day, I was told that I had passed and was "released to the line". John added that the real time for learning was just beginning.

I had now had my allotted time in the Skean Dhu Hotel, courtesy of Dan-Air, and had to find some accommodation of my own. One of the captains who I had met on the HS 748 conversion course, and who also happened to have his home in the Lake District, suggested that we could possibly find somewhere together and share the costs. He would drive home on his days off and join his wife and children. The whole of the area was very expensive, and we eventually found a small cottage on a farm that was available at a not-too-earth-shattering price. We went to have a look at it and found it to be basic but the best we could afford. There was an open fire and hot water with a couple of portable electric radiators. It was about thirty minutes drive from the airport and, under the circumstances, we decided to take it. The farmer and his wife were very friendly and agreed to put a small television in for us.

We were still in April in the north-east of Scotland, and it was still very cold at times. There were still snow showers and whichever of us was flying on the early morning sectors was going to have to be aware that the roads could block very easily. We were issued with "Aberdeen base" parkas which were warmer than the normal airline-style coats. They were lined and offered a little more protection against the bitter cold winds which occurred regularly in the far north of Scotland and the Shetland Islands.

Following my successful final line check with John Smith, my first few days flying were with a captain called Chris Watson. He was a real good guy to fly with, and he started to help and guide me with the realities of flying the line on a commercial operation. All sorts of tips were given, and my knowledge and practical experience started to grow. The HS 748 could not be heated inside until the aircraft was pressurised. This also meant that, in the winter, the aircraft boilers were frequently frozen up, and we couldn't get a hot cup of tea or coffee until we had completed the first sector of the day. The good news was, however, the cabin crew would lay the Aberdeen rolls, which we were given for breakfast, on top of the boilers so when we did eventually get a cuppa, there were hot rolls to go with it!

Another ex-wartime character I flew with during my early days in Aberdeen was a captain by the name of Ron. Although he was a good age, he was as sharp as a tack. He had regular parties at his house and was usually the last man standing in the early hours. He was also a chain-smoker which meant wherever you were with Ron, be it on an aircraft, in a car, or in his house, you were always in a "fug".

Whoever flew with Ron as his first officer knew that they were "by themselves". Ron always shared the flying equally but did not partake in any of the aircraft operation except to start the engines and raise and lower the undercarriage when the first officer was doing the flying. All other duties were left to the first officer. And I mean everything. We had to operate the radios, raise and lower the flaps, read the checklists, get the weather; everything. It would be a sackable offence these days but, at that time, I have to say, it was great fun and youngsters like myself learnt an awful lot. Bear in mind that we had no autopilots in those days, so we also had to hand fly the aircraft extremely accurately. Ron would quite happily, if we had an empty sector, i.e. no passengers on board, "feather" an engine just when we were relaxing and starting to appear bored. This meant he was actually shutting down an engine and turning the propeller blades so that they were "edge on" to the airflow to reduce any unwanted drag. When this happened, he would quite happily shout, "Sort that out!". We would have to push in sufficient rudder with our feet to keep the aircraft "straight" and in balance, as otherwise the live engine would make the aircraft yaw through the sky. Once he saw that we had coped with everything, Ron would restart the engine and all was back to normal.

Initially, we only had three aircraft based in Aberdeen. This meant that there were about four to five crews per aircraft, so we tended to fly quite regularly with the same captain and we got to know each other quite well. As the oil industry was now growing rapidly so did the oil-related contracts, and more and more aircraft were destined to be based in Aberdeen. Fresh faces appeared to join us, and I very quickly became classed as an "experienced" first officer and so my duties also involved flying on the jump seat when other new first officers were being line trained. I also had to fly with new captains when they had finished line training. These duties were boring, as sitting on the jump seat involved no handling of the aircraft and flying with new captains also involved no handling, as they were not allowed to give "legs" away to the first officers until they had completed a certain amount of flying themselves on what was a new aircraft to them. It was tedious but someone had done it for me when I arrived and it was "payback" time.

At an early stage during my Aberdeen flying, I was sent in an aircraft with Chris Watson to Prestwick. All the passenger seats had been stripped out of our aeroplane, and we were to pick up some very long pipes which were being flown in from the United States. Chris very kindly allowed me to fly the aircraft to Prestwick which was an exciting prospect in that we were going somewhere new! When we landed at Prestwick, we were told to park next to a cargo Boeing 747. Whilst the pipes were transferred to what looked like our tiny aircraft, we were invited by the crew of the 747 to have a look around. I remember being amazed at the size of the aircraft, and the way up to the flight deck (up a spiral staircase) was a journey in itself. This amazing aircraft was so impressive, and I did not realise at the time that it would become a major part in my career later in my life. Getting the pipes on to our aircraft took some time using forklifts, winches and other equipment to persuade them to fit through the relatively small rear door before they were lashed down to the aircraft.

Trips like the one down to Prestwick became a pleasant change from the normal Aberdeen to Sumburgh and return flight. Those flights could be very straightforward, but they could also be very challenging if the weather was bad. It could be a beautiful day in North East Scotland, but there could be storm force winds, low cloud or even thick fog for days on end in Shetland and the North Sea. (Or, of course, the other way round.)

Another contract, which was held by Dan-Air, was a weekday service between Glasgow and Scatsta. Scatsta was a wartime airfield which had fighter aircraft based there as part of the northern defence. It sits approximately 40 miles north of Sumburgh. There were also flying boats stationed at the nearby Sullom Voe. During the last war, a 24-year-old, flying boat pilot based at Sullom Voe won the Victoria Cross for sinking a German U-boat.

Sullom Voe oil terminal was owned by BP and work had started to build the terminal in 1975. They also had the runway lengthened and resurfaced in order that we could operate a service on behalf of a company called Foster Wheeler to the big oil terminal. Despite the work, the runway was not overly long or, indeed, wide. It was sufficient for the job, but the only instrument approach aid was a non-directional beacon which, because of its inaccuracies, gave relatively high minima which could give problems in bad weather and cause diversions to Sumburgh. Initially, one aircraft operated the service to Scatsta and the crew night-stopped every time in Glasgow. However, as the oil industry expanded, another aircraft was put on the route, but the crew for this one night-stopped in the executive accommodation at the oil terminal. Executive accommodation it may have been, but it was still in a Portakabin. The food was excellent, but night-stopping there on the coldest and wildest of winter nights was not my idea of fun. The only thing that made it bearable, in my eyes, was the fact that we were on twenty-four-hour expenses which made it financially attractive.

Before the runway at Scatsta had been made ready for our operation, the service was initially made between Glasgow and Sumburgh. At weekends, the aircraft were on standby, and we night-stopped at "Maggie's" near Sumburgh airfield. This was a small bed and breakfast establishment, but it was clean and tidy and Maggie herself was a lovely lady. The Shetland-based aircraft used cabin crew from centres on the mainland. They were usually from Newcastle, and it was great to have the company of someone new. Over the weekends, should we not be needed to operate, we sometimes borrowed the Dan-Air van from the engineers at Sumburgh. They were busy with the aircraft, carrying out the usual maintenance checks. We would ask Maggie for some "supplies" and disappear for the day up the coast. We always had to be near a public phone box to be able to ring the crewing department in case we had to rush back to the airfield to fly. There were no mobile phones in those days! On a nice day, Shetland shows its own beauty. The sea is turquoise and the sands are white. It is clean and unpolluted and, apart from the temperature, one could be in the Caribbean. It really is a wonderful place to be for the peace and quiet. On a bad day, it is wild and untamable.

On one particular detachment to Scatsta, we had very strong crosswinds for several days and had to operate into Sumburgh instead of Scatsta. We night-stopped in Sumburgh for those few days which, to my eyes, was wonderful.

About this time, I had started to go out with Jan, one of the Dan-Air ground stewardesses. I have always maintained that she was rather rude to me the first time that we met. She denies this fact, and it is a source of banter to this day. To cut a very long story short, we married in 1978 and, forty-one years, three children and six grandchildren (to date) later, we are still happily married. We were married in Dyce, Aberdeen by the Reverend Scott. Steve Threlfall, who was one of the first officers who sat on the jump seat during my line training, was my best man. We had a very enjoyable honeymoon in Austria.

I was always very happy in Aberdeen. The countryside is beautiful. There was plenty of fishing which, due to my grandfather, I have always had a passion for, and the flying was challenging despite the lack of different destinations. I had hoped to stay in Aberdeen and eventually achieve a command on the HS 748. It was a matter of building up the required experience and doing well on the six-monthly checks and revalidations that we did with the training captains. However, when Jan and I went on our honeymoon, we flew from Gatwick to Munich on a British Caledonian BAC 1-11. I can remember sitting in the back of this aircraft, looking out of the window, admiring its performance. I knew I had to have a go at a jet aircraft. Jan had completed a course to become an air stewardess, but she has always been happy to go with me wherever my career would take me. And so, a conversion to a jet was put on my bucket list for the future along with a posting to wherever it would take us.

The flying from Aberdeen continued to expand, and sometimes we would get a roster which would show a flight to somewhere new. In those days, the Isle of Man had become a popular destination for tourists and, at the weekends, when the oil industry requirements were very few and far between, most of the HS 748 fleet was found operating from airfields all over the United Kingdom to Ronaldsway, the main airport on the Isle of Man. For example, we would fly Aberdeen - Ronaldsway - Teesside - Ronaldsway - Birmingham - Ronaldsway and back to Aberdeen. Exciting stuff! On one particular flight, my wife Jan was in the cabin with a very senior cabin crew trainer from Gatwick. We had a couple of hours spare on the Isle of Man, and so we all walked down to the beach. The senior girl immediately stripped to her bra and pants to enjoy the warmth of the sun.

"If anybody says anything I'll give myself a bollocking," she said.

The base continued to expand and with it came a lot of different characters. One new captain in particular had a new, young Dutch wife. He was much older, but he insisted that every time he went to work she had to go with him. She had to sit in the car or in the airport all day waiting until he had finished his duty; very odd.

Another new skipper, Pete, was a very professional guy and had been in the Royal Air Force flying the English Electric Lightning. This aircraft had an extremely impressive performance and was used by the military as a front line interceptor. He had joined Dan-Air as a first officer on the BAC 1-11 and had now come to Aberdeen as a new captain. He was a pleasure to fly with and a fount of knowledge. Any tips Pete passed on were most definitely worth listening to.

He told a wonderful story about when he was an instructor on the Lightning. He had some trainees from a certain Middle East air force, and they were doing a conversion on to this aircraft. They put one of the students into the simulator following a comprehensive briefing. He was to get airborne, and Pete decided to feed an engine fire into the simulator. The student was expected to follow the correct procedure which, obviously, involved dealing with the fire.

The student got airborne, Pete gave him the simulated fire, and said, "Identify the failure."

"Hydraulic failure," came the reply in a deep Middle East accent.

"No," said Pete. "Let's try that again." Pete reset the simulator to the beginning of the runway, and said, "Right, off you go. Let's do that again."

The guy got airborne, Pete fed in the failure.

"Identify the failure."

"Hydraulic failure."

"Nooo!" said Pete. "Let's open up the sim and talk about this."

When they opened the canopy, they found one of the hydraulic lines of the simulator had ruptured, and it was spraying hydraulic fluid all over the student!

It was a great story, and Pete always swore it was true.

He was a great chap, a skilled operator, and I learnt a tremendous amount from him. Sadly, Pete was killed a few years later in a skiing accident whilst on holiday.

Jan and I had now moved to an apartment in Dyce which was only ten minutes' walk from the airport. It was quite large, and very comfortable, but not particularly cheap. Life was good in Scotland, and I managed the odd day here and there fly-fishing on the River Don at Kintore. We also walked quite a lot, and there was a pleasant social scene with some of the other crews and their wives. Jan's family also lived in Dyce, a short walk away from where we were living.

The practicalities of both flying for the same company in Aberdeen became evident as the summer went on. We found ourselves passing on the aircraft steps with crew changes. I was going to work as Jan was finishing and vice versa. This didn't happen all the time, but it was starting to happen quite regularly. Of course, there were pleasant times to be had also and one particular work roster showed that we were off together to Bergen in Norway. The captain was "another Pete" who we both knew quite well, so this was going to be a nice day out. This was a slightly different charter by one of the big oil companies. They had decided to transfer the occasional rig crew out to one of their rigs via Bergen. This made a pleasant change from what were the usual bread-and-butter trips between Aberdeen and Sumburgh. Fortunately for us, as we arrived in Bergen on a beautiful, sunny day, we were told by the handling agent over there that there was a considerable delay waiting for the inbound crew on the helicopters in order for us to take them back to Aberdeen. This gave us the opportunity to go to the airport restaurant and enjoy a leisurely lunch at the invitation of the oil company. We spent a little bit of time walking around the area in the vicinity of the airfield. Bergen is a stunning city with a large history. If we flew in there on a nice day, the views of the Norwegian mountains were stunning. If landing on the southerly runway, there is an impressive sight of U-boat pens carved into the rock to the left of the centre line. All very pretty and colourful, but when the weather was bad it could be vicious.

About to enjoy lunch in Bergen

Eventually, the helicopters appeared and, when the passengers had been through the formalities in Bergen, they boarded our aircraft and we set off back to Aberdeen.

Another pleasant outing for us both consisted of a couple of days in Teesside. This again was with a lovely skipper who I got to know very well. Our paths were to cross many times over the next few years. John Hewitt was a giant of a man, both literally and metaphorically, and a joy to have as company in an aeroplane. He was another good friend who sadly was taken from us at a far too early age due to a long illness.

Life went on, and I became quite comfortable on the HS 748. There were many highly amusing incidents some of which I recall. I had flown up to Sumburgh with a relatively new captain, one particular day. He decided to let me fly the aircraft back to Aberdeen. The air traffic control tower at Sumburgh sat at the far end of the north-westerly runway and was slightly off to the left. We were planning our departure from that same north-westerly runway.

The skipper said to me, “Make an early left turn, Pete, and we’ll have a look in the tower!”

I took him at his word and, as soon as we were airborne, I called for the gear to be retracted. As his hand went to the undercarriage lever, I put on a large amount of left bank and the left wing tip passed pretty close to the tower window.

The skipper said, whilst laughing, “Ffffucking hell, Pete, I didn’t mean that bloody close.”

In those days, we got away with it. As the years went by, everything was tightened up in aviation, and now such tomfoolery would involve serious time with the Civil Aviation Authority asking an awful lot of uncomfortable questions.

I was flying with Jan, and a very experienced captain, one morning. We took a load up to Sumburgh and, after the passengers had disembarked, Jan said to me, “Can I sit on the jump seat on the way back to Aberdeen as it’s an empty flight?”

“You’d better ask the captain,” I replied.

"No you can't," the skipper said to Jan.

"Pete... you get in the left-hand seat and Jan, you get in the right-hand seat. I'll bring you a cup of tea halfway home!"

And so, as true as I type these words, that's what we did. I started the aircraft, we taxied out and took off. I had to get Jan to close the dump valve with her right foot and then pressurise the aircraft. We flew all the way back to Aberdeen (with a cup of tea brought to us halfway home) and landed.

As we taxied in, the skipper reappeared and said, "I better get back into my seat before we get to the terminal. Don't want anybody to see what's going on!"

I flew with a captain one day who I hadn't met before. He had retired from what is now British Airways. They had a mandatory retirement age of 55, but he did not want to finish flying. Captains can continue to exercise the privileges of their licences until they are 65. Many, therefore, who had retired from British Airways, looked for other jobs to continue their love of flying. I was rostered to fly with this new chap from Sumburgh to Bremen in Germany. It was another exciting trip; somewhere I hadn't been before and into Germany which was new territory again. The skipper was pleasant company, and we chatted as we went along on the sector which was almost three hours. He had come from the Trident fleet in British Airways, and he told a few interesting tales about that aircraft. It had three jet engines at the back, but its performance was quite limiting in hot weather. Some of the later Tridents had an extra "tiny" jet engine stuck on at the rear to give even more thrust to help with take-off performance in hot and high conditions. (A jet engine becomes less efficient as the temperature increases. Low air density, i.e. high-altitude airfields, also degrades performance. All performance that is calculated for take-off assumes that an engine fails at a critical point during the take-off run. This performance gives the maximum take-off weight that an aircraft is allowed to use for the particular aircraft, airfield and ambient conditions.) An interesting fact, which I still remember, was that the Trident could select reverse thrust on the centre engine, if required, for an emergency descent. This gave it a phenomenal rate of descent.

Anyway, back to the story.

I said to the skipper, "Have you been to Bremen before?"

"Yes, I have... but we didn't land."

I didn't quite understand his comment, but it transpired that he flew during the latter days of the war and was involved with a bombing mission to Bremen.

Stavanger in Norway was another new airfield for me. That was a one-off visit. In those days, the RAF was still operating the English Electric Lightning as front line squadrons and, on that particular day, one of their aircraft had landed in Stavanger for unknown reasons. He was taking off just before us and gave a blistering demonstration of the performance of that aircraft. The Lightning had "reheat" which meant that neat fuel was injected into the exhaust which subsequently ignited to give the aircraft even more thrust. As soon as he was airborne with the wheels retracted, he held the aircraft down just above the runway. Stavanger has a very long runway, and he had built up tremendous speed by the time he reached the end. He then pointed the aircraft vertically upwards, and the thing disappeared like a rocket; very impressive.

There were quite a few different destinations appearing at this time. Some were at the request of the oil companies and some were due to operational reasons. Occasionally, due to snow or fog, Sumburgh was below limits for a landing, and we ended up diverting to Kirkwall. Inverness was also used occasionally; in fact, the whole operation was transferred, at one point, from Aberdeen to Inverness due to a firemen's strike at Aberdeen. If there was no fire cover then we couldn't operate.

The Bergen flights continued, which were nice days, and, as there was no simulator for the HS 748, we occasionally had to travel to such places as Newcastle where there was an aircraft and a training captain available to carry out our six-monthly "base checks" on the aircraft. This involved us demonstrating that we could fly the aircraft safely, not only on one engine but also carry out instrument approaches on one engine, to our decision height, followed by a missed approach. This was simulated on the aircraft by putting up a screen in front of the pilot in order that he or she couldn't see out. Following a simulated engine failure, we had to input a large amount of rudder with our feet. This stopped the live engine "pulling" us or yawing towards the dead engine. After an hour of flying the aircraft around on one engine, despite the fact that we could use a trim facility to help us take off a lot of the pressure required on the rudder, we would get out of the seat with a trembling leg.

About this time, I was considered experienced enough to be checked out by one of the training captains to sit in the left seat, start the aircraft up and taxi it to another area of the airport. Sumburgh was becoming exceptionally busy as an airfield, and there wasn't enough room on the main apron to leave the aircraft sitting for several hours whilst we waited for the helicopters to carry out their rotations to the rigs and back. There were scheduled services to and from Shetland by British Airways and Loganair and room was very tight. So Tom took me out one day, and we did what was necessary to sign me up. We always took someone else, to sit in the right-hand seat, to look out of the window and ensure we did no damage with the wing tip. This felt like another "feather in my cap". Despite being a simple task, it was fun and relieved the boredom of sitting and waiting in the crew room for hours on end.

HS 748 Aberdeen

Photo with kind permission of Chris Wood

More and more new captains continued to pour into Aberdeen. They were mostly from the right-hand seat of the jet fleets and brought with them knowledge and discipline which was of benefit to the young first officers such as myself. Their stories of flying on the jet fleets just continued to whet my appetite to follow them on to such aircraft that they had been flying.

One of the new captains had been promoted from being a first officer, and I flew with him on his first trip as a captain by himself, i.e. having been "signed off" by the training department. It was a slightly different flight in that Sumburgh had been suffering from thick fog for a few days. The oil company, who we were flying the trip for, asked us to go to Sumburgh and see if the weather had improved. Unfortunately, it didn't and, after flying around in circles above Sumburgh for an hour, the fuel we had left dictated that we should divert to Kirkwall. This we duly did and waited in Kirkwall for a couple of hours for the fog to lift. As soon as we saw an improvement starting to take place, we set off again for Sumburgh and eventually landed there almost three hours later than scheduled. The passengers disembarked, and the skipper had a quick word with the engineers regarding a small snag on the aircraft which had to be rectified. This was duly done, and the passengers for Aberdeen were quickly boarded and off we set. Halfway to Aberdeen, the skipper decided to start filling in the aircraft technical log. The technical log is the bible of the aircraft and records all details of every flight. It was a legal document; airborne times, chock to chock times, any snags with the aircraft, any snags which were acceptable to operate with, total hours etc., etc. – everything. The log had to be kept with the aircraft at all times unless it was taken off by engineering whilst the aircraft was on the ground.

"Oh, good God," said the skipper. "I've forgotten to pick up the tech log from the engineer's van."

This was virtually a hanging offence, and we only got away with it by managing to call the operations room back at Sumburgh and asking them to put the tech log on the next aircraft leaving Sumburgh which was only a short period of time behind us. Crisis averted and no bollockings to be issued!

One particular incident, whilst in Aberdeen, was quite a nasty shock. It was something I have never forgotten and could have ended as a fatal accident.

I was rostered to fly with a particular captain to Bergen. Normally, these busy airfields have radar which will identify inbound aircraft and give them headings to steer in order to intercept the instrument landing system. Once established inbound to the landing runway, the crew have all the indications that they require on the flight deck to fly an approach before becoming visual in the last few hundred feet. The ILS will give guidance from right to left, and vice versa, and also show if they are above or below the ideal approach angle i.e. too high or too low.

On this particular day, the radar was unserviceable at Bergen. There was, however, a beacon, more or less on the airfield at Bergen, which gave an indication of its position relative to the aircraft by means of a needle on the flight deck. These beacons could be used to fly a complete approach if necessary, but they could be fairly inaccurate, therefore the minima was higher i.e. we could not let down to as low a decision height as we could using a more accurate aid such as an ILS. As there was no radar on this particular day, we opted to fly over the beacon on the airfield and then, having passed over it (the needle on the flight deck would swing from pointing ahead, as we approached the beacon, to pointing behind as we flew away from it), we would fly a prescribed teardrop pattern. As we were landing on the southerly runway, the teardrop pattern would take us from above the airfield on a north-easterly track (over the mountains) followed by a left turn back towards the airfield. As we flew back on a south-westerly heading, we would then intercept the ILS and be able to follow that and fly our approach. Assuming we were on the correct prescribed track to or from the airfield, we could descend to specific altitudes which were safely above high ground until we were established back in towards the airfield when further descent with the ILS was safe. The beacon (called an NDB or non-directional beacon) had a specific radio frequency. This had to be found on the instrument on the flight deck and then checked with a three-letter Morse code identification unique to that particular beacon. To get the strongest signal, and hence identification, the needle was "looped" i.e. moved to a position of 90 degrees from where the beacon was. As soon as the identification was confirmed then the needle was taken out of the "loop" position, and it would then point to the beacon on the ground. We called this form of instrument a "coffee grinder", as the knobs needed to be turned to find the correct frequency and fiddled with to ensure it was a strong signal. As we approached Bergen, the weather was poor. We descended through thick cloud, rain and turbulence. The skipper was flying the aircraft and had talked about our approach and how he intended to fly it. We flew to the beacon and passed overhead. As we now had to fly away from the beacon, the needle pointed behind us, and we followed a prescribed track whilst starting a further descent.

After about a minute and a half, air traffic control asked us to inform them when we would be turning back towards the airfield for our final approach. After I had pressed the transmit button to acknowledge their request, there was a short pause and the air traffic controller told us we were off track and to check our position. ATC could tell because they have an instrument in the tower that shoots a line out on a screen to show which direction the transmission was coming from. They therefore know approximately which bearing an aircraft is from the airfield, but they do not know the distance from the airfield. We looked to where the needle was pointing and all seemed in order. I then looked up again to the instrument on the roof panel and noticed that the instrument had been left in the "loop" position. Because of that, the needle was "frozen" and still pointing to where it had been left when "loop" was selected. I quickly put it back to where it should have been, and it swung through about 30 degrees. We were way south of where we should have been, over high ground, descending through cloud to an altitude which was below the safe altitude had we been in the correct position. The skipper immediately stopped our descent and turned left towards the correct part of the teardrop. We continued and landed safely.

Looking back, we chatted about what had happened when we got on the ground and the aircraft had been shut down. The NDB is subject to many errors. One of them is coastal effect, which can cause a deflection from where the needle should be pointing, and another is thunderstorm effect, which means the electrical activity in a storm can cause the needle to point to the nearest electrical storm cell. The skipper was aware of these errors and, although there were no storms around Bergen, the weather was bad and there could have been the odd storm cell about. Unseen by me, he had kept occasionally "looping" the needle to check the identification and see that the needle was pulling strongly towards the ground beacon. Unfortunately, on the last occasion, he had forgotten to take it out of "loop" and, as a result, it was frozen, pointing in the wrong direction! Lesson learnt. I have never forgotten that incident. Modern aircraft, these days, have much more modern systems and once a beacon is selected (although they are really no longer needed and there are few of them left in the Western world), it gives an automatic identification to the pilot and lets him know when they are not receiving a signal. Most navigation these days is GPS and, as far as I know, most of the NDB approaches have disappeared. The days of the old "coffee grinder" instrumentation are virtually over.

After two years' service in Dan-Air, the company gave us the opportunity to go to one of the professional organisations and obtain an airline transport pilot licence (ATPL). If we gave up four weeks' annual leave, they would match that with a further four weeks and we could go and undertake an eight-week course approved by the Civil Aviation Authority. I sent off my logbooks again to the Civil Aviation Authority in order for them to check that I had sufficient hours for the course. Eventually, they were returned with an accompanying letter approving my application for the upgrade to my licence subject to passing the required written exams.

Jan had decided to give up her job as cabin crew, as we found ourselves regularly crossing on the aircraft steps. She was finishing a duty as I was beginning mine and the time we had together was less and less. She got a nice little nine-to-five office job which she enjoyed, and it suited our lives much better. We had started our married life buying a brand-new MG Midget. It was a lovely little car, in russet brown, and gave us a lot of fun. Those who own a seventies, soft-top car will agree that they leak like a sieve when it rains but are great in the sunshine. We had also bought a puppy, Jamie, by this time. He was a Gordon setter and totally nuts. In hindsight, it was a big mistake, as we were both working in Aberdeen and it involved leaving him alone for relatively long periods. We also had said goodbye to our flat in Dyce, in which we started our married life, and we had bought a small but new semi-detached house in Westhill. This had taken some time to achieve, as in those days mortgages were "rationed", and we found ourselves having to queue for one. Not literally, just on paper! Fortunately, after getting some local advice, we had taken out an endowment policy with a big, well-known company and they managed to pull some strings for us. The offer of mortgage came through after not having to wait too long.

Through the rumour network, although we were not sure of timescale, we had an idea that a jet course may be on the horizon for me with an associated move south to one of the Dan-Air jet bases. As coincidence would have it, we had received this rumour shortly after moving in to our new house; such is life.

I had booked one of the ATPL courses at the Oxford Air Training School and had arranged "digs" at the same place as a friend of mine had been on a previous course. The accommodation was said to be nice and clean and was with a family just north of Kidlington. Jan was going to go with the dog and stay with my parents in the Lake District which meant I could travel back there from Oxford every weekend to be with her. Had she stayed in Aberdeen, the length of the journey would have been prohibitive.

I was now back into the studying big time! The subjects were similar to the previous ground school I had completed for the commercial pilot licence but in much more depth. There was, again, a great bunch of people on the course. Some were going straight for the ATPL and some, like me, were upgrading. They consisted of ex-military people and civilians. All were in pursuit of this British licence which would give them the opportunity to fly with British companies and achieve a command of a heavy aeroplane. The digs and family I stayed with were nice except the breakfasts were of miserly portions! The studying was tough, and Friday evenings were looked forward to for a quick getaway back to the Lake District and a couple of days off with Jan. I say a couple of days off, but I had to study over the weekends just to keep up. However, I kept Saturday evenings free, and we always had a night out with my old mate Terry and his wife Alison. Sunday evening came around far too quickly and it was off again in the car, back to my digs, in readiness for work again on Monday morning. That was always quite a depressing drive.

Whilst I was on the course at Oxford, I received a message one particular day to ring the administration department at Dan-Air's head office. I got in touch at lunchtime and was told that I was going to be offered a Comet conversion with a new base at Gatwick. I had twenty-four hours to think about it.

"Are there no BAC 1-11 courses coming up in Manchester or Newcastle?" I asked.

I didn't particularly want to go on to the Comet fleet. At the time, the trainers on that fleet had a bit of a reputation amongst us young first officers as being "hard men", and I was slightly dubious. That thought, as I was to find out a few years later, was absolute rubbish, and it turned out that they could not have been better. However, I didn't particularly want to go to Gatwick. It was expensive to find nice property down there, and we didn't know anybody in the deep south of England. Being a northerner, I have always felt more comfortable north of The Wash!

"Well, if you wait another eight weeks, you can have the BAC 1-11 at Manchester."

"That would be great," I said immediately.

I rang Jan that evening and told her the news.

The end of the course approached and the multitude of the exams were taken. It was now back to the Lakes, to pick up wife and dog, and then back to Aberdeen to start work again and await the exam results. I went back to flying the routes out of Aberdeen for a week or two with the excitement of a BAC 1-11 course to look forward to.

In the next few weeks, the results of the exams came through, which I had passed; another hurdle completed.

I also got another phone call from Dan-Air asking me whether I would be interested in swapping my upcoming Manchester base on the 1-11 with Newcastle. This was great news. Newcastle was close to the Lake District, which we liked very much, and would offer escapes over there on my days off. I snatched their hands off at the opportunity to swap.

Over those few weeks, we slowly packed the few bits and pieces that we had and arranged to put our house on the market. We were given the name of a solicitor in Aberdeen who was known to move houses quickly and, sure enough, we had an offer on the house within a few weeks which we accepted. In those days, the oil industry in the north-east of Scotland was booming and houses not only went up in value very quickly but were also bought and sold in a very short period of time.

CHAPTER 11

Dan-Air 1-11 500 series – the next big adventure!
Photo with kind permission of John Barlow

And so we left Aberdeen. Jan was pregnant with our first daughter, so it was very handy to have her move back with my parents whilst I went to undergo the conversion course on to the 1-11. The plan was that she would stay with them, and go to look at houses in the north-east of England, whilst I was in Gatwick.

The first thing I had to do, as part of the conversion, was a supernumerary flight. I had been rostered to report at Gatwick for a Strasbourg and return flight. The captain was an extremely helpful Canadian who, despite me not having started the technical course, tried to show me the various systems on the aircraft. This looked to be a complicated machine after the simplicity of the HS 748. The first officer, Bob, flew the aircraft out to Strasbourg and again showed me what he was doing regarding the first officer duties. (Bob was to go on in his career to great things in the training world, and I met up with him again several times over the next few years.) It all looked very complicated, but for now, it was back to the classroom to spend the next six weeks going through the aircraft to the last nut and bolt (or so it seemed).

The ground school was in Horley, at the main Dan-Air training department. Here the various aircraft conversion courses were run, and in the middle of the building was the Dan-Air Comet simulator. It was a large piece of equipment and, because it was a very early simulator, it actually had a man who sat and operated the radios to simulate air traffic control. He had a reputation of being awkward at times and could make life quite difficult for some of the crews.

We had a small room for the six of us on the course and, unfortunately, there were no windows. The mornings were fine, but the afternoons, after a pub lunch, were quite hard going. Les, who was the knowledgeable gentleman running the course, would rapidly spot anyone with drooping eyelids. They were then asked the most complex question to ensure concentration was maintained. This soon woke us up. Having covered every conceivable system of the 1-11, we then had to go and take the Air Registration Board examination at the CAA. Like the HS 748 exam, this was to ensure we knew everything there was to know about the aircraft (or so we thought), and it had quite a high pass mark.

The next phase of the course was the simulator. This was undergone in Dublin using the Aer Lingus (Irish national carrier) sim. Someone with a sense of humour had christened the sim "St. Thetic" which was painted on the side. We flew across to Dublin, and our hotel was in the airport, so it was a quick walk from the terminal to the simulator block. I was teamed up with Derek who was doing his command course having been a Boeing 727 first officer previously. Our instructors were Clem and Pete. Pete was being trained to become a simulator instructor, and so there would be four of us in the sim at any time with two pairs of eyes watching us carefully. We would not get away with anything. One of the issues with simulators is that they run twenty-four hours a day, seven days a week and fifty-two weeks per year. Because of this, the four-hour blocks for which one could be rostered could well be in the middle of the night. On a conversion course such as ours, we were usually given the most unpopular slots, as we were on the sim course for approximately two weeks. Days off were taken in Dublin and usually meant catching up with lost sleep. Apart from the start and the end of the course, there were no flights to and from our base for the admin department to worry about. Sure enough, all our sim slots were in the middle of the night. This was quite exhausting, as we had to sleep and study during the day with all the distraction of noise and talking from the normal daytime running of the hotel. One of the other problems that we had to deal with was that Clem had a taste for Guinness. We would finish in the sim at some ungodly hour, walk back to the hotel and debrief the session in the now empty bar. Clem would persuade the night porter to organise a couple of pints of Guinness each plus God knows how many Mars bars. All I wanted to do was go to bed, but the debrief was, of course, important, and the Guinness had to be drunk. (It does have a wonderful taste of its own when drunk in Ireland!)

I found the simulator quite hard work. Because of the speed and performance of the 1-11 compared to the HS 748, we had to think well ahead. When things went wrong, they went wrong very quickly. The air system of the aircraft I found quite complex. All kinds of failures had to be dealt with on all the systems. The operation of the 1-11 was highly disciplined, and the training was of a very high standard. Derek and I worked our way through the course and, with the help of Clem and Pete, we progressed well. I had an issue with the memory items on the fire drill. Pete took me to the "cardboard bomber", which was a cardboard mock-up of the 1-11 flight deck, and spent half an hour with me on the fire drill which I then managed to sort out.

The sim course progressed, and a new dimension in flying was slowly introduced to me. By the time the end of the sim conversion approached, I was starting to feel more comfortable with this aeroplane, albeit that we had generally just stooged about the various patterns which we had to learn at an intermediate speed. This was mainly on one engine in the latter stages, and therefore it was easier to keep up with what was going on. Normal operational speeds would be introduced during line training.

The next phase of the conversion course was the base training. This consisted of flying the actual aeroplane, without passengers but with a training captain, around the circuit to achieve proficiency with take-offs and landing. This was usually regarded as the most enjoyable part of the course.

Unfortunately, just at this point, Jan's parents were involved in a bad car accident near Perth in Scotland. I already had a few days off before the base training was due to start, and so we drove up to Perth to visit them in hospital. They were quite lucky in that their injuries were not life-threatening.

After we were certain Jan's parents were in a relatively good shape, I took Jan back to the Lake District and then had to pack a bag again to go base training. The spare aircraft for this exercise just happened to be at Newcastle, and so I made my way across there and checked into the airport hotel where I met up with the other guys from my course.

We had a mixture of training captains, one of which was eventually destined to become the Dan-Air chief pilot and another would become the fleet manager of the British Aerospace 146 fleet where I would eventually achieve my first command and spend eight happy years.

The first day consisted of a little bit of handling, followed by circuits. The aircraft was a joy to fly. This first session was actually on a 500 series 1-11 which was slightly bigger than the 200, 300 and 400. It was a very stable aeroplane to fly and, with the engines at the back, was very quiet. What great fun this was and, with the encouragement of the trainer, I seemed to settle in quite quickly.

A quick debrief followed with nothing worrying written in my training file. We were sent home again until another aircraft became available for the next session of base training. After a few days back in the Lakes, the phone rang again, and I was off back to Newcastle. Here we met up again. The next session was with Laurie Buist who was a gentleman and would become my fleet manager on the BAe 146 in years to come. We spent two hours in the air, some of which was flying instrument procedures and the rest was in the circuit. Again, all went well.

The next day was to be the final training bit followed by a quick check flight. The trainer today was the man who would become the Dan-Air chief pilot. His name was Dick Spurrell. He had a reputation of being firm but fair. As we walked out to the aircraft, we were met by the engineers who explained that there was a fuel leak from the centre tank. The centre tank was in the belly of the aircraft.

Dick turned to me and said, "Were you the last to fly the aeroplane last night?"

"Yes," I said.

"Did you hammer it on to the runway?"

"Absolutely not." I was mortified. "Please, speak to Laurie about my landings, they were fine."

By this time Dick was smiling, and I realised he was winding me up.

It turned out the leak was not serious and was quickly rectified.

Part of this session was to be at night. We flew down to Teesside, which was only seven or eight minutes away in the 1-11, and did all our instrument work and circuits there before flying back to Newcastle in the dark which satisfied the night requirement. After another two hours of flying, this part of the conversion was signed up as complete!

Following the base training, it was back to the CAA to get the aircraft type added to our licences. This was a proud moment to have a shiny jet-type on our licences.

The next phase was line training. I was quite lucky in that most of my line training was to be out of Newcastle. Jan was busy looking around the Newcastle area for a house for us with the help of my dad. They would drive across to the North East, from the Lakes, for the day and get details of property for us to go together and have a look at.

I had been telephoned by the fleet training office who gave me my training roster over the phone for all of my line training. Most of the destinations sounded exotic after the regular "bus run" on the old HS 748 from Aberdeen to Sumburgh. Places such as Palma, Mahon, Rome, Girona and Malaga.

"Where the hell is Mahon?" I asked.

"Haven't got a clue, mate," came the response. "Minorca, I think. I don't fly there. I just sort out the routes for you guys. Enjoy!" he said, laughing.

And so, the first day of line training arrived. It was from Newcastle to Palma with one of the Newcastle training captains. He was an ex-Navy pilot with the patience of a saint. I had a safety pilot on the jump seat watching me closely. There seemed to be so much to do and that was before we even got on to the aircraft. With so much to learn, and the aircraft going so much faster, it was quite a battle to take it all on board.

However, at the end of the day, I got a good write-up, and he seemed pleased enough with how my first day had gone. The next day was with a different trainer. This, again, seemed to go well, and I was starting to feel a little more settled in what, after the HS 748, was more of a Ferrari of the aircraft world.

Training flights all over Europe continued. One of the earlier ones was to Rome. We used the older airfield at Rome which was called Ciampino. This was a military field and was rather a scruffy airport where a lot of the approach aids never seemed to be serviceable. Due to the relatively short runway and obstacles (mountains) on the south-eastern edge of the airfield, we could be very restricted with the take-off weight out of Rome. It was a hot day in July and, no matter how we did the calculations for the take-off weight back to Newcastle, we just could not lift all the passengers, bags and fuel in order to get back to Newcastle in one hop. John, the captain, decided we could carry enough fuel to get back to Paris, and we would stop there for a fuel uplift which would get us home. We were to land at Paris Beauvais, rather than the more busy airfields at Paris, so that we could get in and out relatively quickly and keep the delays down to a minimum. I was given the sector back to Paris to fly.

All went well until the final approach into Beauvais. For whatever reason, I failed to judge my height correctly on the landing, and we "arrived" with an almighty thump on the end of the runway. I was completely crestfallen not to mention embarrassed. There are a certain group of people in aviation who are very quick to remind you of your shortcomings with the quality of your landing, and they are the cabin crew.

"Who the hell did that one?" we were asked when the engines had been shut down.

"Jesus..." said another, "that was terrible."

I was mortified. However, John, the trainer said, "We all do that now and again... now let's discuss why it happened."

The safety pilot on the jump seat was enjoying my embarrassment.

We were refuelled very quickly, and John got me to fly the last sector to try and rescue my confidence. Thankfully, the landing back at Newcastle was much better, and I drove home feeling that I had definitely learnt something that day.

Another early line training flight, out of Newcastle, was with a training captain with a reputation of being slightly pedantic but also somewhat of a bully. Again, I had a supernumerary first officer on the jump seat to keep an eye on the proceedings. On this particular day, the first officer was a highly experienced ex-military pilot who was quietly waiting his turn for a command.

The 1-11 had a procedure which involved the non-flying pilot shouting "positive climb" when he was sure that the aircraft had achieved exactly that, after leaving the ground, by reference to the flying instruments. The pilot handling the aircraft would then call "gear up, lights and ignitors". This meant that the non-flying pilot would then retract the undercarriage and the lights, which had to be done by 185 knots. This was the limiting speed on the landing lights, and should they be extended or retracted above that speed it could cause damage to the electric motors. The call for the ignitors to be switched off was in case they had been used on the take-off roll. This was a procedure if the runway was wet. The ignitors would ensure there was ignition remaining to keep the engine lit in the event of excess water being ingested into the engines.

On this particular day, we got airborne and I called, "Positive climb."

The training captain called, "Gear up, lights in and off and ignitors off."

I duly retracted the gear and reached above his head to retract the landing lights.

As I did so, he shouted, "Don't touch anything!" We continued to climb to our cruising altitude and, when we levelled off, he said, "I can feel vibration through the control column. I wonder what's causing that?"

The supernumerary first officer leant forward and said, "The landing lights are still extended."

The trainer looked at me and said, "Why the hell didn't you retract the landing lights when we got airborne?"

Before I could say anything, the supernumerary first officer leant forward and said, "Because you told him not to!"

Nothing more was said.

My line training continued and, eventually, the safety pilot on the jump seat was signed off as no longer required.

Part of the line training on the 1-11 required a few sectors flying the 1-11 500 series. This was longer, held more passengers and had more powerful engines. I was sent to Manchester to fly these sectors and had my first flights into Girona and Malaga. Both airfields were surrounded by high ground and much more to learn. The last of these two days was my final line check, which I passed, and I was released to fly the line with ordinary line captains. As is always said after these conversion courses... now the real learning begins!

By now, we had found a small house in Morpeth, and Jan dealt with the move and settling in whilst I started flying from my new base at Newcastle.

We only had one aircraft based in the North East, and we therefore only had six crews covering that aircraft. The particular aircraft based at Newcastle was usually a 200 series 1-11 which was lighter than the other series and went like a rocket. In fact, one of the Newcastle routes consisted of flying across the North Sea to Stavanger, then on to Bergen, back to Stavanger and home again. A lot of the passengers on this route were oil workers going out to the rigs from Norway. The service and aircraft provided by Dan-Air became affectionally known as the "Geordie Rocket". Great fun was to be had flying this 200 series 1-11 with its exceptional rate of climb. If we were at a particularly low weight, the cabin crew would complain that they couldn't push the trolleys up the aisle as the angle was too steep.

Over the first few weeks, I got to fly with the Newcastle captains. The same captain that I had shared a cottage with in Aberdeen had also converted back to the 1-11, and he ended up at the same base. We tended to fly a Gatwick service twice a day with the addition of Norway between the Gatwick flights. At weekends, however, we were chartered by a large holiday company to fly holiday routes around the Mediterranean. This was all interesting stuff for me.

One of the Newcastle captains, who I met and flew with, was an interesting character. He had a slightly eccentric trait but was a superb guy to fly with and was happy to sit back and let me get on with it. I learnt an awful lot from Mike Hamilton, and we are still good friends to this day, over forty years later. We speak every week, swearing and cursing at each other (because it's what real blokes do) and generally put the world to rights. He has always been a fount of knowledge, on all subjects, from fixing cars to laying tiles. Over the years, I have always had an interest in restoring classic cars and have spent hours on the phone seeking his advice about various technical problems, particularly electrical. I always looked forward to flying with Mike. He was generous with allowing first officers to choose which sector they would like to fly and, as my experience grew, we would always try and outdo each other by choosing the most difficult sector. This was particularly evident if there was a cheeky crosswind to deal with. We both wanted to deal with it, and Mike would always let me have a go.

We had two training captains at Newcastle. One of them was a slightly pompous chap who usually managed to upset either one of the crew or one of the ground engineers. This was the man who I had the "landing light incident" with. The engineers got tired of his ranting and raving and, one particular day, managed to get their own back. The external power (the aircraft could be powered electrically on the ground by a ground power unit) was plugged in to the aircraft at a socket near the first officer's feet on the right-hand side of the aircraft. The socket was about half the size of a biscuit tin with approximately 30 feet of cable attached to it which, in turn, was attached to the GPU itself. This was basically a diesel engine powering a generator. The engineers had a spare plug with cable attached and, on the day in question, we arrived back from Stavanger and parked the aircraft "on stand". After a while, the engineers came on to the flight deck.

"Are you sure that you disconnected the ground power unit in Stavanger before you left?"

"Yes," said the captain. "Why do you ask?"

"Well, I think you should come outside and have a look. The plug is still in the socket, and there is 30 feet of cable lying down the side of the aircraft."

By this time, I had realised what was going on. A wink from one of the engineers had tipped me off, but it was very obvious that, in the extremely unlikely event that this had really happened, somebody, particularly in air traffic control (ATC), would not have noticed as we taxied out. The noise in the aircraft, had the plug and cable remained attached after take-off, would have been horrendous along with the risk of the whole thing coming adrift and going down one of the rear-mounted engines!

The captain got out of his seat and rushed down the forward stairs, with the blood draining from his face, at the realisation of a possibly massive faux pas. I watched him from my seat, as he stood looking at the evidence at the front of the aircraft. Eventually, the penny dropped and, although I couldn't hear him, I could lip-read the expletives coming from his mouth. He saw the funny side, and the engineers had their revenge on somebody who was known as a bit of a bully.

The summer arrived with large ATC delays and many a turnaround down the route was spent waiting for improvements in slot times. These were ATC times that were given as a time to be airborne. If not due to congestion along all the routes, they could be given due to weather along the journey with aircraft having to deviate from their track due to large thunderstorms or, more likely, French ATC was on strike and the flow of aircraft through French airspace was severely restricted, as only a fraction of the normal ATC officers had turned up for work. We could end up with delays of three to four hours which meant we had to keep a close eye on our duty periods (how long could we fly without being required to take more rest, i.e. go to a hotel). If we did manage to get away, and the flight was delayed arriving back at base, then we required twelve hours' rest, and it was more than likely that a new crew would have to be found for the next day's duty.

Crewing rang me up one day with a roster change. I was to fly, with one of the Newcastle training captains, down to Cognac in central France. This trip was a charter for licensed victuallers from the pub trade. This was different and sounded like fun. We departed early in the morning and arrived at Cognac which, certainly in those days, was a very quiet airfield. People from Hennessy were giving the victuallers a tour of their distillery, lunch and a cruise down the river. Fortunately for us, they had very kindly laid on the same for the crew. We had a very good day and, as we prepared to leave, the crew were given a bottle of Champagne cognac each. This was not a cheap gift, and I took the bottle home making a mental note to open it at some large celebration in the future. It was not to be wasted!

A few years later, I came home from work a few weeks before Christmas, and Jan said to me, "I've made the Christmas cake."

Excellent, I thought. "I didn't think we had any brandy," I remarked.

"Yes," she said, "I opened that stuff you brought home from work years ago." Wasted in a cake!

In those days, we could also come across the problem of not being able to land due to weather limitations. Today, aircraft can make an automatic approach in zero visibility assuming they are fitted with all the modern equipment. Back then, on the 1-11, the minimum that we could accept to make an approach was a visibility of 600 metres. Should we have that requirement, then we could descend to 200 feet on the ILS which was our decision height. (Again, that depended very much on the airfield but was typical at Newcastle.) The last part of the approach and landing also had to be done manually, which required a good standard of aircraft handling; transferring from monitoring the instruments on the flight deck during the approach, to looking outside and achieving a visual reference, disconnecting the autopilot and manually landing the aircraft whilst doing in the region of 150 miles per hour took a bit of concentration.

One particular day, Mike and I were sent down to Teesside airport to pick up a 1-11 which had been unable to land at Newcastle due to thick fog. Ops at Gatwick told us to fill the aircraft with fuel and go to Newcastle with the aim of making as many approaches as necessary in order to try and get the aircraft back on the ground at the home base. They were desperate to get the aircraft back, as the programme was slipping badly behind schedule and flights out of Newcastle were beginning to pile up. We duly went down to Teesside, in a taxi, and put as much fuel on to the aircraft as we could before launching off on the seven-minute flight to Newcastle. We then took turns in flying approach after approach down to the minimum height of 200 feet before climbing away and trying again. I think we flew about ten approaches before the fog lifted just enough to see the approach lights and land. These days, flying so many consecutive approaches is not allowed, but there was not the same restriction back then and it was certainly good practice!

I flew with new faces, mainly from Gatwick, who would come north to fill in for people who were either sick or on leave. They were all very nice people, but one or two had their own idiosyncrasies. One in particular, who I remember, used to fly wearing his uniform cap all the time. He then wore his headset on top of his cap and looked just like an "Airfix" pilot. He was a very quiet chap, and I was slightly taken aback when I was criticised for taxiing the aircraft too fast. When I mentioned this to a fellow first officer, I was told that he had a "bee in his bonnet" about taxiing speeds and most people who he flew with received a comment about this.

Dan-Air started a scheduled service on the 1-11 from Newcastle to Jersey. The runway at Jersey was (and still is) quite short for jet aircraft. The 1-11 was not world-renowned for being able to stop over a short distance, and so the aircraft had to be flown accurately and landed in the right place to stop safely in the available space. The same applied to the take-off, in that should there be a malfunction on the take-off run, below a specific, calculated speed, then it would be necessary to be able to reject the take-off and stop the aircraft before the end of the runway. All these calculations were made carefully before take-off, and the speeds were called out during the take-off run so that the flying pilot could either decide to stop the take-off or continue and take the aircraft in to the air. Because the runway was so limiting at Jersey, the captains would usually elect to fly the sector in. As my experience grew, I was then trusted with flying the aircraft into Jersey more and more. This was a great confidence booster.

There were a lot of perks with the routes we flew from Newcastle. We regularly brought boxes of frozen prawns and fish from Bergen. We would send a request by telex before departure, asking the handling agent if he could organise this for us, and we would place the boxes on the airstairs at the rear of the aircraft for the trip home. The airstairs were not part of the pressurised hull and, as such, the temperature was way below freezing in the cruise which kept the boxes of fish and prawns frozen all the way home! Other uplifts were large tins of olive oil from Mahon (Minorca), beer from Faro and also beer from Palma. In Faro and Palma, there were crew shops that used to drive between arriving aircraft and offer the crew not only beer, but garlic, other vegetables and cigarettes.

I went to Rimini, on a night flight, with one of the Newcastle captains. There were terrific thunderstorms over Italy. The approach into Rimini, in those days, was a non-precision approach. This meant that there was a beacon on the airfield which we could use as part of the procedure. It had its limitations and was not anywhere near as accurate as an instrument landing system (ILS). Because of this, the height to which we could descend was much higher and, therefore, the chances of seeing the runway in order to land were slightly less. Rimini was known as "the black hole" in those days. There wasn't a mass of lights, as the area was still being developed as a tourist area. There was only the one type of approach, which had a high decision height, and on a night flight it could very much feel as if we were descending into a "black hole". The procedure involved flying to directly above the beacon and then flying away from the airfield for a certain amount of time (usually between one and two minutes) whilst starting the initial descent. With the timing complete, we then turned back towards the airfield (following a specific inbound track) and descended to our minima. At this point, if we didn't see the runway, we would carry out our missed approach procedure, climbing away to a safe height in a safe (specified) place to consider whether it was worth another attempt or divert to another airfield where the weather was better.

As we approached Rimini, we picked our way around the

massive thunderstorms as best we could. The rain was torrential on the windscreen, the lightning was flashing away constantly and we had to be very careful where we were in relation to the airfield due to high ground to the west of us. The needle, which was pointing steadily towards the airfield, was more or less all we had to orient ourselves. Eventually, the needle went from pointing ahead to pointing behind us, indicating that we had passed over the airfield. We started our descent, on the outbound track, and started the stopwatches to check we were flying away from the airfield for the correct amount of time. The noise and bright lights of the storm were as bad as ever, and we were being thrown about in the turbulence. Eventually, we turned back inbound to the airfield and started our final descent towards our decision height. We could not see a thing through the windscreens, at this point, due to the massive torrent of water. As we descended towards our minima, I made all the necessary calls to the captain in order that he knew we were approaching our decision height. I called the decision height and, again, we could not see a thing due to the rain. To my horror, the captain seemed oblivious to the fact that we were starting to descend below our decision height into the "black hole" with no visual reference apart from a very blurred few lights. I told him again that we were now below our decision height, but he seemed transfixed with trying to find the airfield ahead. He increased the power on the engines, and I thought he was going to commence the correct missed approach procedure, but he kept going down. We were now completely out of sync with what we should be doing, as the speed was increasing rapidly and we were descending. I reached forward for the control column, to put the aircraft into a climb, and pushed the throttles forward.

At this point, the captain seemed to realise what was happening and said, "OK, sorry. I have it. I got disorientated."

We carried out the correct missed approach and, fortunately, we were carrying quite a lot of extra fuel just in case the weather prohibited us from landing. After half an hour, the storms still had not cleared enough for us to think it was worthwhile making another approach. We made the decision to divert to Venice and wait until the weather had cleared. After an uneventful landing, we had a bit of a tense discussion on the ground as to what had happened on our approach into Rimini. He kept apologising profusely, but this was the captain who had a bit of a reputation for being a bit of a bully and, to this day, I wonder if he was initially "trying his luck". Breaking limits on an instrument approach is an absolute "no-no" and could involve severe consequences. I did not like being taken for granted, but I decided to take him at his word. Eventually, we received a weather report from Rimini showing the weather was clearing, and so we put on some more fuel and took the passengers to where they wanted to be.

Life carried on flying the 1-11, and there were lots of relatively long sectors throughout the summer with a lot of tech stops for fuel! The performance of the 1-11 could be very limiting, and we just could not get from A to B at times, due to the weight restrictions taking off from certain airfields. The tech stops mainly involved Rome and Faro. Unfortunately, this would put a delay on to the next planned services from Newcastle which was frustrating.

Another captain, who was quite a good friend of mine, was a terrible man for worrying about the most unlikely things. We went to Malaga together one day. One of the engines was using quite a lot of oil. The 1-11 carried spare oil in cans along with an oil gun. The can was attached to the gun, and then to the engine, with a long, flexible hose.

We arrived at Malaga and I said, "I'll just nip out and top up the oil on that engine."

"No… I'd rather do it myself."

Fair enough. I'd made the offer, but I knew this would happen as he was a "belt and braces" man, and I knew he wouldn't be happy with me doing it.

We agreed that I would organise the boarding of the passengers and off he went.

Fifteen minutes later, he was back and we were ready to go. He was flying the aircraft back to Newcastle, but his hands were covered in oil.

"I'll clean my hands properly when we get going."

I need to explain the starting sequence of the Rolls-Royce Spey engine at this point.

The small jet engine in the rear of the aircraft supplies electrical power and air conditioning, whilst the aircraft is on the ground, until the main engines are started. It also supplies air pressure to start spinning the main engines during start-up. When the flying pilot starts the main engines (one at a time), the air is directed through a starter motor and the engine starts to turn.

When it reaches a certain RPM, fuel is then introduced to the engine through a handle in the flight deck which opens what is called an HP (high pressure) cock. If the outside air temperature is below 15 degrees centigrade, the HP cock goes to a "rich setting", until the engine has been started, and then to a "run" setting. If the temperature is above 15 degrees centigrade, the HP cock goes straight through to the "run" position. When fuel has been introduced, then ignitors ignite the fuel/air mixture and the engine accelerates to idle. Unfortunately, the starter motor on the 1-11 has a weak point which is the driveshaft.

On this particular occasion, we found ourselves sitting on the ground in Malaga ready to start up, with the captain in a hurry and with greasy hands! It was a winter's day in Malaga, and the temperature was below 15 degrees. We had been given a slot time, by air traffic control, and didn't have time to spare. As the engine started to rotate, he should have opened the HP cock to "rich". With his oily hands, he took the HP cock past the "rich" setting and tried to bring it back down to "rich". Had he just left matters and gone straight to "run", the engine would have started albeit perhaps more slowly. As he brought the HP cock back down, there was a loud scream from the engine, which I recognised as the starter motor driveshaft shearing. This was not an unusual occurrence, as I had come across this problem before.

"What's happened?"

"I think you've sheared the driveshaft on the starter motor."

"No!"

"I'm afraid so."

"The oil on my hands made me miss the 'rich' position."

"Yes, your round!"

"What do you mean?"

"Well, I think this may be a night stop. They will have to get the bits down from Gatwick which will take some time. They will also have to get engineers down to do the work. By the time that is all done, we won't have enough crew duty time left to get back. Night stop I think! Your round!"

I seem to remember, at this point, his head was placed in his hands. He was never keen to delegate jobs and always in a hurry.

A hotel was found, and the girls managed to relieve the free bar of a few drinks for us.

As we made our way into town on a minibus, the captain said, "I suppose all that we can do now is go to bed."

"What? We've got a few drinks with us; we're not going to bed. Don't be a misery!"

"Well, maybe just one."

We checked in to the hotel and agreed that the whole crew would meet in one of the girl's rooms in ten minutes for a drink.

I went to my room, dropped all my stuff and made my way to the "gathering" for a drink. As I did so, I met the captain walking the wrong way.

"It's this way… You're going the wrong way."

"Yes, I know. I'm checking to see where the fire escapes are."

Maybe it's just me, but I have never lived my life like that. I think that kind of worrying just might send one to an early grave.

I flew the 1-11 for over three years. At about this time, the holiday company that we flew for at weekends was taken over by a much larger company, and it was decided the requirement for holiday flights to Europe would increase considerably from the North East. Dan-Air made the commercial decision to base a Boeing 737 at Newcastle for the holiday work and a British Aerospace 146 for the scheduled service work. The more senior of the crews got a choice of which fleet to join and, as I was in this position, I decided to go on to the Boeing 737 fleet.

So, on 8th October 1982, I did my last flight on the 1-11 which was a good day out, because it was with my old mate Mike Hamilton.

CHAPTER 12

Earlier in my career with Dan-Air, I had turned down a Comet conversion course for two reasons. One was because I did not want to go to Gatwick, and the other was because the Comet training and management team had a reputation for being quite tough with quite a high failure rate. The Comet had retired by now, and the management and training team were running the Boeing 737 fleet. I need not have worried in the first place, as I found, without exception, all of them to be very encouraging and helpful.

The simulator work was to be completed with a Norwegian company, Braathens SAFE, using Dan-Air training captains. Initially, however, we set off to Gatwick for a month of ground school to learn about this new aircraft.

One of the early Boeing 737 series, the 200, had a reputation for reliability, comfort, economy and performance. It could carry almost 25% more passengers than the old 1-11, using almost the same amount of fuel, and without many of the restrictions on take-off weight that we had become used to. The days of having to stop en route to pick up fuel on the same routes that we had to on the 1-11 were virtually (but not completely) over.

Once established in a hotel at Gatwick, we started the daily commute to and from Horsham in order to complete the ground school and pass the required exams. Mike Hamilton and I travelled to and from Newcastle together at weekends, as we had both been selected for this course. There were other guys, mainly from Manchester, but also Geoff, who was a HS 748 captain from Leeds, who I was destined to be teamed up with in the simulator.

Following a month of purgatory in ground school, we passed the required exams and, after a few days off, we found ourselves on the way to a bitterly cold Oslo. Here we were put into a good hotel courtesy of Braathens whose simulator we were using for the next two weeks. Geoff and I were to be trained in the simulator by the fleet manager who, in turn, was being trained as a simulator instructor/examiner by the chief training captain. No pressure then! However, it turned out to be a pleasant couple of weeks and, after flying the 1-11 for over three years, once I got used to the relatively stunning performance of the 737, I found it fairly straightforward.

Jan was staying with my parents again for this fortnight along with Becky our daughter. Wanting to take something home for Becky, I found a "Snoopy" toy along with a few outfits for him in the airport. This was received enthusiastically, and Becky has treasured Snoopy right up to this day.

Following a couple of days off after the simulator course, we were told to report at Newcastle for base training. This involved a couple of sessions of day and night flying with the chief training captain and another senior trainer. Following a successful completion, it was off to the Civil Aviation Authority in Gatwick to have the Boeing 737 stamped in our licences.

I did all my line training out of Newcastle, mostly with one of the Newcastle training captains who had completed the conversion several months previously. I was familiar with most of the routes out of Newcastle except for a new destination which I had not been to previously. This was Tenerife. Tenerife, or Tenerife South as it was called, lies on the south of the island. Charter companies used to operate into an airport at the northern end of the island (Tenerife North), but the airfield was approximately 2000 feet above sea level and, if the weather was anything but good, the airport was covered in low cloud, which appeared as fog, and prohibited a lot of aircraft from making an approach. It was at this airport where one of the world's worst aircraft accidents occurred when two Boeing 747s collided on the ground. One of them was trying to take off, whilst the other was backtracking the runway, and visibility was so bad that they could not see each other.

The newer airfield at the southern end was at sea level, and the only significant weather normally were strong gusty winds which could result in a very bumpy approach. Generally speaking, a flight down to the Canaries was quite a pleasant day out if the weather was favourable.

Tenerife South could provide challenges with performance on certain days. If the weather conditions at Newcastle were not in our favour, we could have problems getting the required fuel on board and meeting our take-off performance criteria.

This could result in a tech stop en route to enable us to uplift fuel in order to reach Tenerife. Our usual places to stop were Santiago, in north-west Spain, Faro or even Porto Santo which is a small island north-east of Madeira. It was a similar problem to the 1-11, but the 737 could go further before this problem presented itself.

The flight down to Tenerife was usually in the region of four and a half to five hours. It could be a pleasant, but long, day if we didn't have any performance issues and the weather was good. Tenerife could usually be seen well over 100 miles out with Mount Teide, an extinct volcano, over 3700 metres in elevation, being one of the first landmarks to be seen. Once on the ground, the caterers usually gave the cabin crew a Spanish potato tortilla which was shared out on the journey home. It was riddled with garlic and much appreciated.

I finished line training and, as all the crews in Newcastle were very new to the 737, we all found ourselves restricted to flying with people from Gatwick or Manchester who had been flying the aircraft for some time.

I set off for Tenerife, one particular day, with a Gatwick captain and, after a couple of hours, as we approached the southern end of the Bay of Biscay, one of those "annoying" little lights came on to show that one of the two main hydraulic systems had dumped all its fluid. This had all sorts of repercussions with the loss of half of certain aircraft systems, and we therefore thought it prudent to divert back to Gatwick where there was lots of engineering backup and a resource of spare crews. It would be unlikely that we would have sufficient duty hours to get the aircraft fixed and continue to Tenerife and back to Newcastle.

It was a long day and, after sitting around at Gatwick for some time, we travelled back home on the evening schedule as passengers. It was a fairly rare occurrence to have a significant technical problem on a new Boeing.

After a couple of months, we all started to achieve the experience requirements that enabled all the Newcastle crews to fly together. The base became "self-sufficient", and we only saw the odd visitor if there was a problem with sickness or too many people on leave. A few more destinations appeared on my roster, and I visited Naples for the first time. I went with the chief training captain who had come to the North East for a few days. As we touched down, a dog strolled across the runway and narrowly avoided losing his or her life. Apparently a very normal occurrence in Naples!

We also started going to Corfu. It was an awful flight, as it departed just after midnight and got back at breakfast time. Corfu could give all kinds of weather problems from thunderstorms to mist and fog. The approach aids were not particularly good and, at times, we needed to circle. This entailed flying an approach, levelling off, flying a circuit at a set altitude and then descending, as we turned back towards the airfield, eventually landing on the reciprocal runway. Our decision height was higher than if we were landing "straight in", in order to take into account any high ground around the airfield and give us the required clearance above it. At certain times of the night, with either thunderstorms in the vicinity or if it was very misty, it could give us big problems.

Mike Hamilton and myself

Mike and I set off for Tenerife, one day, knowing it would be a very tight trip on fuel. The winds during the cruise were against us, and the margins got less and less. We had friendly banter all the way south as to the advantages of dropping into Porto Santo for more fuel. My vote was to do exactly that, but Mike felt we could carry on to Tenerife and still land with the minimum we needed.

It really was the minimum, and I said to him, "What about potential delays? We may be OK without any problems rearing their ugly heads but, should that happen, then we will have to go to Las Palmas and the delay going on there will be even worse."

He grudgingly agreed to go to Porto Santo. Thirty-six years after the event, he has still not forgiven me. "We should have carried on to Tenerife" is all I get when the subject arises. And so the banter goes on.

The next couple of years were great fun flying the 737. It was quite a Ferrari compared to the old 1-11. As the time went on, I found myself in line for a command. These were exciting times and, as Dan-Air had so many different fleets, it was guesswork as to where I would be offered a command and on which fleet.

After a lot of anticipation, the phone call came through, one day, offering me a command on the BAe 146 fleet. Dan-Air had bought a couple of these regional jets and was, in effect, one of the first customers. The idea was that they were cheap to operate, cheap to maintain and had excellent short field performance so would be a good replacement for the old HS 748 on routes with short runways such as Bern, Switzerland. This destination, in particular, was quite a long flog for the HS 748, and the company wanted to put a jet on the route but the runway was too short. This was where the BAe 146 would be ideal.

Initially, I had hoped for a 737 command at Newcastle, as we were happy living in the North East and were reluctant to move. We had another daughter, Louise, by now, and Becky had started a preschool toddler group and would shortly be starting school. Fortunately for me, there was a BAe 146 based at Newcastle with another one possibly coming in the future. This was good news for the stability factor in our lives.

My last flight out of Newcastle on the 737 was with a local captain. He had a wicked sense of humour and, unknown to me, he had given a PA to the passengers telling them it was my last flight. When we landed back at Newcastle, he told me that there had been a message from the cabin crew telling him there was a problem with opening one of the front doors. He asked me to go and look at it and, when I opened the door into the cabin, I got a loud cheer and round of applause from the passengers wishing me well on my command course. Bastard!

CHAPTER 13

There were two of us on the BAe146 course; myself, undergoing command training, and a new first officer who was joining the company. The course was to be a manufacture's course, i.e. completed by the company who built the aircraft. In this case, it was with British Aerospace at Hatfield. We were to stay in the Clock Hotel in Hatfield which, in itself, had quite a history.

Hatfield airfield was originally owned by Geoffrey de Havilland who was an early aviation pioneer. His company produced, among others, the Mosquito, one of the best aircraft we had during the war, and also the Comet which was the first jet airliner. After the war, the airfield got a hard runway and became well known as a test airfield for aircraft such as the Comet and the Trident.

Hawker Siddeley took over the de Havilland Company in 1960 and, in 1978, Hawker Siddeley, in turn, was merged with the British Aircraft Corporation (BAC) and Scottish Aviation to form British Aerospace. Hatfield was now the home of the 146.

Many years ago, I recall the long journey by road from the Lake

District to central London where my grandmother lived. My dad had been winding me up, for hours along the journey, telling me that he had requested John "Cat's Eyes" Cunningham to conduct a fly-past. (John Cunningham achieved fame during the war as a night fighter pilot and was now test flying the Trident aircraft.) As we drove past Hatfield (there was no M1 motorway in those days), a Trident flew past us making his approach into Hatfield; a fortunate coincidence.

I was now returning to Hatfield. Who could have known?

From the early days of the 1930s, there were a lot of art deco buildings around Hatfield, and the area was full of aviation history. The Clock Hotel, where we were booked to stay for the duration of the course, appeared old but still had an atmosphere of all those years ago with many old pictures and photographs on the walls recalling the early days of aviation.

I had driven south, to Hatfield, and met up with my "partner" on the course. We met and had a beer whilst discussing what we had been doing throughout our careers so far. John had come out of the military and had been flying Hercules transport aircraft. This was his first experience of a civil airline.

The next morning, we drove to the ground school and introduced ourselves to the British Aerospace instructors. We were given several large manuals and started work. There were films to watch and briefings from the ground instructors covering the many different systems.

We were taken for a tour of the production line of the 146. It was great to see the manufacturing process of a modern aircraft, but I was amazed to see the production stopped totally in the morning for a tea break as it did in the afternoon. Lunchtime was also an hour's shutdown. We were invited to the British Aerospace executive canteen for lunch every day. This, again, was a bit of a time warp. We sat at enormous round tables, which were covered with large, spotless, white tablecloths, and we were waited on by waitresses dressed in black with white aprons. It was a complete throwback to the 1930s.

The 146 was the UK's latest project in aircraft design and manufacture. As such, it was doing well initially, with plenty of orders from around the world, and the future looked promising. There were lots of orders, and airline management, from various airlines, were present receiving "all the treatment" plus demonstration flights from the British Aerospace test pilots.

After three weeks of fairly tedious ground school, we passed the various exams and made our way up to Newcastle where the base training was to take place. Although the 146 was new, there was not a simulator available, as yet, and the initial training on the aircraft actually took place on the machine itself and not in a simulator.

The first session out of Newcastle was with the fleet manager, Laurie Buist. On a bright afternoon in December, we took off and climbed out over the North Sea for some general handling exercises. The high-altitude work was to end with an emergency descent from 30000 feet. The aircraft was very pleasant to handle, and the rate of descent from high altitude, using the large air brake on the tail, was impressive. We finished that day by flying a few circuits back at Newcastle. Clive Fleming, the chief training captain, flew the remainder of the base training with us. All went well, and John and I were sent back to the Civil Aviation Authority at Gatwick to get the 146 endorsed on our licences.

Line training was mainly from Gatwick. There were lots of new, interesting destinations which were virtually all scheduled service routes as opposed to the charter network which I had been used to on the Boeing 737. I really enjoyed "running the show" as a new captain, and it was a great experience to be flying passengers, including business passengers, on these routes. Dan-Air had places such as Toulouse, Montpellier, Dublin, Berne and the Channel Islands on their network; short but busy sectors with quick turnarounds and off again.

I completed the required number of sectors and then underwent an intermediate line check. Having passed this, the training captain then moved out of the right-hand seat, and I was supervised with him in the jump seat and me flying with a "real" first officer. My first trip with a first officer in the right-hand seat was a lady who went on to become a 747 captain with British Airways.

The day of my final line check arrived. The senior girl in the cabin was a highly experienced individual, and I pulled her to one side before Clive Fleming appeared.

"Angie, I don't care what happens down the back of the aeroplane today. You deal with it! Don't give me any problems!"

"No worries, Pete."

I had been rostered with a notoriously difficult, older first officer, and I really didn't want any more problems than I could see I already had!

BAe 146-100 flight deck

The line check was passed without problems, and I was released to fly the line as a new captain. The routes out of Newcastle were mostly an hour or less and were great fun. As a new captain, I could only fly with experienced first officers initially, and they were helpful in passing on even more knowledge about the aeroplane. The daily scheduled services took us north to Bergen via Stavanger and south on a night stop at Cardiff. That particular schedule took us through Teesside, Amsterdam and Bristol with a very short hop across the Bristol Channel to Cardiff. The next day consisted of seven sectors routing Cardiff, Guernsey, Jersey, Cardiff, Bristol, Amsterdam, Teesside and finally Newcastle. There was also a twice daily scheduled service to Gatwick.

Within a week of being let loose by myself, we had a technical problem with a hydraulic leak passing through Stavanger. This involved a rather lively night stop in Norway while we waited for an engineering team to arrive and rectify the fault. Unfortunately, the 146, in the early days, suffered from technical problems which involved a "rescue" by the engineering teams. Although this was one my first experiences of problems on this type of aircraft it was by no means my last.

My first winter on the aircraft passed and, as we arrived at the beginning of the summer, Dan-Air had sold a series of charter flights to the Mediterranean on the 146. Not quite what the aircraft was designed for, as it was ideal on the shorter, quick turnaround sectors. We therefore found a couple of crews were sent to Teesside, at the weekends, to operate the flights from there. The aircraft flew from Friday night, throughout the weekend, to the various (mainly Spanish) destinations and, unfortunately, one of the crews would find themselves doing the Friday and Saturday night flights. This meant that most of the day was spent recovering in the airport hotel. For the crews operating the daytime flights out of Teesside a gentle drink could be enjoyed in the hotel bar in the evenings.

One particular weekend, a Gatwick captain had been sent to Teesside to operate a couple of the Spanish flights. After the first trip was completed by the early afternoon, the crew had a few drinks in the hotel bar. The captain, who was a delightful but slighter older gentleman, eventually declared he had had enough to drink, was really tired and went off to bed for an early night. The rest of the crew remained in the bar and, by the early evening, the first officer, who had a wicked sense of humour, decided to liven things up. It was now 7.00 p.m., and he rang the captain's room telling him that he had slept in for the flight which reported at 6.30 a.m. the following morning. Instead of telling the first officer to politely "fuck off", the captain put the phone down. The crew, who were still sitting in the bar, saw the captain run out of the hotel, in full uniform, towards the terminal. The guilty first officer ran after him telling him it was still 7.00 p.m. and not 7.00 a.m. He was then told to politely "fuck off" and the captain went back to bed.

A lot of the Mediterranean destinations had their own perks. There was usually a crew shop (old van) that appeared at the aircraft after landing, and we could buy anything from crates of Spanish beer and tobacco, to fresh fruit and vegetables to take home. In Mahon, on the island of Minorca, we could pick up five litres of olive oil by sending a fax to the lady who ran the company station down there.

A lot of the young first officers I flew with on the 146 went on to continue with their own careers in aviation. I am still in touch with several of them to this day – more about them later.

In those days, it could be a regular occurrence to have a Civil Aviation Authority check ride thrust upon one with no notice given. My first experience of this was one afternoon when we were just about to depart from Newcastle to Gatwick. An ID card was shown to me which showed the details of one of these inspectors. He said he was purely there for one sector, just to ensure the company procedures were being adhered to. I had not had one of these inspections previously so, with slight apprehension, we got him strapped into the jump seat ready to go. He spent some time checking all the aircraft documents, along with our licences, and then off we went. It had already been decided that the first officer I was with was going to handle the aeroplane on this sector, and Pete was a very sound chap, so I knew he would put on a good show. Unfortunately, the weather in Gatwick was fairly foul with large thunderstorms forecast all around the airfield. We got down there and were told to "take up the hold". This means flying a racetrack-shaped pattern around a ground beacon. There were lots of aircraft in the area, including ourselves, who were taking what is called "avoiding action" to remain clear of the storms, so there were delays in making an approach in Gatwick. After a fairly long delay, and with good use of the weather radar to keep us clear of the storms, our turn came to make an approach which we completed without further incident. Having arrived on the parking stand, the CAA man thanked us and got off without any further comment. We never heard another thing about the flight and so assumed all had gone well. I came across the inspector several more times in my career with Dan-Air. It turned out, unknown to me, that he was great friends with a captain who I used to fly with on the 1-11. This captain lived in Northumberland, and so the inspector could combine a visit to his mate with a company inspection. I was also to meet him again, sometime later, on Dan-Air business.

Just before midday on the 29th February 1964, a Bristol Britannia aircraft left the stand at London Heathrow Airport bound for Innsbruck, Austria. The aircraft was owned by British Eagle International Airlines and registered under the British authorities as G-AOVO. The flight number was flight 802/6 and there were 75 passengers and eight crew on board. Sadly, the flight would never reach its destination, and all on board perished.

Innsbruck was generally regarded as one of the most difficult airports in Europe due to the extremely high terrain around the airfield and the accurate handling required to maintain the required separation from the high ground. On the day of the accident, the flight had passed over Kempten, which was approximately 50 miles north-west of Innsbruck, and was routing to a point overhead of the airfield. The minimum altitude, at their position, was 11000 feet, to keep them safe, unless they had good visual contact with the ground below, in which case they could ask air traffic control if they could carry out a visual approach and maintain their own clearance from the mountains.

The last communication from the crew was received at 2.12 p.m. reporting that they were at 10000 feet. A few minutes later, the aircraft crashed into the eastern slope of the Glungezer Mountain (east of Innsbruck) at approximately 8500 feet.

The impact caused an avalanche, and the debris slid 400 metres down the mountainside. Due to the snow flurries at the time, the crash site was not found until the following day.

It was concluded that, as the crew had asked to change their flight plan from instrument flight rules to visual flight rules as they neared Innsbruck, their intention was to descend through the cloud as quickly as possible to continue the flight with the airfield visually instead of using the full instrument procedures. This would save time and fuel. Other aircraft were operating in and out of Innsbruck visually which may have been a factor in their thinking. By descending below 11000 feet and not following the full procedures, the obstacle clearance was not assured.

This accident was the worst aviation disaster in Austrian history.

The British Civil Aviation Authority would not give any airline the required clearances to operate in and out of Innsbruck for a considerable period of time.

With Dan-Air now operating the 146, ideal on short runways and in mountainous terrain with its four engines, it was an opportunity to recommence a prestigious route. This was an ideal destination for winter sports and summer breaks. The company already had a lot of experience flying in and out of Berne, Switzerland, so the decision was made to apply to the British and Austrian authorities for a licence for the Innsbruck route.

After quite a long period of time, with paperwork, questions and many meetings with the regulator (CAA), the approval was given.

One of the requirements was for crews to be trained in the aircraft, at Innsbruck, with a CAA inspector, to go through all the various procedures including simulated engine failures at critical times. These days, all these checks are carried out in a simulator, without the need to leave the UK, until the first flight into one of these difficult airfields under the watchful eye of a training captain. At that time, we still did not have a 146 simulator.

The company selected a handful of crews, and I was fortunate to be included. On the 28th October 1985, we left Gatwick for Innsbruck.

Crews to be checked in to Innsbruck

A CAA inspector came with us along with two senior cabin crew members, the fleet manager and chief training captain.

There were two main approaches into Innsbruck. The more commonly used approach commenced at a beacon to the west, Kühtai. From here, we would commence a descent towards the east, flying above the airfield to a point where we turned 180 degrees in the valley to face west. From here, we would either land on the westerly runway or fly past the airfield again to the south, then turning right and landing back on the easterly runway.

The other main approach commenced at Rattenberg, to the east of Innsbruck. The approach from here was usually when conditions were really poor, as it gave us a lower decision altitude and a better chance of achieving a landing and not having to divert. All these procedures had to be flown at specific speeds and very accurately, for obvious reasons.

It was a glorious day, and we all enjoyed the flight into Innsbruck whilst also getting an appreciation of the mountainous terrain. Our first approach was from Kühtai and gave us our first good view of the valley. Upon arrival, half of us were to be checked out that afternoon whilst the other half were to be completed the following morning.

The Inn Valley taken from the west.

The airfield lies just beyond the eastern view of the river.

I flew with the chief training captain, Clive Fleming, along with our friendly CAA ops inspector who was watching everything from the jump seat. We had all been sent a "brief" of the procedures for Innsbruck which included all the flight paths to be followed particularly in the event of losing an engine at a critical time. I made my own cards for these procedures which could be clipped on to the control column in front of me for immediate reference. We each did our "bit" and, whilst the next pilot was going through the various requirements, the rest of us sat down at the back of the aircraft and enjoyed the spectacular view of the scenery around Innsbruck. Following an afternoon's flying, we parked the aircraft and made our way into Innsbruck town to find the hotel. After a few beers, we all ate together and eventually, after many "war stories", all disappeared off to bed.

The plan for the next day was for the remaining crews to fly with Fleet Manager Laurie Buist in the morning and, when everybody had been signed off, we were to fly on to Chambéry. Generally speaking, the big, new destination for the company was Innsbruck, but they had also decided to start a winter only route between Gatwick and Chambéry. Nestled in the mountains, to the south-west of Geneva, Chambéry was another airfield well suited to 146 operations which had its own problems with terrain and procedures. It was therefore decided that pilots would require an individual check out at this airfield.

It was a fairly quick hop over to Chambéry. Again, we entered a holding pattern to the north of the airfield. This was where all approaches started from. The runway was at the end of Lake Bourget on a north/south axis. The approach was from the north. It was a fairly steep approach down the valley and involved landing straight ahead, on the southerly runway, or at a point before the runway making a 90-degree turn to the left followed by an immediate 270 turn to the right. This would position us to land on the northerly runway if the wind dictated that was what we had to do.

After landing at Chambéry, we were welcomed by the airfield authorities before jumping on to another bus and making our way to the hotel in Chambéry itself.

The date was the 29th October 1985. The following day was my thirty-second birthday. I happened to mention this fact to someone, and it was then decided that we should partake of a few drinks in celebration! That was a mistake. When lots of aircrew get together on a night stop, things tend to get out of hand. There was a lot of alcohol consumed that evening. The plan was that, the next morning, a group of us were to meet as the morning team for training at Chambéry and the rest would follow to continue with their flying in the afternoon. I was on the morning team and, fortunately, had been quite modest with the amount I had consumed. When we met in reception, to get on the crew bus, a couple were missing including the CAA inspector!

Arrival at Chambéry.

Picture taken from the north with Lake Bourget in the distance.

Laurie decided that he would observe the training, as the CAA man had been formally required for Innsbruck but not for Chambéry.

Crews and various wives at Chambéry

Early departure from Innsbruck

146-300 G-BPNT

Photo with kind permission of Chris Wood

Training completed, we set off back to Gatwick. I was hoping to get home that evening, but there was a change from the crewing department asking me and a first officer to travel to Cardiff to ferry an aeroplane to the maintenance base in Lasham. The aircraft had landed in Cardiff and, due to an issue, had ended up with all the main tyres burst. The engineers had changed all the tyres, but they now wanted a full inspection made of the aircraft at Lasham. We were taken by taxi to Cardiff, the following morning, and had to fly the aircraft with the undercarriage in the down position. This entailed more fuel than usual and a fairly noisy flight due to the wheels being left extended.

Lasham lies to the west of London in East Hampshire. Built as a military airfield in 1942, it was used by Dan-Air as a maintenance base from the 1950s onwards, after the RAF had closed the military side of things. It became a large gliding centre and, in those days, there was even a small, moveable radar unit which could be used as necessary should the weather be marginal. We duly landed at Lasham, which was a first for me, and there was a taxi waiting to take us back to Gatwick. There we caught the evening schedule back to Newcastle and then home.

After a few days at home, the phone went, and I was told that, as well as getting checked out into Innsbruck and Chambéry, I was also to be checked into Berne.

Stunning geography around Chambéry

So it was back to Gatwick and a rostered check out under the careful eye of our CTC. This was great news as far as I was concerned, as Berne was another very interesting destination and had just as many challenges.

Berne, the capital of Switzerland, had a regular service to London with Dan-Air using the HS 748. The runway was quite short and, initially, the use of a jet was not practical. That was until the BAe 146 came into service. By using the BAe 146, the company could cut down the flight time considerably, giving the comfort of a jet as well as carrying considerably more passengers.

The approach into Berne involved a "shuttle" between three non-directional beacons. As previously mentioned, these types of beacons had their fair share of errors, and so caution was of the utmost importance. The initial part of the approach involved arriving at the "Schupberg" non-directional beacon where we could hold, if required, until cleared to make an approach. When so cleared, we then continued to the next beacon which sat more or less at the threshold of the south-easterly runway. From here, it was either a case of landing ahead, on the south-easterly runway, or tracking away from the beacon to put us in a suitable position to land on the reciprocal runway. The runway was rather short, and so it required care and a bit of precision.

There was fog at Berne on the particular morning of my check flight and, by the time we got down there, the fog had lifted slightly but was forming into a layer of low cloud and reduced visibility. On this particular day, we were intending to land on the south-easterly runway. We tried two approaches, to no avail, and had to divert to Basle. This was disappointing for me, as I wanted the check flight out of the way. Nobody likes to have a flight under the watchful eye of the boss.

Just over a month later, however, I was rostered for another check with Clive and, this time, all went to plan. In the meantime, I'd completed the requirements for Innsbruck and Chambéry by having another check flight with Clive and Laurie with passengers on board. Both of these went well, and I was now checked out into the three Alpine airfields.

The winters now consisted of most weekends spent in Gatwick to fly the three routes for which I had been qualified. These airfields required an annual check with the management trainers, and they would use the requirements for any other check flight by watching the crews into these particular airfields. The weather at these airfields could be beautiful, but it could also be horrendous in the winter with lots of snow and strong winds. The people in charge of the fleet kept a close eye on us all.

Very soon, after completing my check out into Berne, I was due for an annual line check which was just a normal flight with passengers whilst being watched by a line training captain. This was a CAA requirement in order to ensure crews were operating in accordance with the company manuals to a legally required standard. Sure enough, I found myself undertaking this annual check into Berne, so there were plenty of opportunities for comment from the guy (in this case Clive) on the jump seat carrying out the check.

I knew the first officer, Cliff Newton, as we had flown together before. He was, and still is, a very able chap who went on to become a training captain with Virgin Atlantic. We are still good friends to this day.

One of the many issues to deal with at Berne was the runway length (or lack of it). If conditions such as high temperature or a wet runway were present, it could reduce the calculated weight at which we could take off. The loads out of Berne back to London were usually fairly full and, at this time of year, there was normally a lot of skiing equipment to carry. As Cliff calculated the take-off performance, I could see that we were going to have problems lifting the weight out of Berne. We could use an increased engine power setting (known as a "bump" rating) to help matters but, as we contemplated the problem, it started to rain. This was going to make the take-off impossible without either leaving skiing equipment or possibly passengers behind. This was a line check and would leave us open to all sorts of comments and criticism about commercial issues if we didn't make the right judgement. Very fortunately for us, Clive leaned forward at this moment in time and made a comment about the runway not being wet as far as he could see. It was only damp. This was gratefully seized upon by me, and we now declared that we had just enough performance to get airborne with everything on board.

Incidentally, the local Swiss pilots christened the 146 the "Jumbolino" (baby jumbo). This name was also seized upon by air traffic control, and it was not unusual to hear ATC come out with expressions such as "follow the Jumbolino to the apron" or "there is a Jumbolino ahead of you on the approach". It was a term of endearment!

"Jumbolino" at Berne

Regarding Innsbruck, there is a mountain which lies just 4 miles to the south of the airfield; Patscherkofel. Innsbruck, in those days, had its own special weather report frequency which enabled us to get, not only the weather at the airfield but also, the weather at various points around the airfield which would give us an idea of the general situation in the surrounding area. Should there be an area of low pressure in the Gulf of Genoa, this could set up a föhn wind in the area around Innsbruck. A föhn wind results from the warming of air that has dropped most of its moisture on windward slopes as it rises and cools. The air on the leeward slopes becomes warmer than equivalent elevations on the windward slopes. This is due to the different rates of warming and cooling of air as it is forced up a slope followed by the descent on the other side. Föhn winds can raise the ambient temperature by as much as 14 degrees centigrade very quickly in the Alps. Switzerland, southern Germany and Austria have a warmer climate due to the föhn, as moist winds off the Mediterranean Sea blow over the mountains. When these conditions are found in the Innsbruck area, it could be spotted very quickly on the weather reports. Not only was the temperature in Innsbruck surprisingly warm for the winter, but the weather report from Patscherkofel usually gave a wind from the south or south-east of in excess of 100 knots! As soon as we saw this, we knew that the descent into the valley was going to be extremely turbulent.

My first experience of this was the day following my line check into Berne with Cliff. We were on an afternoon flight into Innsbruck, and the weather reports suggested it was going to be rather turbulent during the approach. We ensured the cabin was secured, with all passengers and crew strapped in, and started the descent down the valley. Turbulent it certainly was, and it only started to become smooth at very low levels. Unfortunately, we got a rough ride on the way out as well, but at least it didn't last too long, as we shot up through the rough air quite quickly on departure.

As a new route, the Austrians were as excited about our schedule into Innsbruck as Dan-Air was. They would shower us with gifts, at times, particularly when we managed successfully to land when the weather was marginal and a diversion looked to be a distinct possibility. On one such an occasion, we had made an approach in heavy snow. We did not expect to see anything at our decision height and had made plans and briefed for a diversion. However, as we approached our decision height, the runway lights appeared through the blowing snow and we landed. Having taxied in and shut down the aircraft, I was busy filling out the aircraft tech log when we noticed someone walking across the apron towards the aeroplane. He was leaning heavily into the wind and snow and appeared to have several items that he was struggling to hold on to. He walked up the steps and introduced himself as the airport manager.

"I congratulate you on managing to land today and, as a token of our gratitude, I have a few small gifts for you."

He handed over chocolates for the cabin crew and a bottle and a small box for me and Cliff. The box contained a glass etched with a picture of a Dan-Air 146 and the name of the airport underneath.

I still have the glass today which sits in my study.

The night stops in Gatwick continued throughout the winter, and my experience of Innsbruck, Chambéry and Berne grew. It was always a delight to fly into those three destinations when the weather was good, as the views of the mountains were stunning. I never got tired of looking at them, and it was just as thrilling for me as it was for the passengers. We could give them a thorough brief on what they could expect to see during the approach, which they all seemed to appreciate.

Of course, there were bad days regarding the weather, and there were diversions occasionally to airfields such as Munich and Salzburg. Although Salzburg was classed as a category C airfield, which meant it required a jump seat ride for the captain, initially, followed by a flight with a training captain in order to be qualified to land there, we were allowed to go there without the requirements being fulfilled if it was a diversion. Strange, but that was the rule!

On another early visit to Innsbruck, I was rostered to fly with a first officer by the name of Tony Foote. In the early days of the operation, Innsbruck was a "captains only" airfield which meant that the captain always did the approach and landing there. This changed as the company experience grew with the airfield and, as time went on, subject to the captain's approval, the first officer could fly the approach. Generally speaking, the handling of the aircraft was shared between captain and first officer and, if the weather was suitable, I always tried to give the first officer the choice of which leg he wanted to fly.

This particular day, we were planning on making an approach from Kühtai, to the west of Innsbruck, down into the valley. Having passed over the airfield, we made a 180-degree turn and, due to the wind on the ground at Innsbruck, we then had to "circle". This meant passing to the south of the runway and, at a specific point (it was a church spire in this case), we made another 180-degree turn back towards the easterly runway. As we passed directly to the south of the airfield, I asked Tony for the next stage of flap. We passed the church spire and, as we turned back towards the runway, I called for the final stage of flap.

"Flap 33."

"Flaps have jammed," said Tony.

We were now below 1000 feet, and I had to make a quick decision on what to do.

With the flaps stuck in the position that they were, the question was, could we land on the runway? It would entail landing at a higher speed which, in turn, meant more runway used. I couldn't remember for the life of me how much more runway we needed in this configuration. The alternative was to abandon the approach, climb out of the valley, try and sort out the problem and make another long, drawn-out approach if we had enough fuel to do so. If not, a diversion with all the problems that entailed would be needed.

"Twenty per cent," said Tony.

He was reading my mind.

A quick mental calculation showed we had enough runway to land on, which we did.

Tony was, and still is, a good friend and, as the reader will see, was with me on future flights where we encountered problems. I think he was a jinx and have never let him forget it!

Tony also went on to become a training captain with Virgin Atlantic, and we also speak regularly in order to put the world to rights!

From memory, at least two of the 146 aircraft which Dan-Air acquired from British Aerospace were pre-production models. They were, therefore, delivered at a much lower price! Unfortunately, we tended to have more technical problems with these aircraft than we should have had. The problems could be spurious warnings on the flight deck of conditions which did not exist but, nevertheless, caused delays and engineering problems. Another of the issues that we had were the engines. There appeared to be problems with quality control on the production line of the engines, and the company had to change over 100 engines in the first year of operation with three aircraft.

My first experience of serious problems with an engine came on a Sunday morning on a quick trip from Newcastle to Jersey. We were over Bristol at the time, and I remember I was having a quick read of a Sunday paper. Suddenly, there was an almighty bang, and the aircraft yawed to the right. My newspaper was thrown over my shoulder whilst I took in all the information about what had happened. My immediate thought was that we had actually collided with another aircraft. The noise had been terrific, but very quickly we could see that the number three engine (right-hand inboard) had failed. However, it was not a straightforward run down, because the engine instrument for the big fan at the front of the engine was not showing any rotation. If an engine just runs down with a fault such as lack of fuel, the engine will slowly continue to rotate in the airflow. This one was not rotating, and I decided the best course of action would be to divert to Gatwick where we had the main engineering base.

Once on the ground in Gatwick, the engineers quickly gathered around and one said, "Come and have a look at this."

I went outside to where they had placed a set of steps in front of the offending engine.

"Try and turn the fan."

It was seized solid.

The aircraft required an engine change, and the passengers were duly disembarked to wait for another aircraft to take them to Jersey.

About three months after this incident, I was sent a confidential engineering report about the engine and the findings. It appeared that a lubrication channel was actually missing and had never been "milled" into the metal, which was most worrying, and was another finger pointed at the quality control of the engine production. This was the first of four engine failures which I had to deal with in my time on the 146 fleet.

We were now approaching the autumn of 1986. Becky was six years old, and Louise had arrived three years previously. We had decided it would be a good idea to buy a bigger house, and we were quite enthusiastic about a property that need some work. We hoped we could do as much as possible ourselves. We had found an old farmhouse in the middle of the village of Hebron, just to the north of Morpeth. We didn't have a large amount of spare cash, but I was earning a good salary and times seemed to be fairly good. We looked at the old house several times and could see there was a terrific amount of work to be done. Most of the windows were either rotten or had woodworm, the concrete floors were damp and a large extension had been added at the back which had the most awful flat roof which was leaking. We paid what was then a large sum of money to have the building surveyed. The survey was quite a disaster, but Jan and I could see the possibilities. Unfortunately, we could not raise enough money to give the asking price. The farmer, whose mother lived in the house until she died, wanted £70000 for the property. We added up the cost of repairs, which local tradesmen had supplied, and offered £56000 which, after much discussion, was eventually accepted. I had to sell a kit car that I had built to help raise the deposit, and we eventually received an offer of a mortgage from one of the building societies.

The great day eventually arrived, and we moved into our new home with the help of a van, which I had hired, and some good friends. Anything to save money! We slowly started to realise the enormity of the project we had taken on, but we had already booked tradesmen for a few of the really important issues. Damp concrete floors were replaced, walls were injected with damp-proof chemicals, electrics were replaced and new windows were ordered for the old part of the house. We decided that the windows in the extension would do for now and aimed to replace them with uPVC windows at some time in the future.

When the major work had been done, Jan and I started with more cosmetic work to try and slowly turn the property into a proper, warm, comfortable home. Wallpaper was stripped and replaced, rotten skirting boards were removed and new carpets were fitted, room by room, as and when we could afford them. We were amongst the first "Sarah Beenies"!

We had decided we would like a new, pine fire surround in the small sitting room that we spent most of our time in. We spent a while looking around various places, where we found most surrounds were beyond our budget. Eventually, we found something we liked on display in a large antique shop in Newcastle where a range of vendors worked together and arranged their products for sale in a wonderful, old building. There was a small pine furniture outlet. The lady in charge of this pine business took our details and promised her husband, who did the woodworking, would be in touch.

A couple of weeks passed, and we got a phone call from a gentleman, by the name of Sid, who asked for directions to the house so that he could come and measure up and give us a firm price for our surround. We were now into the late winter and, one particularly cold night, Sid knocked at the door.

"I've come about the pine fire surround. Is it OK to leave my van at the end of your drive?"

Sid turned out to be a very amiable sort of guy and, after he had done the measuring and we had agreed a price, we offered him a beer. After a couple of drinks, we got chatting and got on really well. He told us all about his wife and how he got into the pine furniture business. Two hours later, he said he would have to leave. It was a very cold evening, and he wasn't sure if he would have a problem getting his van started.

"When you come back bring your wife with you," we suggested. "Where is she tonight?"

"Oh, she's waiting in the van at the bottom of the drive!"

Sid and Sue became really good friends over the years, and she never let him forget the story where she was left freezing to death in his van whilst he had a few beers with us in front of a warm fire.

As time went by, we spent all of our spare time renovating "Stonecroft". By increasing the size of our mortgage, we had a garage built and Jan slowly got the garden into shape.

Life continued with work and many weekends still spent away in Gatwick. I bought an old car to restore, a Triumph Stag. Sid and Sue were regular visitors at the weekends and, as he was a panel beater by trade, he managed to help me with replacing some of the bodywork on the car. We would potter away with the car during the day, and Jan would make a meal which we enjoyed together in the evening. My old friend Mike Hamilton, who lived just fifteen minutes away, was always available for advice with the car restoration. There was very little he hadn't seen or done mechanically, and his knowledge of electrics was much better than mine.

Although our crazy Gordon setter (Jamie) was still with us at this time, we decided to add a golden retriever to the family, as we thought Jamie's days were numbered and we didn't want to be without a dog. Jamie kept going for quite a while before the inevitable one-way journey to the vet occurred and, by this time, Fudge had grown considerably. We had noticed that Fudge was limping quite a lot after moderate exercise, and the vet advised us that he was suffering from hip dysplasia. After a recommended surgery he was much better but was to suffer from arthritis when he got older. Fudge was an extremely gentle character, and we found that we could leave him alone in or outside the house should we need to go shopping or away for a few hours. When we returned home, he was always lying by the back door usually enjoying the sunshine.

What we didn't realise, for a year or so, was things were slightly different than we thought and Fudge had not always remained in the garden. Our neighbours, out of the blue, relayed what was actually happening. There was a blacksmith in the village where we were living. The blacksmith's shop sat on the corner in the centre of the village. As soon as we had disappeared, Fudge would wander out of the drive and through the gate, along the road to the blacksmith's shop. Here, the blacksmith (a lovely old gentleman) would share his sandwiches with our dog at lunchtime. We always wondered why his appetite was not that good on certain days.

There was also a church on the hill adjacent to the village. On certain summer days, when there was a wedding or a funeral, our dog would walk up the hill and sit at the back of the church to watch the proceedings. He became quite well known for his wanderings, but as far as we were concerned he was at home. He was always at the back door when we drove back to the house. He was a great character who we still talk about regularly.

About this time, Dan-Air started a new route between Manchester and Amsterdam. It just so happened that I was rostered for this first flight, and myself and one of the Newcastle first officers flew an empty aircraft down to Manchester well in advance so that the new service was guaranteed to depart on time. We had a couple of managers on board and some people from the press. This was still winter and it was dark as we left Manchester. As we climbed out towards Ottringham on the east coast, one of the engine instruments started to fluctuate wildly. We also got a call from one of the cabin crew.

"There are sparks coming out of the back of the number two engine!"

We shut down the engine and, as we were still nearer to Manchester, we asked for an immediate return. We obviously had to inform ATC as to what was going on and landed, fifteen minutes later, back at Manchester with fire engines to accompany us. Calling out the fire service when an aircraft has to shut down an engine in flight is normal procedure. This obviously didn't look very good for an inaugural scheduled service, and we made the newspapers but for all the wrong reasons; another failure of a 146 engine.

I was scheduled, one morning, to fly the Newcastle to Gatwick and return service. Newcastle and Teesside were both suffering from thick fog, and it put our ability to carry out the return sector to Newcastle in doubt. Newcastle was well below limits to even start an approach, and Teesside was much the same. I wandered up to operations when we got to Gatwick. They had already been discussing the weather and, always being a believer in getting someone else to make the commercial decision, I asked "Skid", the duty manager (his surname was Marks!), if he had any thoughts about where we should go should the weather in the North East remain "clamped".

"We've decided to use Carlisle. We'll bus the crew and passengers back to Newcastle."

I didn't argue. This was going to be a nostalgic trip back to where my career started, and I was looking forward to it.

We got airborne from Gatwick having duly explained the plan to the passengers. Some of them decided not to travel, but the majority stayed with us. We called Border Radar as we approached Pole Hill, a beacon just to the north of Manchester. As we listened on the frequency, and just before we called them, a British Airways aircraft called.

He gave his details to Border Radar, and the controller then said to him, "What's your aircraft type?"

"We're a 1-11. Actually, we're a Super 1-11," said a rather arrogant voice.

This last piece of information was totally superfluous to anything the controller needed to know. A Super 1-11 was a British Airways' name for the slightly stretched 1-11.

I said to Jim, the first officer, "When you call him, don't tell him we're a 146, tell him we're a Super 146."

Jim duly obliged and, before anything could be said, an AirUK small turboprop came on frequency and duly announced to the controller that he was a Super F27.

The controller at this point said, "OK, gentlemen, I think that's enough."

It was all great fun, and it gave us something to snigger about.

Sure enough, the weather in the North East didn't give us much of an option, as there was no improvement. We duly turned west for Carlisle. The weather was better there; no fog, but fairly low and overcast cloud. The approach procedure is basically a cloud-break procedure which gets one into a position, hopefully below cloud, as the decision altitude was fairly high. The last bit could then be carried out visually. I had carried out this procedure many times previously but not when operating for an airline. We approached the beacon at Carlisle, the "Charlie Lima", and descended to the west before turning back towards the field. I got the occasional glimpse of the railway marshalling yards just to the north of the city and, sure enough, just as we broke cloud, there was the airfield in exactly the expected place. A slight turn to line up with the runway in use, and we landed towards the east.

Carlisle was very much a "sleepy hollow" now. The Oxford Air Training School had moved back to Oxford, as the need for pilot training at that time was very much reduced. Gone were the days of half a dozen aircraft flying around the circuit with another half dozen or more out in the local area undergoing rigorous training in preparation for a job with one of the many airlines.

We taxied in and shut down. Steps arrived, and the passengers were quickly ushered on to their buses for their hour and a half journey back over to the North East. The next crew had arrived, and their passengers were also on their way over to be flown across to Stavanger and Bergen.

It was all a bit of an anticlimax really. As good as it was to return to Carlisle, I felt it a great shame that Bill, who had helped me so much, wasn't there to see it. He had been made redundant and he was not in the best of health.

Return to Carlisle 7th April 1987

Reproduced with kind permission from the Solway Aviation Museum

By now, British Aerospace had introduced a simulator for the 146. We could, therefore, dispense with doing our six-monthly checks on the aircraft and were rostered for two days' training and checking at Hatfield where the simulator had been installed. At first, the simulator was quite hard work to fly and, in certain circumstances, did not bear much resemblance to flying the actual aircraft. The simulator kept getting taken offline, at times, in order that the engineers could make more modifications. At one point, we actually had to go back to flying an aircraft for our check, and British Aerospace provided one of their demonstrator aircraft. At one particular check, we used a camouflaged aircraft with massive tyres. This was for any prospective purchases for the military of various foreign powers to use on rough airstrips. It made a change!

My training record to date was good and, out of the blue, I received a phone call from Clive, our chief training captain.

"Peter, we need another training captain. We hope to add more aircraft to the fleet. Your training record is very good, and we think you would fit in with the training team. Would you be interested?"

He didn't have to ask me twice.

"OK, I'll make the arrangements, and we'll be in touch."

The plan was for me to be trained as a line training captain in order to train captains and first officers to fly the line with passengers on board. I got a phone call from the training department with my "adjusted" roster. I had to go back to the simulator in order to get checked in the right-hand seat. We were qualified according to our seat on the flight deck but, as a line trainer, I had to be qualified for both seats. I would sit, as normal, in the left-hand seat to train new first officers but would need to sit in the right seat to train new captains.

I now had to observe a certain amount of sectors with a new first officer being trained. Following that, I then conducted the training of a new first officer whilst being observed by a senior trainer. This was also then covered with the training of a new captain. Finally, a similar amount of training took place in order that I could conduct line checks on captains and first officers as required every thirteen months.

In between all this, I was still flying the line as normal and going down to Gatwick regularly at the weekends to fly the routes from there. It was during one of these weekends when my third engine failure, on the 146, took place. We had departed Berne and had just levelled out in the cruise. We had a sudden "bong" from the master warning system, and I looked down to see that we had lost all oil pressure from the number three engine. The checklist led to an in-flight shutdown, and we decided to continue to Gatwick which was the acceptable option on a three engine aircraft.

The 146, being a four engine aircraft, was certificated to fly three engine ferries. This meant that, should the aircraft have suffered an engine problem, it could be flown to an engineering base on three engines only. This, of course, was without passengers and involved certain different safety procedures. It happened quite regularly in Dan-Air, as we seemed to suffer with engine problems relatively regularly, and the aircraft needed to be flown to Gatwick for an engine change. My first experience of one of these flights was with my old friend Cliff Newton. We travelled, by taxi, down to Leeds where we picked up the aircraft and flew it south. Despite the aircraft only having three serviceable engines, it still performed well, as there were no passengers and we were at a low take-off weight.

The company were dabbling with a few innovative ideas to try and make more money. One of these ideas was to operate flights from Lydd to Innsbruck for the skiing fraternity. Part of this scheme was to use a quieter airfield but, although we operated a few flights from Lydd, they were never a success. I went down there with Clive Fleming one day, and we found that the journey to Lydd from Gatwick was not only long, but the road network to get there was definitely going to put people off. Nothing came of that idea.

Another idea was to start operating the 146 from Glasgow to Ibiza. Unfortunately, we couldn't get enough fuel on board the aircraft with a full passenger load to reach Ibiza! The company, in its wisdom, decided to reduce the maximum passenger load from eighty-nine to eighty. This enabled us to get the fuel on (just) but, again, was not a commercial success.

My training to become a training captain started with the observation flights, and these were soon followed with me conducting training flights whilst being observed myself. I enjoyed this part of my flying and hoped to give the benefit of my experience to the new guys who were joining the fleet. I was soon also checked out to be able to conduct the annual line checks on crews. By now, we had four 146-100s in the fleet and the crew numbers were growing rapidly.

We also continued to have numerous technical problems. Another regular issue were problems with the hydraulics. One particular afternoon, we landed at Bristol with an indication that we were losing hydraulic contents on one of the systems. I got off the aircraft and wandered around to have a look in the hydraulics bay. I opened the door and, as soon as I stuck my head in the hydraulics compartment, got a face full of hydraulic fluid which was escaping as a "mist" as there was still some pressure in the system. A recommendation, to get the stuff out of one's eyes, was to wash them with milk. I staggered back on to the aircraft and asked the cabin crew to pour milk into my eyes. An unusual request, but it seemed to work. By the time the engineers had sorted the technical problem, I felt fit enough to continue and off we went. My logbook for that time showed various problems from hydraulics to cracked windscreens and, on one occasion, we were unable to retract the flaps after departure which meant a quick landing back at the departure field (in this case Newcastle) to get yet another technical issue sorted.

Of course, there were more engine failures. My fourth engine failure on the fleet was approaching Gatwick. The arrival took us towards Gatwick via Lydd. At this point, there was a speed restriction of 250 knots. The first officer was flying the aircraft and, as he closed the throttles to achieve the speed restriction, all the engines reduced power except one which just kept decelerating until it stopped completely. More paperwork!

I was doing a large amount of training by now. We had also received approval from the Civil Aviation Authority to be able to carry out approaches in much reduced visibility. We had to undergo more simulator training to qualify to be able to do this, and we were encouraged to fly practice approaches whenever possible. All records of these went to the Civil Aviation Authority to ensure there were no issues with the aircraft equipment which could provide problems. This was a big step for the fleet which enabled us to fly an approach with reduced visibility, such as fog, instead of having to divert to somewhere else where the weather was clear.

After the Second World War, the city of Berlin was divided into American, British, French and Soviet zones. Berlin itself was surrounded by East Germany. In 1948, the American, British and French powers announced that they would unify their zones. This caused alarm with the Soviets and, as a result, a blockade was imposed on road and rail transport into and out of Berlin. The Berlin airlift began in 1948, as the Western powers were adamant that they would ensure supplies reached West Berlin. The Russians lifted their blockade the following year, but in 1961 built the Berlin Wall that remained until 1989. West Berlin was left as an "island" within East Germany, and the only way to access the city by air was through three recognised air corridors from West Germany to the city.

In 1968, Dan-Air had started flying services from Berlin-Tegel Airport. They were using the fleet of Comets to start flying package tours in partnership with a West German tour company. The following year, a base was set up at Tegel. German cabin crew were recruited and flight deck personnel were sent out to Berlin on detachment. Eventually, the company decided to introduce the 146 to the Tegel operations which meant week-long detachments for the flight deck crews. For those of us based in Newcastle, this usually meant operating through Amsterdam initially and then on to Berlin, as we had a scheduled service between those two cities. It also meant that the Newcastle cabin crew came with us to Berlin. Services flown by us were between Berlin and either Amsterdam, Saarbrücken or Gatwick.

Due to our arrivals into Tegel being usually from the west, we had to descend to an allotted altitude to be level at a beacon named Hehlingen which was one of the entry points for the westerly corridor. In our case, this was usually a maximum of 10000 feet but sometimes considerably less. The corridor was approximately 100 miles in length and 20 miles wide and could cause us problems in the summer, as we could not deviate to stay clear of thunderstorms. Should we do so, we would stray into East German airspace and risk being intercepted or, at worst, shot at by Russian fighters. We could regularly see Russian fighters flying right up to the edge of the corridors to try and antagonise us. On the ground below, there were massive areas where Soviet forces appeared to be practising for World War III with enormous barren areas of land covered in tank tracks and which were obviously used for manoeuvres.

Life in Berlin was interesting. The West Berliners had a beautiful city with no evidence of shortages of money. The food and beer was excellent, and the operation from Berlin seemed to be thriving. On a weekly detachment, we could not only enjoy the sights but also the food and beer. Much care had to be taken, as an increase in our weight was virtually guaranteed. We usually stayed in the Berlin Pentahotel which was fairly central and full of aircrew. One particular story was of a crew who were enjoying a room party in a hotel which got slightly out of hand. For some strange reason, mainly due to the amount of alcohol which had been consumed, they decided that the wardrobe in the room should go out of the window. This task was enthusiastically undertaken, and the wardrobe crashed several floors to the ground. Unfortunately, the window that it went through was at the front of the hotel, and the wardrobe went through the large awning over the hotel entrance and narrowly missed people who were going through the front entrance. Airline management were informed, and the culprits were severely reprimanded, as the company were banned from that hotel for several weeks.

The 146 kept us on our toes, and we were having problems around this time with starter motor failures. The company decided that each aircraft would carry a spare starter motor along with instructions on how to change it. I ended up changing one in Berlin one particular day in April. It was a pain of a job, but at least the weather was relatively mild. Working on an aircraft in Berlin in the depths of winter was not an exercise to be welcomed. The 100 series of the aircraft were really causing a lot of technical issues but, by now, there were rumours of the company acquiring the 300 series of 146, with a rapid expansion to the fleet, which was something we all welcomed.

Eventually, the first 300 series appeared. I had to go down to Manchester for my check flight on the new aircraft with Clive. It was a pleasure to fly the aeroplane, all shiny, brand new and smelling as if it had just come out of the factory which, of course, it had. Although the aircraft had slightly more powerful engines it carried more passengers but, because of the increased weight, it still ran out of puff climbing at the higher altitudes. They were clean, quiet and very few "snags" appeared in the aircraft log. It was always disappointing to find we were flying an old 100 series when we turned up for work now that we had these new aircraft.

A fairly rare sight; two 300 series 146 at Innsbruck
Photo with kind permission of Chris Wood

I was permanently busy at work, and my time off usually was spent at home with Jan and the family. Kay had arrived by now, and the girls were happy around the house and garden at "Stonecroft" whilst Jan and I continued working on the old house. Each of the girls had a room of their own, and Jan was slowly transforming the garden into some form of respectability. I had built a tree house for the girls to play in, and many a happy hour was spent eating their meals in it during the warmer weather.

I had again been approached by Clive Fleming to ask if I would be interested in becoming a simulator instructor. Again, I accepted the invitation, as I thought it would help further my career and it would lead to becoming an aircraft examiner and instrument rating examiner on behalf of the Civil Aviation Authority. This involved travelling down to Gatwick regularly, getting a hire car, which was provided by the company, and driving around the M25 to spend up to a week at a time at Hatfield where the simulator was based. The simulator work involved a lot more studying for me. I also had to discover the ins and outs of how to operate the sim. I spent time with Clive, Laurie and another trainer, Dave Reiss, who gave me the benefit of their experience and knowledge whilst I learnt "the ropes".

Dave Reiss became a good mate on the fleet but sadly passed away a few years later after a battle with cancer.

Eventually, I was checked out on the sim and became heavily involved with conversion courses for those people joining the fleet. I didn't particularly relish the weeks away in Hatfield. Apart from the time spent in the simulator with the new guys, I was pretty much by myself. They would spend time studying, apart from meeting up for an odd beer and a bite to eat in the evenings. It was always good to go home at the end of the week.

Another of the new destinations for me was Gibraltar. This airfield had its own problems and required a trip on the jump seat as part of the requirement to be qualified to operate into this category of airfield. Gibraltar is adjacent to the Spanish border and any infringement, without prior agreement, was likely to stir up a hornets' nest. There were also considerable issues with the "Rock". With the wind from certain directions and only of moderate strength, the turbulence could endanger the aircraft, as it could become virtually uncontrollable. I went down there on the jump seat of a 737 whilst the crew gave me the benefit of their knowledge. The first time I went down there with the 146, we landed without any problems and, as the 737 crew had told me to do, I dutifully collected all the newspapers which had been left lying in the cabin to take them up to air traffic control, as they much appreciated any newspapers of the day. I wandered up and had a chat with them. It was then end of 1991, and Robert Maxwell had been found drowned after it appeared he had fallen off his boat in the Atlantic. One of the ATC guys pointed to his boat, the Lady Ghislaine, which was moored in the harbour. The boat looked impressive.

"It's a bit like its owner," he said, "top-heavy, overweight and not very good in the water."

Storm clouds now seemed to be starting to appear in the package tour business. There was considerable competition regarding the selling of seats, and the cost of borrowing was high. It seemed as if it was going to be a monumental battle between Air Europe and Dan-Air as to who survived.

146-300 at Gibraltar

Photo with kind permission of Chris Wood

The International Leisure Group (ILG) was run by Harry Goodman, which was a rags-to-riches story in itself. He set up Intasun and, following the demise of Court Line and Clarksons in 1974, he had a team of people who picked up over 65000 of their customers and many cheap hotel rooms. Dan-Air was already flying charters for Intasun in those days, but inevitably Harry Goodman thought it would be cheaper and more efficient to do the flying with his own airline. Air Europe was launched flying not only to Europe but also to the United States.

ILG expanded rapidly, with a large fleet of new aircraft in its stable, but the Gulf War of 1990-91 proved its undoing. In 1991, ILG collapsed owing £500 million and 4000 people lost their jobs.

The Dan-Air staff breathed a sigh of relief, as it seemed as if it could well have been Dan-Air rather than Air Europe who collapsed first. Lack of a link up with a tour operator meant that more emphasis was being put on scheduled service routes and, as a result of Air Europe's demise, Dan-Air took over several of Air Europe's scheduled service routes from Gatwick. Times were still tough despite Air Europe having disappeared. Several tour operators had set up their own airlines, and Dan-Air were still operating a hugely varied fleet of aircraft many of which were nowhere near fuel-efficient. The writing was on the wall.

I was still spending most of my time training other pilots on the 146 which included a lot of time away in the simulator at Hatfield. A large amount of my flying was out of Gatwick, and by mid 1992 we had taken delivery of a total of four 146-300s. The new aircraft were also "glass cockpit" aircraft, and all crews required a check flight to help with the differences and ensure they were happy with all aspects of the slightly different displays. The "glass cockpit" just meant having a small screen, similar to a television screen, rather than the separate instruments on the panel in front of you. Having undergone a check flight, I found myself sitting on the jump seat more and more to check other crews. With the increase in the size of the fleet, the training department was becoming very busy.

The new year of 1992 was a tough one for the company, and everybody was now starting to fear for the future. Dan-Air decided to consolidate and try to control their budget more efficiently. A decision was made to move the two 146 aircraft based in Newcastle to Gatwick along with the crews. This was a major blow to Jan and I, who had spent the last six years restoring our old farmhouse near Morpeth, but we felt it would be more sensible to make the move together rather than me trying to commute. The three girls were still very young, and maybe there would be more opportunities for my career in Gatwick. With heavy hearts, we put our house on the market and starting making plans to move.

We made several trips, over the next few weeks, to Gatwick to look round the surrounding area and try to find a new home. We didn't find anything that we liked in East Sussex and, after searching West Sussex, we eventually found a superb home just outside Storrington. Built in the Sussex-style, it even had a swimming pool. It was close to Becky's godparents, Julian and Alison, and despite the forced move south we were starting to feel much more enthusiastic.

Very quickly, we had a buyer for our house in Northumberland. However, matters seemed to be dragging with our purchase, and communication from the estate agents seemed to be virtually non-existent. It was now only two weeks until the expected move. We could not understand what was going on but, after what appeared to be very "shady" dealings on behalf of the estate agents, they informed us that the house we had set our hearts on was no longer available. I'm still somewhat confused over what happened back then, but it is enough to say that I didn't have anything complimentary to say about the agents, as their actions were dubious to say the least. When we are in Sussex and see one of the agent's boards there are a few choice words heard. We had to return to the search for a home and found a nice house, eventually, which we settled on along the road in West Chiltington. No swimming pool this time!

The day of our move came and, after a sad farewell to friends and neighbours, we made our way south to Sussex.

A company doctor, by the name of David James, had by now been brought in to try and improve the outlook for Dan-Air. He came to talk to us, and we received a "questions and answers" letter from him. Rumours were flying thick and fast, and eventually the news came that the company was to be wound up with a sale to British Airways for £1.

As seems to be the norm for situations like this, we actually heard that Dan-Air had stopped trading on the BBC news. Other friends and colleagues were in the same position. The media had the information before the employees.

It just so happened that the day we received news of the total collapse of the company was the same time that our old friends Sid and Sue had arrived to stay with us. I shall always remember them saying to us that they had £1000 in savings and, if we needed it, we should make use of it. They were great friends, who in years to come, we sadly lost contact with due to their divorce.

Julian and I went to the Wena Hotel at Gatwick one evening, where our union, BALPA, had arranged a meeting for Gatwick pilots to present to us the details of our fate. Unfortunately, this was not a proud moment for various parts of our industry, and most of the ex-Dan-Air staff have strong opinions on what we considered a wrongful outcome of the Dan-Air demise. The union told us that they had agreed reluctantly with British Airways that seniority, a traditional method used to decide redundancy, would not be taken into account, as they did not think the situation warranted it. This meant that, eventually, pilots who had been in the company for twenty-five years were made redundant and some, who had only been in the company for two months, were kept; it all depended on which fleet the individual pilot was on. British Airways wanted to keep the more up-to-date Boeing 737 aircraft, together with the crews who were qualified on that type, and everybody else would go. Furthermore, they were only prepared to pay a paltry amount of redundancy payment. The union claimed that, by doing this, they were at least saving some jobs. There has been much written about the demise of Dan-Air and, no doubt, it will still be discussed in years to come. Suffice to say that it was a sad and stressful time for many and a victorious time for others.

The flying programme was due to finish mid November 1992. That left a couple of weeks of "normal" flying operations before we were to hand in our IDs and other bits and pieces. We were left in no doubt that there had to be no unusual manoeuvres carried out, and a colleague was severely reprimanded for carrying out a low pass at Gatwick in his fully loaded Boeing 727. In hindsight, we should have never been allowed to operate during that last two weeks. All of those who were destined for the dole queue had a tremendous worry about the future and it was, without doubt, a safety risk.

I got a call from Laurie, our fleet manager, who told me to make my way to Hatfield where the senior trainers were putting us into the simulator to renew our instrument ratings. The hope was that this left us another twelve months or so with a current rating which might help in the pursuit of another job. It was the quickest renewal I have ever done, but it was legal and the fleet management had done their best to try and help us all in the future.

CHAPTER 14

On the 6th November 1992, I carried out my last flight for Dan-Air. Myself and the first officer, Chris Wood, took a 146-300, registration G-BUHC, from Gatwick to Bristol Filton airfield. We were ferrying the aeroplane back to a British Aerospace airfield, as they were being returned to the manufacturer. Having landed at Bristol, we were told to park and close the aircraft up. It was a sad day, and we drove back to Gatwick in the taxi in virtual silence.

So what would happen now? We had only moved to Gatwick, a few weeks previously, and had bought a house which entailed taking out a large mortgage. I had also taken out payment insurance for the mortgage so, as I was now to be made redundant, at least the mortgage would be covered. Or so I thought. Having contacted the building society, they informed me that there was a "cooling off" clause in the policy which meant that it would not be valid should I lose my job in the first 90 days, and we were still within the first 90 days.

The flight deck of G-BUHC as Chris and I left it 6th November 1992
Photo with kind permission of Chris Wood

We received five months' salary from the company, as well as the statutory redundancy, so we had a little bit of breathing space, but it was time to start chasing another job.

Julian and I went to the unemployment office to see whether we had any entitlement to any financial help. I shall always remember the two of us turning up at the office in a suit, shirt and tie. This was something that we had not had to deal with in our lives, and we were very much out of place dressed like this. We sat opposite a rather dubious-looking gentleman who was reading a pamphlet entitled Claiming benefit for those with a criminal record. We had hit rock bottom.

Yet again, Laurie Buist came to my rescue. He rang me up one morning.

"Peter, I have just been chatting to a friend of mine at British Aerospace. They need a simulator trainer at Woodford to conduct conversion courses on the 146 to Makung crews, one of the Chinese airlines. There's a little bit of work for you if you want it."

Having thanked Laurie profusely, I rang the number he had given me and was given details of a meeting in Woodford with the gentleman who required a trainer. I drove up, and we met at a hotel near Manchester Airport to discuss all the details. It was a "no-brainer", as I would have done the work for a lot less money than I was being offered. It involved a couple of weeks' work every month for the next two months. In those days, British Aerospace were paying fantastic allowances which included mileage, hotel, lunch and dinner, and even an allowance for drinks in the evening. I ended up earning as much in two weeks, as a simulator instructor for British Aerospace, as I was in a month for Dan-Air.

I remember turning up at the simulator block for my first session and being introduced to the other simulator trainers. A lot of them were retirees, but some had lost medicals and were enjoying keeping in touch with flying by teaching others in the simulator.

I remember saying to the chief sim instructor, "I don't think I'll ever fly again."

"Don't be ridiculous," he replied, "of course you will."

He was right.

After a week's work, I would drive back to Sussex, and we would take Julian, Alison and family to the pub for drinks and a pizza; some light-hearted relief during those dark days.

The crews that I was given responsibility for were from a company called Makung or China Northwest Airlines. Officially, they didn't use English on the flight deck, and so I was given an interpreter. The interpreter was a very young lady who translated my every word into Chinese. This all made life very difficult. Not only was I trying to teach Chinese pilots how to fly a brand-new type of aircraft, but I had to use the most simple and straightforward phrases in the English language to try and get my teaching points across to them. The interpreter knew absolutely nothing about aviation, and so I had to explain certain things to her before she could pass them over to the pilots. I was earning my money here. There were other issues which were completely different to the aviation norms of the Western world. The two pilots consisted of a very senior captain and a very junior first officer. The captain would undergo his two hours of training in the left seat. After a ten-minute break, halfway through the session, it was the turn of the first officer. Instead of him flying from the right-hand seat, he also climbed into the left seat to fly the aircraft from that side; very unusual, as crews are normally qualified by the seat. It was also common practice, with one particular crew, to see the older captain starting to hit the first officer on the shoulder if he was struggling with certain parts of the exercise. I had to explain, through the interpreter, that this was not the way we did things, and I didn't appreciate his physical interference!

During my time at home with Jan and the girls, I was desperately applying for a new flying job. Jan's parents used to work for a paper company in Aberdeen who manufactured top-class writing paper. Due to this, we had a good supply of nice paper particularly in a shade of blue. I handwrote many letters to many airlines trying to find another flying job. Although my writing is not the best, I always felt that it gave a personal touch. The reason I mention the writing paper will become apparent a little later.

One of the companies that I applied to was Saudia or Saudi Arabian Airlines. I received a letter back from them asking me to come for an interview in London. The day came and Jan dropped me off at the station, and I made my way up to the Saudi Arabian Airline office in London. There, I was introduced to a gentleman called Geoff Uren who was the senior pilot on the Boeing 737-200 fleet. I was taken into a room and introduced to half a dozen Saudis who were in traditional white Saudi dress. These were all people connected to the airline but only one of them, plus of course Geoff Uren, asked the questions. If successful, they wanted me to join Saudia as a captain on the 737s to fly with inexperienced first officers around the Gulf but also into airstrips with no air traffic control and poor runway surfaces. I was more than happy to do this. My base would be Jeddah. The only problem was that I had three children and, for whatever reason, they would only allow me to take my wife and two children to Saudi.

I went home and told Jan about this issue. However, as soon as it was mentioned in front of the girls, our eldest, Becky, declared that she would be delighted to stay in the UK. We knew there was a good girls' boarding school in Keswick, near my parents, where she could go at the weekends. Problem sorted.

A few days later, I received a phone call telling me that I had got the job. I was still uneasy, however, about splitting the family up.

Dave Reiss, one of the senior trainers on the Dan-Air 146 fleet, rang me up.

"Pete, I've been asked to set up a 146 operation with a company called Business Air flying between London City Airport and Frankfurt. If you're interested in joining me, come and have a chat with the man in charge."

London City Airport had opened in the docklands of London. The runway was short, and there were a lot of obstacles on the approach (buildings in the City). It was ideally suited for the 146, and the idea of the service was to give business people a quick connection between financial capitals without all the issues of getting out to Heathrow or Gatwick. A quick trip on the Docklands Light Railway from the city centre was all that was needed.

I went to meet Dave and the man in charge. He was a retired, senior military man who I didn't particularly take to but, nevertheless, the job was mine if I wanted it.

I now had two job offers, one of which meant we could stay together as a family. The job with Saudia was potentially more secure and the money was better. However, the other meant we didn't have to go to Jeddah. I had never been to Jeddah but wasn't exactly keen to go.

At this time, I had been sent a reply to my letter written to Virgin Atlantic asking about potential vacancies for pilots. Unfortunately, they informed me, they were not recruiting pilots but would keep my letter on file. Not long after receiving that letter, I was out of the house getting some shopping for Jan one day. When I got home, she told me that Virgin Atlantic had been on the phone and I was to ring them back as soon as possible. This I did and was told that they wanted me to come for interview in a couple of days. How things had changed in such a short period of time! The day, 3rd February 1993, arrived, and I drove up to Crawley and found my way to Virgin's head office. I was taken to a room where there were five other ex-Dan-Air captains all waiting for interview.

Virgin Boeing 747-200. The next step.
Photo with kind permission of Chris Wood

We all chatted away and eventually my turn came, and I was taken through to an interview room where there were half a dozen people waiting to talk to me. They were all introduced, and there was a lady present who I recognised as ex-Dan-Air. She was now head of the HR department. There was a very senior training captain, who was ex-British Airways, and the others included the chief training engineer and senior people from flight operations. It was a rather nerve-wracking experience, as I really wanted this job and didn't want to make a mess of the interview. However, they were very understanding and told me that they knew it was a long time since I had undergone an interview. I didn't mention Saudia. I noticed a pile of application forms in front of the HR lady, and there on the top was my handwritten letter on that blue paper. There were lots of questions over the next thirty minutes or so, and they explained that, although they had originally not required any more pilots, they now required experienced captains due to unforeseen expansion. The idea was to employ successful applicants as first officers for eighteen months, to learn the routes and the Boeing 747, after which they would move to the left-hand seat as captains. I didn't think, at the time, that it would happen like that... but it did. They were as good as their word. I made my way home, after the interview, for the long wait and telephone call to give me the result of my full application.

After two days, the phone rang. I had been successful, and my starting date was 1st March. Things were looking up, and we celebrated the news by going to the pub! Julian had managed to get some help with his application to Virgin by using one of Virgin's flight managers who he knew. He had no further news about his application, but his turn would come before too many weeks had passed.

I wasn't quite there as yet, because I still had to pass a simulator assessment on the 747. We were sent details of the exercise and details of all the flap and power settings along with the speeds they wanted us to fly. This was obviously not an exercise on how to fly the 747, as we knew nothing about it, but it was to see how well we could take in information and apply it to flying this aircraft as well as we could under the circumstances. The simulator block was in Burgess Hill, and I made my way along there on the specified morning. There I met virtually all the guys who had been at the interview in Crawley. There were two training captains who were to run the exercise, and they briefed us before going into the sim. Fortunately for all of us, the briefing went something like this...

"We are ex-Laker Airways. We have both been made redundant in the past. Don't worry too much about this sim assessment."

That was such a great attitude, as our futures were hanging on the next few hours. All went well, thank goodness, and success and starting date was confirmed a couple of days later with a phone call from Virgin.

I now had to contact the various people who had made me the offer of a job and who I was going to turn down. I started by contacting Geoff Uren. He was absolutely charming about the whole situation. He said that he fully understood my decision and, should I ever be in need of a job again, I was to contact him. Lovely guy! Unfortunately, I could not say the same about the "gentleman" in charge of the 146 operation. He proved to be rather unpleasant over the phone and, in the end, I put the phone down to end the conversation. Thank God I wasn't going to work for him.

CHAPTER 15

I only had to wait a couple of weeks before starting my course, and we discovered that another friend of mine, Nigel Barnes, who had flown as my first officer on the 146 several years previously, was teamed up with me on the course. Marvellous! Nigel had taken a command on the Boeing 737 fairly recently and was still based in Newcastle. Unfortunately for him, this meant that, although he was flying the correct aircraft, he was at a base other than Gatwick and was not offered the opportunity to join British Airways. Ridiculous really, but such was the mindset of BA at the time.

The 1st March soon arrived, and I picked up Nigel and we made our way to the first day of ground school in the Burgess Hill sim block. We drove across there, delighted at our fortune for having secured a job with Virgin Atlantic but slightly subdued at the demotion to the right-hand seat as a first officer. We were going to miss all the aspects of command but, according to the people at Virgin, we were told it would only be for eighteen months.

There were six of us on the course, and the ground school was to be run by training flight engineers. The first day was run by Allan who was the senior training flight engineer. We were given an immense amount of paperwork to fill in for our new employer plus a desk full of manuals to learn about the aircraft and the Virgin Atlantic operation. Within an hour, we had started the 747 technical course. All the aircraft conversion courses I had completed, over the years, started with the electrical system of the particular aircraft and this was no exception.

Over the following days, our heads were filled with all the new systems of the aircraft and the facts and figures which we had to learn. Every morning started with a quiz around the classroom to make sure we were keeping up with everything we had to know. It was always a slight worry that one didn't know the answer as the training engineers went round the room asking questions. One could easily be made to look a complete idiot! There was always friendly banter between the flight engineer fraternity and the pilots.

We were given example questions and answers for the Air Registration Board examination which would come at the end of the first four weeks. There was a colossal amount of things to learn about this aeroplane and, when we got home in the evenings, there was lots of homework.

We were taken to Gatwick Airport for an aircraft visit. This was to help tie in with what we were learning about the aircraft. We were shown around the outside looking at the various bits and pieces as we went. All the numerous systems could be viewed as we walked around this monster. Eighteen wheels, brake packs, flaps, flight controls, leading edge flaps, four enormous Pratt and Whitney engines, lights, compartments for this and that, baggage holds and so forth. Then, of course, there was the inside of the aircraft.

This was an aircraft with just under 400 seats, but Virgin had aircraft which held more. These were known as "Florida config" aircraft. These were aircraft mainly used for the Orlando and Miami routes which were high-density holiday flights. We were shown everything that we needed to know at the aircraft visit, from the crew accommodation at the base of the fin to the flight deck at the "pointed end". This was a flight deck which I had last seen in Prestwick when an American crew had shown us the inside of their 747 freighter. Having spent the last fifteen years in the flight deck of "normal" size aircraft, the view from the flight deck was just totally different. The flight deck sits just over 30 feet above the ground and gives one the impression of sitting on the top of a building. It was just totally different to anything I had experienced in the aeroplanes I had flown so far.

After the first four weeks, we were presented with the exam for the Air Registration Board. We could not afford to fail this and, within a few days, the company had received the unofficial "nod" that we had all passed; first hurdle completed.

The next few days covered all the items such as emergency equipment and performance (calculations of take-off and landing weights and other aspects of what the 747 could actually do on four, three and even two engines). We also approached new subjects including the North Atlantic Track system and how it worked.

The North Atlantic Track system is used twenty-four hours per day, three hundred and sixty-five days per year. It has devolved over the decades to provide a safe system for aircraft crossing the North Atlantic. The air traffic control authorities on either side of the North Atlantic, or "pond" as it is affectionately known, decide every day where the tracks will run usually dependent upon wind and any very nasty significant weather. There are somewhere in the region of six to eight tracks (parallel and 60 miles apart) which usually have the entry point somewhere to the west of Ireland and the exit point somewhere in the area of Newfoundland. In those days, the tracks were agreed upon by Shanwick ATC (on our side of the Atlantic) and Gander (on the other side). They had a reporting point every 10 degrees of longitude. They were organised to take into account the prevailing winds where possible. The prevailing winds, in this part of the world, are usually westerly and so the tracks for the westbound aircraft were usually constructed to keep out of the stronger headwinds. In some cases, the miles flown could end up being longer, but if the headwinds were significantly less then the flight time would be less. It was all about saving fuel. Sounds odd but it's true.

Most westbound departures are early morning to midday, so the flight planning department for each airline, and each flight, would look at the weight and capability of the individual aircraft and request a particular track on the north Atlantic, at a particular speed, which was usually a combination of economy and flight time. If you got the requested track at the requested altitude and speed then lucky you! If not, the crew had to set about a "track change" calculation to see what the penalties in time and fuel were. With the aircraft approaching the new entry point for the new track at 8 miles per minute, the calculations had to be quickly checked by each other on the flight deck and then entered into the inertial navigation systems to enable the aircraft to navigate over several thousand miles accurately.

With me so far? Good! It's not rocket science!

Conversely, most eastbound flights leave the United States in the evening (local time) to arrive back into Europe between breakfast and lunch. The track system was then planned and altered to allow aircraft to now take full advantage of the prevailing winds. At higher altitudes, very strong winds called jet streams are present. These can vary in strength and, in some parts of the world, they can exceed 200mph. Towards the edge of these jet streams, the air can be very turbulent. The situation regularly presented itself for an eastbound flight to be relatively short in time but could also be quite a rough ride. Crews reporting for a flight coming eastbound through the night would sometimes look at the track that their flight planning department had given them and then look at the forecasted levels of turbulence. It was not unusual for them to ring flight planning and ask for a reroute, as the level of turbulence on the planned route was too great.

There were other routes, in those days, too. It was not unusual to find your flight had been planned to Florida passing to the north of the Azores and within a few miles of Bermuda. Flights to the west coast took a much more northerly route. Generally speaking, if the earth is a sphere then the shortest distance between two points is to cut that sphere in half with the cut passing through the two points; much like cutting an orange in half. The same applies to the earth. The shortest distance between two points is to imagine the earth has been cut in half with the shortest distance being along the cut. In navigation and flight planning terms, this is called a "great circle" route. A quick look at a great circle route between the United Kingdom and San Francisco or Los Angeles will show you that the great circle route takes you approximately over Iceland, Greenland, northern Canada and over the Rocky Mountains. This, again, can vary due to winds and forecast turbulence.

All this, and more, was information that we had not come across in our aviation careers, as none of us had flown long haul previously. It all seemed way above our heads initially but, with practical use in the coming weeks, it was all to fall into place.

Eventually, Nigel and I received our simulator programme. We were again teamed up together, which was a very pleasant prospect, as we could talk to each other about the simulator exercise before we went into the "box". We could also do a post-mortem, when we came out, after any debrief from the training captain. We were allocated a training captain who was a true gentleman. He was a retired British Airways captain who was now flying with Virgin Atlantic. He was full of knowledge regarding the 747 and an excellent trainer. Unfortunately for us, we couldn't say the same about the training engineer! He was a rather aggressive gentleman who we didn't take to at all.

Overall, Nigel and I worked extremely hard with the sim conversion, and the feedback from our training captain was good. It had to be. The prospect of a command in eighteen months time meant we had to have a sound training record. At the briefing and debriefing, the training engineer seemed desperate to try and trip us up with his technical questions. They became more and more in depth.

Nigel was asked one particular question.

"If you don't give me the correct answer, I shall take the checklist and shove it up your arse!"

"Well, having removed the checklist from my bottom," said Nigel, and proceeded to give the correct answer.

We both survived the 20 simulator sessions and, when we came to the end, we were both complimented by our trainer and received a nice report. Fortunately for us, the nasty, aggressive, little git had been replaced by a much more pleasant training engineer who did his best to be constructive. What a refreshing change.

The next stage was to proceed to base training.

May 5th 1993, we assembled at the Gatwick Virgin Atlantic crew room for a briefing from our base training captain. He spent an hour over the briefing and then told us that he planned to carry out the detail at Châteauroux in central France. One of the new guys was "volunteered" to fly the aircraft out to Châteauroux and then fly the requisite number of circuits before the rest of us took our turn. The weather was good, and we left Gatwick for the flight of just under an hour. Like a bunch of overexcited schoolboys, we spent the time making tea for the people on the flight deck whilst eagerly awaiting our turn for what is the most exciting part of any type conversion course; the first time we would actually handle this large aircraft.

It was still a lovely sunny day when we arrived and, after the first pilot had completed his circuits, we taxied to the apron. We had a handling agent at Châteauroux for any problems that should occur, but he was also there for another purpose. Following the completion of the first pilot's circuits, he and the ground engineer who was with us (in case of any technical problems that needed to be dealt with) were thrown out of the aircraft for a trip to the local supermarket. The handling agent drove them the few kilometres into town and back. They took a "shopping list" and returned in time for the flight back to Gatwick.

My turn came, and I completed the required number of "touch-and-goes" to the satisfaction of the training captain. What a pleasure to get back to handling an aeroplane, particularly this one. The power from the four engines is immense and had to be brought back to a training setting. As we had no passengers, freight or bags, the weight was exceptionally low and should we have used normal settings the aircraft would have been exceptionally lively.

All the other guys completed their turn, and we eventually returned back to the deserted apron to pick up our "shopping". It had been a good day and with only a couple of landings that we could laugh at and make rude comments to the perpetrators!

Everybody had completed the detail successfully, and we arrived back at Gatwick ready for a trip to the CAA the next day to have the luxury of a Boeing 747-type rating entered into our licences.

I had to wait a month for my first line training flight. It was a warm June afternoon, and I had made my way up to Heathrow to meet my trainer, Jim, for my first trip to Newark, New Jersey. Paperwork was completed, and the handling agents, British

Midland, gave us a lift out to G-VGIN which was sitting on a stand with a hive of activity going on around her. Baggage pallets were being loaded along with freight, and fuel was being pumped in at a much larger rate than I had been used to. We climbed on board, said hello to the in-flight supervisor (IFS) who was in charge of the cabin and made our way upstairs to the flight deck. I still was taken aback by the height of the flight deck and the view of Heathrow. I'd never had anything like this in the aircraft I had flown previously. Frank, the flight engineer, sat down at his panel to start his preflight checks before going outside the aircraft to check all was in order there. I sat down in the right seat and started with my various chores. Jim and Frank had checked the technical log, and we had discussed the various "deferred defects" which we were allowed to dispatch with. Jim started to load the triple inertial navigation systems which would take us along our planned route. In the meantime, I was busy calculating the take-off performance which would be checked by Frank.

Eventually, the standard time of departure arrived and, with all doors confirmed closed and locked, I asked Heathrow ground for pushback clearance.

The starting engine procedure on the Classic 747 is done by the captain and flight engineer. The captain can see the flight engineer's panel from his seat just by turning and looking over his right shoulder. Therefore, the first officer, who sits directly to the front of the flight engineer's panel, is left to monitor the radio and start the stopwatch to ensure any time limitations are not exceeded.

All engines started, Jim cleared the ground engineer, who was outside monitoring the pushback and engine start, and I requested taxi clearance. This was the first time I had flown from London Heathrow and, although different, was fairly straightforward.

We departed from runway 09R (right), one of the easterly runways, and following a fairly early right turn which included the noise abatement procedure, we were vectored out to the west. Flaps retracted, we accelerated to 250 knots and, eventually, the radar controller told us to route direct to Trent which is a beacon in the Manchester area. I was just about keeping up with matters, as it was all very new, but Jim was patient and was monitoring the change in fuel tank configuration which Frank was dealing with. It was all going very quickly and, before I knew it, we were passing the Manchester area having achieved our minimum flight level which air traffic control had given us as a restriction at that point.

Our Atlantic crossing had been planned at 35000 feet and a speed of 0.84 Mach (speed relative to the speed of sound. This is how speed is measured at high altitude). We were planned to cross on track W (Whisky). As the entry point to our requested track was now less than an hour away, Jim told me to use the other radio and get our crossing clearance. I called Shanwick Radio and was told to stand by. Would we get the requested routing, altitude and speed, or would we get a change which would involve recalculations and track change books being shuffled quickly around the flight deck as new time estimates were made?

After five minutes, the Shanwick controller came back with a clearance which, fortunately for me, meant we were given exactly what we had requested. We were told to route direct to our entry point and climb to our cleared level. Having checked that the aircraft was not too heavy to climb straight away to 35000 feet, we didn't have to wait to burn off a few more tons of fuel before being able to achieve it. We settled down and kept an eye on the ETA for the entry point. We were expected to achieve that ETA with no more than a three-minute discrepancy. If we were going to be early, we could slow down; if we were going to be late then we would have to check with ATC and make sure they were aware. We couldn't give problems to any aircraft behind us which would then reduce separation.

For the first time in my career, we were now starting an Atlantic crossing to go and see the United States. The great unknown lay ahead.

The cabin crew brought us a menu to choose our meals. Luxury! This had been unheard of in my previous life. We had already been supplied with a large tray of sandwiches, on the ground at Heathrow, just to "keep us going". If we were lucky, the cabin crew would also let us have a look at the upper-class chocolates should there be any left by the passengers. This was all before afternoon tea and, of course, anything else that we could always request. We were also asked what drinks we would like to take off the aircraft at Newark. Virgin had a generous policy of allowing us to take a small amount of alcohol off to drink at the hotel. I was never a big drinker and always asked for a couple of Budweisers. Some of the older generation were quite hard Scotch drinkers and would ask for that.

The navigation was being done now by the triple inertial systems which were linked to each other. They were a similar system to that which took Apollo 11 to the moon in 1969 and were still in use. The three systems "talked" to each other, and should one of them lose the required accuracy it would be disconnected. Upon reaching the other side of the Atlantic, they would be checked again in relation to the position of a known ground aid and, if necessary, disconnected if accuracy was not good enough.

As we approached our entry point, I made a check call on the HF radio. (High-frequency radio was used crossing the Atlantic, as the normal communication was VHF which is only good for line of sight.) The Shanwick controllers could hear us on HF, and we crossed the entry point at 10 degrees west in the knowledge that the rest of the reporting points crossing the ocean would be made using the HF.

The middle of the Atlantic is traditionally 30 degrees west. An hour or so later, we were to make our position report to the Canadians with Gander ATC. This we duly did having said cheerio to the Shanwick controller. We were now being looked after by the Canadians. Jim had, by now, pulled out my training file and started to go through the mass of questions and subjects to be covered during line training.

He signed off the first half dozen or so and eventually said, "That'll do for today; we'll do a few more tomorrow."

We continued to chase the sun which was streaming in through the left-hand window of the flight deck. It had been a smooth crossing so far. I had completed the Atlantic chart which showed our critical point and also our point of no return. The critical point is the point at which it is the same time to continue to a planned diversion, close to landfall on the Canadian side, as it is to return to a safe airfield back on the eastern side of "the pond". Should we have a serious technical issue, or passenger with a serious medical problem, these issues needed to be kept in mind. The point of no return is the point at which we only have fuel to continue to destination and are unable, due fuel, to return back to departure point.

Eventually, Newfoundland appeared on the horizon. I felt a bit like an early explorer with land appearing way over in the distance! We were now talking to Gander on VHF, and there was the airfield itself in the middle of what could be, in the winter, a wild landscape. Gander had been used over the decades as a "staging post" in aviation. It was used, along with Goose Bay, for aircraft to refuel before starting the long and, what were then, dangerous oceanic crossings. Most aircraft, in the early days, were not pressurised and were thrown against the elements at relatively low levels. There, they were subjected to all weathers most of which were experienced due to poor quality forecasting. Due to the leaps forward in science, we can now sit in a warm flight deck, in shirtsleeves, whilst stuffing our faces, with an autopilot connected to inertial navigation or GPS. That is not to say that we don't earn our money when there are problems to deal with.

This was my first time on this side of the Atlantic and the view was tremendous. We coasted down the eastern side of Canada, passing the massive estuary of the St. Lawrence River and Nova Scotia, whilst enjoying a light snack for afternoon tea. Jim briefed Frank and I on the arrival into Newark. It was basically going to be a bit of a "bun fight", with the last 100 miles or so done at low level, with other traffic flying freely in our area with them possibly not talking to ATC. He also warned me that ATC was at a "machine-gun" pace, and they didn't take it lightly if they had to repeat anything as it would be incredibly busy.

ATC finally gave us our initial descent and turned us right, direct to Albany. We had to be level just before Albany at flight level 240 (24000 feet). After this point, we were given further descent and were way below an ideal descent path therefore using copious amounts of fuel. The ATC was indeed rapid fire which got worse as we eventually approached the airfield at Newark. There were, what seemed on the radio to be, dozens of aircraft in front of us and behind us, and ATC continued to give us speeds to fly in order to keep their traffic patterns where they needed them. So far, so good. I had managed to keep up with them and not been given a "tongue-lashing". Jim continued to keep a close eye on me and, eventually, after much radar vectoring, there was the runway ahead of us. We were landing on runway 22 left. Newark has two parallel runways and the right-hand one was being used for departures. Several aircraft ahead of us had been told to "go around". It seemed as if someone was not flying the speed allocated by ATC and had "cocked-up" the separation. He was suffering the wrath of ATC. Eventually we landed, and Jim had warned me that this is where the fun would really begin. During rush hour, the airfield was incredibly busy on the ground. Routings were fired at each aircraft, and should they go the wrong way they were put in the "sin bin" by ATC. It didn't matter if you were departing or arriving. If you went the wrong way on the ground, you not only suffered the embarrassment of ATC letting you know, in no uncertain terms, where you had made the incorrect turn but also were placed in the "sin bin" (which was a parking point where other aircraft could taxi past you) for five or ten minutes until you could be given new taxi instructions to put you on the right path.

We waited for clearance to cross the right-hand runway, until there was a gap in the departing traffic, and found our way to the "gate" where Jim asked Frank to shut down the engines. Whilst we secured the aircraft and completed the paperwork, the passengers were all disembarked. We gathered our bits and pieces, and made our way down the stairs, to wait until the cabin crew were finished with their various bits and pieces before we all got off together. We passed through the terminal, on to immigration, and then picked up our suitcases at a particular point in the baggage hall where crew cases were all left together in the crew area. Then it was outside, on to the bus and the journey into New Jersey. The five-hour time difference had placed us right in the middle of rush hour, and the journey could take us more than an hour despite the hotel not being that far away.

Once in the hotel, we were given our allowances for the twenty-four-hour stopover. This was paid in cash, as the long-haul airlines were aware of the fact that crews might not want to eat at particular times due to jet lag. If we were paid in cash, we could eat when and where we chose.

All our hotels had a room allocated as the crew room. It was agreed that those that wanted to would meet in the crew room in an hour; time for a shower and quick reflection on the day. After a quick drink, we decided to adjourn to a local hostelry for another beer and a bite to eat. Jim was extremely pleasant company, and it turned out that he was chief pilot at Virgin in the early days.

We eventually decided to call it a day and agreed to meet the next morning for breakfast (early afternoon back in the UK). There was a system in place whereby the captain would receive a fax from London, as soon as the outbound flight had left Gatwick, to let him know that everything was running on time or if there were any delays. The crew would each receive a phone call from hotel reception an hour before the bus was due to pick us up. Should anybody be asleep, this would give them ample time to get ready. With all this in mind, we agreed to do some shopping. All bases, in the early days at Virgin, had a crew car. Each car had one of the flight engineers delegated to keep an eye on it regarding oil levels etc. They were fairly old machines, but those that wanted could join the crew car club and subscriptions went towards upkeep.

It was through this scheme that one could be introduced to the joys of Costco, Home Depot, Sears and other great places to buy "toys". Like others, I regularly received a shopping list from my wife and children to bring items home from the United States.

We made our way back to Newark Airport that afternoon. My mind was full of the various procedures with the 747, as it was my turn to be the handling pilot and fly us home under Jim's supervision. After getting to the aircraft (G-VRGN this time), we checked the weather, aircraft state and the planned routing home. I managed to load the INS, which Frank double-checked, and gave the take-off briefing to Jim. He then added a few tips of his own. All advice was very welcome. This time Jim was using the radio, and we taxied out to runway 22R (right) for our departure without any problems. Soon after take-off, it was a quick left turn followed by a right turn, and we were then given radar vectors before being released on our way. It was dark by now, but the large area of New York was quite easy to make out before we climbed into the cloud and all below disappeared. The flight home was a quiet event as night flights usually are. We talked about various subjects, and Jim signed a few more items off on my training file. Our track across the Atlantic was more southerly to take advantage of the jet stream. Our outbound flight was an airborne time of six hours and fifty-five minutes compared to six hours twenty minutes on the way home. The only issue here is that being closer to the jet stream can give a turbulent ride. Such is the trade for trying to save a bit of fuel. The 747-200 burns approximately 12-13 tons of fuel per hour depending upon weight!

We eventually approached the west coast of Ireland and, with the help of ATC, got a few direct routings towards Heathrow. Apart from the fact that I was totally knackered due to the adrenaline required for my first trip in the aircraft, I had enjoyed the new experience. Heathrow was using one of the westerly runways today, and we were vectored with no delays into Heathrow. We had missed the rush hour. I went through the landing procedure in my head... 100 feet radio altimeter call announced by the flight engineer, at the 50-feet call look at the far end of the runway, at the 30-feet call raise the nose by a couple of inches (gauged on the windscreen frame) and close the thrust levers. Hold it there and keep the wings level! Not the smoothest of landings but perfectly acceptable. We taxied in, and I handed over control to Jim to park the aircraft, as the guidance system is set up for the left-hand seat. After a quick debrief from Jim, it was on to the crew bus, back around the M25 and home. I was desperate for sleep!

It was just under a week until my next flight which introduced me to the delights of JFK Airport. Even busier than Newark, we had to join the holding pattern at Calverton, on the eastern end of Long Island, before getting cleared onwards to the airfield at the other end of Long Island. The extremely pleasant training captain who I was with embarrassed himself by thumping the aircraft on to the runway which drew adverse comments from the cabin crew well after we had arrived. He was highly embarrassed, but I said nothing just in case fate would catch up with me which, at some time or other, was inevitable.

Our twenty-four-hour stopover in JFK involved the crew bus to our hotel on Long Island. This sits on Mitchel Field which is literally a stone's throw from Roosevelt Field where Charles Lindbergh took off for his solo crossing of the Atlantic Ocean in 1927. There is a small museum now where Mitchel Field once was. I never seemed to have the time to visit it. We had the usual meeting in the bar for beers and a plate of wings before retiring. The flight engineer on that trip was a particularly interesting chap. He was probably older than average but had crossed the Atlantic many times, over many decades, and had many "war stories" about flying the route in very old propeller-driven aircraft.

The next morning involved another trip for various shopping requests from wives and, by the time we'd all had a couple of hours' nap in the afternoon, it was time to set off on the journey home.

I again flew the sector back to London Heathrow, and all seemed to go well. The landing, although safe, was still "by numbers" rather than any finesse, but I was told that would come with more experience on type. It couldn't be any worse than the landing we had experienced back in JFK!

My third trip was back to JFK with the chief trainer. The flight engineer on this trip was an ex-Cathay Pacific man; lovely bloke, highly experienced and knew every nut and bolt on the aircraft. He was meeting his mate in JFK, who was already over there, and was also ex-Cathay Pacific. He was a great character in himself and, it was fair to say, that they both enjoyed a good time on a night stop. At one point, after we had landed in JFK, I was pulled to one side and advised not to try and keep up during the evening as it could be a costly affair. I wasn't sure whether he meant costly in terms of financing the drinks or costly in terms of a hangover! I quickly found out what he meant. It was another thoroughly enjoyable few days away, and I was starting to feel a little more comfortable with this "big bird".

I was not looking forward to the next two training trips. I was rostered to fly with a guy who had a reputation as a "hard man". Every airline has these characters, and it is a known fact that should someone's confidence be broken it is very hard to bring it back up. The first flight was down to Orlando, and it gave him a flight of over nine hours to ask the most awkward questions.

At one point, when he had left the flight deck, even the flight engineer leant forward and said to me, "I don't know where that bastard finds these questions. I've been flying long haul for years, and I don't know what he's talking about!"

The second trip was to Miami. I would normally be quite happy to take any criticism "on the chin" but, on the way back from Miami, I had had enough.

"Where do you expect me to find the answer to that last question?" I said.

"Well, you need to read the airman's information manual."

"I've never heard of that. What is it?"

"It's an American publication."

"That's all well and good, but you've flown for an American carrier and lived in the States. Where are we supposed to source this material? Is there a copy at head office?"

"Well no... but you can always go and ask around when we night-stop in the States."

His argument was pathetic, but I let it go at that point. He was a known quantity.

My next two sectors were my final line check and were to be undertaken with George, the fleet manager. Everybody spoke highly of him, but I was just slightly concerned that word had got back to him about my difference of opinion with the previous guy. I met George at the bus stop in the staff car park. He introduced himself.

"Hello, you must be Pete. I think we're off to Orlando together. How's it all going?"

"Well, George, I thought it was all going well, but I had some issues on the previous trip."

George was about to open my training file for a quick perusal whilst we waited for the bus.

"Who were you with? Oh, yes, I see. Him! Ignore him."

I immediately felt at ease.

George asked me to fly the first sector out to Orlando, and we had plenty of time for him to ask me questions and get to know each other. He had a cracking sense of humour and was a highly experienced pilot. He had flown long haul for many years. He was excellent company, and I could immediately see why everybody spoke highly of him.

At that time, we stayed in the Peabody Hotel in Orlando. It was a beautiful hotel, and they had a large fountain and pond in the reception area. Way up on the roof of this large building, they had quite a large collection of ducks. I'm not sure if they were wild or tame, but every day they would bring all the ducks down to reception in the lift and they were allowed to swim in the pond and enjoy the fountain. It was a tradition and went on every day ad infinitum. However, at some point, one of the crews decided to "kidnap" the ducks and hold them to ransom. They were very much the worse for wear and, having found the ducks on the roof, they were taken to one of the crews rooms whilst the particular demands were made. It was most likely a request for free beer, chicken wings or something similar, but it didn't go down well and, from that point, our days in the Peabody Hotel were numbered. It's a great story, which as far as I understand is true, and very typical of aircrew who have had one too many!

When we got back to Gatwick, George told me that he was very happy with my performance and I was released to the line.

As with any conversion course, the "meat is added to the bones" when one gets signed off at the end of the official training course and one starts to fly with the ordinary line captains. This is where you get more tips, to add to your knowledge, without the stress and formality of flying with a trainer. I was eager to increase my knowledge and listened to every item of interest that was given to me.

Within a few weeks, I was rostered for my first Tokyo trip. This was done with a "heavy crew" i.e. an extra first officer and an extra flight engineer. It's a hell of a long way to Tokyo! The route took us east from London to pass north of Moscow. From there, we routed across what was known as the great Siberian f**k all. Leaving London just after lunch, the flight ended up in the dark fairly soon, flying away from the setting sun. Altitudes had to be converted from feet to metres as that's how it's done in Russia. Exceptional care had to be taken with the conversion. The figures were double-checked and checked again. Way over on the other side of Siberia, when in contact with the Japanese, the clearance reverted back to feet. In more modern aircraft than the 747 Classic of those days, there is a button on the altimeters to automatically change the presentation from feet to metres. No such luxury back then. The other issue, regarding flying in Russian airspace, is the fact that the airways were of short sectors between turning points. In most parts of the world, ATC were happy to give shortcuts and clear one direct over long distances to cut out the smaller dog-legs. This saved time and fuel. Not so in Russia. The inertial navigation systems that we used would hold only nine waypoints. As there were so many waypoints that we had to fly over, we were forever adding new waypoints to the INS as we made our way along the route. No shortcuts there. One of our flight engineers made a small handout, which I regret I no longer have. In it he wrote details about the various towns and cities (not that many as we were way up in the frozen wilderness) and the wildlife in the areas that we passed. It was really interesting, and the only thing I remember was detail about the diamond mine at Mirny. In the handout, he claimed that the Mirny mine was the largest man-made hole on the surface of the planet.

We passed airfields such as Irkutsk, Novosibirsk and Vladivostok. The weather reports, particularly in the winter, could be dire, and we had to bear in mind exactly where we would divert along the route with a serious problem should the situation arise. We took turns with crew rest during what could be an eleven-hour flight to Tokyo. There was only one captain and so, at times, two first officers were working together, one of which was delegated as pilot in command, until the captain was back from his rest. He was never far away should he really be needed.

As the flight progressed, we decided to ask one of the Russian air traffic controllers what the weather was like where he was.

The answer came back, "Cold."

Narita Airport is about 50 miles outside Tokyo. The town of Narita is not that big and centres on life at the airport. We stayed in the Tokyu Hotel which was clean and smart and centred around aircrew. They had a crew restaurant and a large stock of DVDs available to crew that couldn't sleep. This sounds odd but, with the long flight east from London, I and many others found the jet lag very difficult to deal with. Many lost souls were seen at various hours of the night making their way down to reception to pick up a video to watch. I found the food in the restaurant quite good, but the portions were very small. On later trips, I would take a few snacks with me in my suitcase to keep hunger at bay.

Having landed at Narita, which is a large and very slick airport, we got on the crew bus to the Tokyu Hotel. Bear in mind that departure from Heathrow was at 2 p.m. and the flight was eleven hours long. It's now 1 a.m. UK time in Japan, but the time difference is nine hours so the local time is 10 a.m. By the time we reached the hotel, it was nearly midday local time. My body clock was totally confused! Experience over the years had told our crews that the best thing to do was to go to bed as soon as we arrived and set the alarm to catch the 5 o'clock bus into Narita. That is what we did. Having dragged myself out of bed, I got downstairs to find other loyal devotees to the plan awaiting the bus. Off we went into Narita with all sorts of plans in mind for me, as it was my first trip there and we had to do something special. I felt this may well be a bad idea.

One of the attractions of Narita for aircrew is the "Truck". The "Truck" is exactly that. It is the rear of an articulated lorry which has been converted into a bar. For whatever reason, people enjoyed going there and, after a long flight with a high rate of dehydration on the body, the alcohol took effect very quickly. There were all sorts of stories about people using the outside toilet (which was a Portaloo) and other groups of aircrew turning it upside down whilst the victim was still in it. Fortunately, I did not succumb to that treatment. I had been warned about the effects of a certain Japanese beer and the chemicals involved in the brewing. It seemed fine to me, but it caught up with me at some point later in the proceedings. Having experienced the delights of the "Truck", we then had to go to the "singing bar". This was a seedy bar with a karaoke where the new guy (or girl), arriving in Narita for the first time, had to give a rendition of their choice. In my case it was "New York, New York", but I do remember a member of another crew giving such a superb example of "La Bamba" that he wasn't allowed to leave until he had repeated it several times, much to the appreciation of the dozens of crews joining along with him. After a few more beers, we went to one of the Korean restaurants to eat. By this time, I had drunk far too many Japanese beers but, despite the warnings, it didn't seem to have much effect on me. I'm not sure what or whose pet we ate at the restaurant, but I didn't remember much about the journey back to the hotel. The next morning, I felt as if death would be a pleasant release and spent most of the day drinking water and examining the menu of the restaurant, again, as I brought it all back. Just as well we had the day off.

The expenses were very generous for a Tokyo trip and, when the crew arrived back at the airport for the trip home, there was a rush to the foreign exchange to convert what expenses we had left into sterling. Generally speaking, we did well as, unless one made the effort to go into Tokyo itself, there wasn't much shopping to be done in Narita.

Over the months, I did quite a few Narita flights. I was still very much learning the ropes. On one particular trip, I was flying eastbound with a very nice captain of Scandinavian descent.

He looked towards Scandinavia, as we passed to the south, and said, "In the summer, up there, we hunt and we f**k. In the winter, we just f**k."

I had learnt to take things easy in Narita by now, and he suggested a walk into Narita on our day off, instead of the usual trip around the bars, which I agreed to. It was towards the end of the summer and was very hot and humid. As we walked along the edge of the paddy fields, I could see things wriggling at the edge of the path. The place was littered with snakes, or so it appeared. I hate snakes, and we came back to the hotel on the bus. There were other eating houses in Narita, one of which was "Ken's". This was a tiny room about the size of an average lounge in a new, semi-detached house. You were lucky (or not) to be able to get a seat but, once in there, the food was tasty and seemed to be of good quality until I noticed, one day, Ken happily cooking the orders in his wok with a cigarette hanging out of his mouth. As he dealt with the food in the very hot fat, the ash from his cigarette was regularly falling into the wok. The other alternative was McDonald's, where the local speciality was a McTeriyaki burger.

I really didn't enjoy the Narita trips and was fortunate enough that I managed to swap most of them, as people were keen to take the trips as the expenses were so good. I did manage to do a couple with old Dan-Air mates which made them good fun. One was with my old mate Julian. We ended up doing a duet in the singing bar. Yet again it was "New York, New York", which we still laugh about to this day. The other was with Tony, who I flew with many times in Dan-Air. We did quite a bit of walking on that trip admiring the blossom trees of Japan. We were flying with a flight engineer who joined us for the walks and a gentle beer or two on that trip. Unfortunately, he was suffering terribly from haemorrhoids, and we had to find a chemist to buy some cream to help relieve his symptoms. Unfortunately, our childish sense of humour was not subtle, and we had to remind him not to mix up the haemorrhoid cream with his toothpaste. We told him he didn't want receding gums or the ring of confidence.

I conducted my first trip to the west coast of the States. Any trip to the west coast involves stunning views if the cloud permits. Having left Heathrow, we made our way up the western side of the UK passing the Western Isles of Scotland. From there, the route took us over Iceland, which can look slightly barren but, nevertheless, is an interesting place which I made a mental note to visit one day. Then over the Denmark Strait which saw a lot of action during the war with the search for the German battleship Bismarck. Well before crossing the east coast of Greenland, one can usually see the mountains which reach up to over 12000 feet. The colours of the sea around the coast, along with the ice and icebergs in the area, are amazing. Crossing Greenland shows mile upon mile of mountains covered in snow and ice. We kept an eye on the weather at Sondrestrom on the west coast, and Thule way up in the north of Greenland, just in case we needed somewhere to go in the case of a severe problem. It was rare for us to be as far north as Thule but, just occasionally, we routed up towards those latitudes depending on the jet streams. Thule is an American air force base with a nice long runway; a good place to have up one's sleeve if required.

Leaving the turquoise ice on the western side of Greenland, we routed over Baffin Bay towards Baffin Island. Iqaluit was now lying a few hundred miles off to our left. There were full hospital facilities in Iqaluit which was good to know. With Hudson Bay off to our left, we checked the weather for Churchill, just in case. It was reduced visibility, in blowing snow, that day but, nevertheless, it was open.

We were now really up in the frozen wastes of Canada. In this part of the world there can be navigational issues. The magnetic pole is a long way from the true North Pole, and a magnetic compass is not of much use. Although we use inertial navigation systems, we were now in an area with very few useable airfields in case of emergency. We had been given ground tuition about flying in this part of the world, and the ship's (aircraft's) library contained a file with full details of landing strips available to us and the approach procedures to be followed. Some of these strips, such as Hall Beach and Coral Harbour, which were almost at 70 degrees north, had gravel runways of not much more than 5000 feet in length. Should we have had a catastrophic problem that required an immediate landing, it would have necessitated extremely accurate flying assuming the weather was good enough to make an approach. We did practise the slightly different types of approach in the simulator should we be presented with this situation. If all had gone to plan, we would have, no doubt, ripped up most of the gravel runway which was not designed for an aircraft as large and as heavy as a 747. Any fire services required would have been minimal and, again, assuming all had gone to plan, we would have almost doubled the figures of the local population with a full 747 load of passengers. It was all a worst-case scenario problem and would have been better than the alternative! It would also require a Boeing test pilot team to have the aircraft stripped down to a light weight and fly it out of there if the runway surface was still up to it.

As we proceeded further south and enjoyed the pleasures of afternoon tea, the landscape slowly changed from snow and ice to fairly barren, flat landscape with very large lakes and eventually masses of forest. This was Saskatchewan and Manitoba. As the miles go by, the never-ending landscape now changes to the Great Plains. ATC cleared us direct to Moose Jaw. Winnipeg lies way over to the east. As the weight of the aircraft reduced with the fuel we had burned, we kept requesting a climb to a higher and more fuel-efficient level.

Eventually, we got clearance towards Great Falls, Montana, named after the five large waterfalls on the Missouri River. The Rocky Mountains could be seen over to the right; my first sighting of them and everything else in this part of the world! We continued south, passing Boise in Idaho, and on towards Carson City in Nevada. Eventually, I could make out the Pacific Ocean to the right of the nose; another first. The captain had briefed both of us, and we were now thinking about the approach and landing into Los Angeles. There are four parallel runways at Los Angeles. They would eventually give us a runway which we could expect to land on, but this was likely to change at short notice and we might have to "sidestep" to a different runway when we were within just a few miles. We would be approaching the airfield from the north-east and passing over high ground, so we needed to be very much aware of the safety altitudes. The air traffic control would be the usual "rapid fire", and they didn't want to have to repeat themselves! There would also be light aircraft in the vicinity, who might not be listening out on the radio so, all in all, we needed to be on the ball.

After just one "sidestep", we landed and then we found our way to the "gate" without any further issues. The engines were shut down and, for the first time in over eleven hours, all went quiet. The ground crews and baggage handlers approached the aircraft like ants. The 747 is a beautiful, graceful aircraft but, despite wearing a headset, it's bloody noisy on the flight deck. The aircraft cruises at a higher speed than average, and the noise of the air around the flight deck windows when cruising at .85 of the speed of sound is considerable.

We eventually disembarked, and I followed the rest of the crew to find the crew bus. The cabin crew were chatting away to each other about their plans for the next forty-eight hours. A quick beer on the bus, and we were at the hotel. With the eight hour time difference, it was only mid-afternoon despite being late at night back at home. Plans were made to meet in the crew room for an hour and then we were off for some shopping to finish a very long day. I tagged along, just to have a look at the area and enjoy this new part of the world. The next day involved a visit to Home Depot for the flight engineer to buy some gadget or other. Jan had given me a list for Costco and asked me to buy a quilt for our bed. I couldn't find exactly what she wanted and made an executive decision to buy one with a pattern that she would consider suitable. Needless to say, I got it wrong, and it is still a bone of contention over twenty-five years later. We still have it, and I consider it a masterpiece.

As usual, we had a full day off in LA, and I enjoyed been shown the various popular places with the crew (i.e. cheap!)

for breakfast and for eating and drinking as the day went on. What a pleasure to have breakfast at a restaurant on a pier with dolphins splashing about all around us. The flight engineer decided to take the crew car to a shop he wanted to visit up in the mountains. He asked me if I wanted to go with him and off we went for a pleasant afternoon. We had a look at the areas where the wealthy lived and stopped at the edge of the Pacific Ocean on the way back to town and had a bite to eat in the sunshine.

The next afternoon, we set off for the long journey home. We were back into Heathrow at midday and, after the bus journey round to Gatwick, I arrived home knackered! Although the longer flights such as these allow for crew rest of maybe two and a half to three hours, it is not the same as being in one's bed at home. The eight hours' time difference doesn't help.

I continued flying my roster and meet other very pleasant people in Virgin. I, eventually, was given a "reserve" month which came around about two or three times per year. This was basically just a month on standby where one was at the beck and call of crewing to fill in and cover things such as sickness. Having spent the first ten days of the month at home, the phone eventually rang, and they asked me to report for a Tokyo trip. I wasn't enthusiastic about Tokyo trips, but that's how it went. I got on the bus at Gatwick, to travel around to Heathrow, and another first officer introduced himself to me.

"What are you doing today?"

"I've been called out from reserve for a Narita (Tokyo)."

"Is this the first time you've been called this month?"

"Yes."

He said, "You've got the wrong idea. You need to call crewing every day. You need to push them to give you a trip."

"But I'm a lazy git who would rather be at home," I said.

We were on a different wavelength. That was the truth of the matter!

The first year with Virgin went very quickly, and it was a great pleasure to fly with the different characters that made up the airline. The flight engineers were also a new addition for me, and they were very knowledgeable members of the crew. They were good company on the layover and generally had a good mental map for the best bars and restaurants in town.

I continued to learn the ins and outs of the 747. The aircraft that we flew did not have a great deal in the way of flight management systems. The more modern aircraft were fitted with computers that would give us information such as when to start a descent taking into account the upper winds. No such luxury for us! We had to multiply our cruising altitude by 3 i.e. if we were at 35000 feet then the descent had to be started at 35 x 3 = 105 miles from the arrival point. We also had to make further allowances for the headwind or tailwind during the descent. It was a little more complicated than that but involved mental calculations rather than a computer. We also kept the calculations going during the descent to ensure the profile was remaining correct and we were not drifting too high or too low. I remember making a complete cock-up of a descent into Heathrow with one particular captain. We were far too high on the profile, and I had not spotted it. It didn't help being so tired but that was all part of the job. When the captain eventually pointed out my error, it took all of the speed brake and pointing the nose rapidly downwards to regain our correct descent profile.

I was highly embarrassed, apologised profusely, but he just laughed and said, "We've all done that."

CHAPTER 16

Virgin had told those of us joining from Dan-Air, on the early courses, that we would get the opportunity for command after eighteen months. Sure enough, as the eighteen-month anniversary of our joining date approached, we were notified that we would be assessed for the left-hand seat. We were given a simulator assessment initially, with everything but the kitchen sink being thrown at us, to see how we coped. That went well, and I then had to fly four or five trips on the line with a training captain whilst my performance on the line was also assessed. We were asked to make all the decisions on the trip and deal with any eventualities that should occur.

One of those fights was rather unusual. I was with a training captain on a trip to Boston. The flight across to Boston went without any problems. It was always pleasant going to Boston, as the flight was relatively short and around the time of the "fall" the views and colours of the landscape were stunning. We stayed at a hotel in the city, at that time, so it was easy to shop, and we frequented a bar which served the most wonderful chowder that came in a hollowed out sourdough loaf. This place was a favourite watering hole of the crews. We met for breakfast the next morning, and then did our shopping, before making our way back to our rooms for a quick nap before the pickup.

I had just got back to my room when the phone went. It was the training captain ringing to tell me he had received the fax, and the aircraft that we were going to operate the return service with had left London. There was a note on the fax saying that the aircraft had an autopilot issue. There were two autopilots, one of which had failed during the westbound sector. This meant that, in practical terms, the aircraft had only one autopilot. The second autopilot also had a history of failing in flight. This left us with the possibility of getting airborne and being left to manually fly the aircraft should both autopilots let us down. This had all kinds of associated problems which could possibly mean we should not enter oceanic airspace without an autopilot. One could only hope that, if both autopilots decided not to cooperate, it would happen within a few minutes of landing at our destination! If the engineers at Boston had done their level best to remedy the problem and presented us with an aircraft with a serviceable autopilot, then it seemed sensible to accept the aircraft for service, as there was no reason not to. This was the issue that I, as a future commander, had to make the decision on.

Fortunately, I knew that the training captain was as enthusiastic as I was to "get the job done", and I suggested that we accept the aircraft but put extra fuel on board in case we ended up hand flying the thing through the night. Should this situation occur then the aircraft would be easier to fly at a lower level, hence the extra fuel required.

G-VMIA in Boston

A long night ahead awaited with this aircraft

Sure enough, one autopilot refused to connect just after departure and the other failed at a rather inconvenient point. We took turns, for about twenty to thirty minutes at a time, to hand fly the aircraft and complete the sector. We sent a message to operations to ask air traffic control to try and avoid any holding at Gatwick, as we were going to be fairly knackered! Unfortunately, the message didn't get through, and we had to hold before being allowed to make an approach. It was probably not quite the correct thing to do, but we wanted to get the service done without incurring another massive delay in Boston with an aircraft with a fault that was proving difficult to find.

I got a good write-up, and I was given the required grades and full reports that I needed for a command conversion course. The simulator requirement was completed without any problems, and I then went on to the line training. I was very lucky in that I was rostered to fly with some very senior trainers. They were virtually all ex-British Airways training captains who had retired from BA at 55 years of age and joined Virgin for a few years more flying. Some of them had been flying 747s since the aircraft first arrived in the UK and had a vast amount of knowledge. My final line check was conducted under the supervision of one of these gentlemen. I was also very lucky to have my old friend Tony Foote rostered as my first officer.

Off we went to San Francisco which was the first time I had been to that destination. All went well, and we had forty-eight hours to have a look at somewhere new and enjoy a few beers. It had been decided, on the flight across, that the training captain would spend his full day off at Point Reyes watching the whales from the beach. Tony and I decided that we would walk to Sausalito and have a couple of beers and a plate of chicken wings. Jack, the flight engineer decided to join us.

A brisk walk to Sausalito 24th November 1994

My trusty crew! Slightly concerned?

Following our walk across the Golden Gate Bridge, we enjoyed a spot of lunch and then we caught the ferry back to town having quietly celebrated my successful sector to San Francisco. There was only one more sector to complete with Tony acting as the handling pilot. This sector was to go well, and the command course was completed.

I spent the next few weeks consolidating my new position. This included several trips to San Francisco. Another of my trips was with Tony, and this time we took our wives along. We had a superb flight engineer with us, Brian. One of his little idiosyncrasies was to adjust the power in the cruise himself in order to keep the aircraft speed at the correct target. He preferred matters if the pilots didn't touch the thrust levers (an American-built aircraft refers to throttles as thrust levers) in the cruise, and he amused our wives when he gave us a jestful "tap on the knuckles" with his ruler if our hands ventured anywhere near those thrust levers. He said it was his job to maintain the correct speed in the cruise, and he didn't want the pilots interfering; all done in good fun! Our wives were lucky enough to get upgraded to upper class, and I went down to see them both during the flight. They were enjoying all the freebies including the champagne and upper-class food.

As I left them, Claire turned to me and, whilst giggling, said, "Pete, don't fuck up the landing!" They'd had enough to drink.

I always enjoyed going to San Francisco. At that time, we were staying in a Holiday Inn in Union Square. They had a very nice bar, on the top floor, where we could have a drink and get a reasonable view of the city. It was a pleasant place to wind down at the end of a long day's flying.

Tony and I did yet another San Francisco trip together. This time we flew with Brian again who had suggested to us both that if we all bid for a trip together he would take us sailing. He had his own boat in the UK and was an experienced sailor. (We were allowed to bid every month for trips or particular days off that we wanted and, every three months, we were at the top of the list for our preferences. The system, generally, worked well and this meant everybody who wanted it could get a good "bite of the cherry" for holidays such as Christmas once every third year.)

Sure enough, on this occasion Tony, Brian and I had managed to get a San Francisco trip together and, after discussion in the bar on the evening of our arrival, a plan was made. Some of the cabin crew decided that they would like to come along, and we met the next morning, after a good breakfast, and made our way down to the place Brian had organised the boat rental. Fortunately, the girls who came with us had decided to bring "supplies" which included some food and a vast amount of booze. We had a great day sailing around the San Francisco Bay under Brian's guidance. None of us knew the front end of the boat from the back, but a good time was had by all, and the only issue at the end of the day was sunburn. We finished the day by having a meal together in the "Stinking Rose", a restaurant where all courses contain masses of garlic. I am led to believe that, at some point, the company put a letter out to crews asking them not to eat there the evening before departure if possible, as there were complaints from passengers about excessive garlic fumes from the crews.

There were times, on the longer trips, that some crews preferred to do their own thing during the forty-eight hour layover. That was absolutely fine with me. Some people preferred to save their expenses and others had plans of their own. I was always quite happy doing any shopping that Jan had asked me to get and then browsing the many second-hand bookshops which could be found particularly in San Francisco. I was usually looking for old books by Ernest K. Gann. Aviation enthusiasts will know that, amongst many others, he wrote Fate is the Hunter. It is a classic aviation book, and it used to be said that if a young, aspiring pilot had read the book he could put another thousand hours in his logbook!

I have a good collection of Ernest K. Gann books which were bought back in those days.

There were also liaisons formed during some layovers. Some of the younger first officers "dallied" with certain members of the cabin crew. This either formed long-term relationships or could end with, what we called, the "thirty west divorce". Thirty west was regarded as, more or less, halfway across the Atlantic. Occasionally, one of the cabin crew would appear on the flight deck halfway through the flight home and discuss any potential future relationship with the young man in question. Should he prove uninterested then the flight deck door was closed (or slammed) and the divorce was complete! This, of course, worked both ways. The young man may ask if he could go for a walk around the cabin and come back twenty minutes later with his tail between his legs. Such is life!

After a very pleasant few months of consolidation in the left seat, the "Tony Foote fickle finger of fate" was about to make itself known again. Tony and I had been rostered for a trip to Orlando together which, in itself, was to be looked forward to. Tony had opted to fly the sector to Orlando and, after an uneventful flight, we duly adjourned to the bar with several other members of the crew for light refreshments, as was the usual. The next day, we met up for breakfast and took the crew car for our usual shopping for the wives and family. That evening, we met in the hotel foyer and eventually made our way on the crew bus back to the airport. All was on time. The weather forecast for the route was reasonable but with thunderstorms forecast all the way up the east coast of the United States which was nothing unusual for July. We had a full flight, as the aircraft was in the "Florida config" with 500 passengers and a few babies. It was a humid evening and dark, as we lined up the aircraft on runway 18 left at Orlando. Due to the high weight and the ground temperature, we were expecting a long take-off run and the engines needed a high power setting. (Should conditions allow, we could reduce engine power settings from maximum during the take-off. This is all calculated carefully and saves engine wear.)

Tony gave the usual speed calls during the take-off and, at his call of "rotate", I eased the control column back to achieve the necessary attitude for take-off. The nose wheel had just come off the ground, when there were two almighty bangs and the aircraft yawed to the right. There was a large flash from the right-hand side of the aircraft. My immediate thought was that we had hit something on the ground, as it was dark and we could only see runway lights. As I assumed the landing gear could be damaged, it would be prudent not to retract it. Any damage could further damage the undercarriage bays which, in turn, could give us more problems when we tried to extend it again.

"Leave the gear down," I said.

"Understood."

At this point, we were airborne, climbing away. I still had a rudder input, as the aircraft was definitely trying to yaw to the right.

Phil, the flight engineer, then called, "Engine failure number four."

We looked down, and the exhaust gas temperature gauge had not only exceeded the maximum but the needle was well and truly against the stop on the instrument.

"OK, gear up." It wasn't a problem with the gear. We had some form of engine compressor stall. (The airflow through the engine has been disrupted and can slow down or even reverse in direction.)

"In-flight shut down number four engine," I requested.

Air traffic control had been watching our departure and asked if we were OK.

"Yes, we're good. Please stand by." We could leave all the chit-chat until we had secured the engine and the aircraft was climbing away safely going where we should be going.

"Florida is yours," said ATC. In other words, you can go where you like until you are sorted out.

Tony and Phil carried out the checklist whilst I flew the aircraft and, once I had it all trimmed out and everything was where I wanted it, I engaged an autopilot.

Once the initial problem had been dealt with and the aircraft was secure, we decided on a plan of action. Under normal circumstances, the company preferred an aircraft with a technical problem to be taken to New York (JFK) where they had a large engineering facility. The forecast showed thunderstorms right up the east coast. There was no way I was going to take a heavily laden 747 on a one and a half hour flight, dodging thunderstorms, with reduced performance, to JFK. The safe and sensible thing to do was to land back in Orlando and get the problem sorted out there. Looking at what had happened, it could well require an engine change.

The maximum take-off weight of the aircraft was 362 tonnes. However, the maximum landing weight was 265 tonnes. In an absolute emergency, the aircraft can be landed at max take-off weight, but we now had the situation under control and, again, it would be sensible to dump some fuel to reduce to the correct landing weight. This we conveyed to ATC as, in the United States, there are specific areas that one can dump fuel, not just anywhere. However, this time they were extremely helpful and asked us to climb to 6000 feet and let us dump the fuel there and then. This all takes time, and we needed to stay well clear of any thunderstorms which we could see slowly approaching in the far distance.

I spoke to the passengers and explained what was happening. We also briefed the in-flight supervisor so that she could prepare the cabin for our arrival back into Orlando.

After thirty minutes or so, the thunderstorms were starting to drift in our direction and were getting a little too close for comfort. We decided to stop the fuel dump and land at the weight we were at. This meant we had to aim for a smooth, gentle touchdown (didn't we always?) and there would then not be any further issues for the engineers regarding an overweight landing.

We were vectored back to the longest southerly runway by ATC and landed amidst a mass of fire engines. Normal procedure is to come to a halt after landing so that the fire crews can inspect the engine before we carried on to the gate to disembark the passengers. This way, they can check visually that there is definitely no fire or damage to the aircraft that could give any problems on the ground. This duly took place, and we eventually got back to the point we had started from.

The engineers came up to the flight deck.

"We were watching your departure. There was about 150 feet of flame which came out of the front of that engine. We genuinely expected to look into the number four pylon [where the engine is mounted] and see nothing. We thought it had fully come apart and disintegrated!"

Thanks to the professionalism of the cabin crew that night, we did not receive one complaint. There are always whingers and moaners amongst passengers but, as they were kept fully informed all the time, they were in extremely good spirits. They were also going to receive another free night courtesy of Virgin Atlantic in Florida. That may have helped!

We spent another night in Orlando and, after a mass of paperwork, I received a call from the engineers saying the FAA (American version of the British CAA) were at the airfield wanting a complete internal inspection of that engine. I fully expected another aircraft needing to be flown over to take the place of ours but, during the following morning, received another phone call to say that our aircraft had been pronounced serviceable and we would be taking it back to Gatwick. The engine had been given a borescope inspection which meant the internal parts of it had been looked at through a camera on a flexible extension. The engineers found one of the bleed valves had been the culprit and adjustments had been made. That evening, we departed for the UK with three sets of eyes firmly attached to the number four engine instruments during the take-off to ensure there were no further problems.

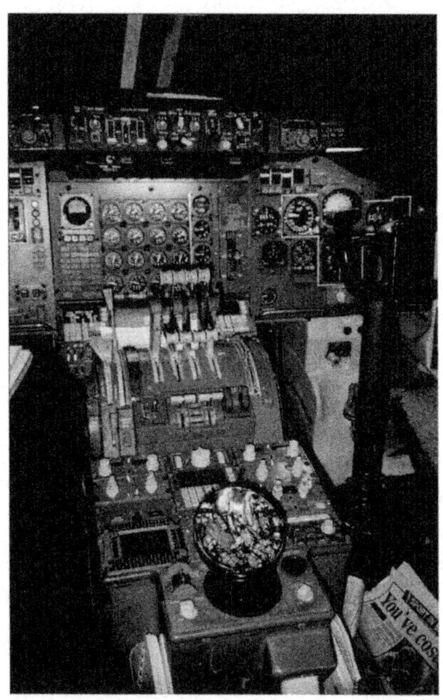

Sweeties with kind permission of Virgin Atlantic cabin crew

Photo with kind permission of A. R. Foote

With mates somewhere over Greenland

When I lost my job with Dan-Air, it had been a big bone of contention that we had been made redundant on the basis of the type of aircraft we were flying and not with regard to time in the company. We had also only received a statutory minimum redundancy payment which was a rather paltry amount. Over a hundred of the redundant pilots, including myself, had got together and paid £1000 each into a "fighting fund" in order to employ a QC to fight our case in court against British Airways in order to receive the rightful amount that we felt we were entitled to. A thousand pounds was a lot of money to find in the days following the loss of our jobs, but we had been advised that our home insurance would possibly cover this. It had done so, and the whole process that we followed had taken the next few years to go through the courts and reach a decision. We won the case, and my payment increased from the statutory minimum of £205 for every year of employment to over £15000 in total which was a marvellous result. We had used the smaller amount to buy a trailer tent, as we were not sure whether or not we would be in the position again to be able to take the girls on any form of holiday. This proved to be a worthwhile buy, and we had some wonderful holidays with our old friends Terry and Alison in the Lake District.

At around this time, Jan and I were thinking about moving back to Northumberland. West Sussex did not hold good memories. We had been forced to move there by the initial circumstances of Dan-Air moving the aircraft type I was flying to Gatwick and, within three weeks of actually moving to Gatwick, I had been made redundant. Although we liked the house we had bought, it was by no means an ideal house for us, and we were used to the wide, open spaces of the north. Sussex is very leafy. The girls had more or less settled into their schools but, whenever we visited the north, it was always a big wrench to pack up the car and have to drive south again. There were many people who commuted in Virgin and, with up to 15 flights per day between London and the North East making the commute viable, we decided to go back to the north of England.

We put our house on the market and left the girls with friends for a few days to go house hunting. Jan and I had been invited to stay with our old friends Ray and Neeta from the village of Hebron which we had left three years previously. We found the market poor at that time in the North East and decided we would rent a property, as we couldn't find a house with the qualities we were looking for. Our house in Sussex sold quickly, and the day eventually arrived when we left the south of England to return "home". The rented property we had decided upon was lacking in insulation and cost us a fortune in LPG to heat. We almost froze to death over the few months we stayed there.

We eventually bought a property to the north of Morpeth which turned out to be a mistake. It was a very pretty old farmhouse we had bought from a farmer who ran a go-kart business next door. The karts had two-stroke engines and were very noisy. Racing took place every couple of weeks at the weekends. We did not want the noise around us and only agreed to buy the house if the farmer accepted a covenant in the paperwork that restricted karting to once every three months, that karts with four-stroke engines only raced and all proceeds went to charity. This was duly agreed to and we moved in. We found a superb old-style builder who came and started the modernisation work that we required.

Unfortunately, the relationship with the farmer did not go well. He was used to having everything his own way and did not appreciate the fact that it was his obligation to maintain our access road properly along with various other issues. Our close friends, Cliff and Sandra, had moved into one of the barn conversions next door, and we all had issues at some point with this rather awkward gentleman.

After a month or so, he approached me and told me he was going to start the karting again, as he needed the money. My response was that if he did, I would sue him for every penny he had! Needleless to say, this didn't go down too well and relations continued to deteriorate. It was time to move on, as I really didn't need all this hassle every time I came home from work tired and jet-lagged.

We found a house that we liked on the edge of the town of Morpeth and were very pleased when we sold the house and could finally move out and away from the problems associated with it. We had very pleasant neighbours at our new home and none of the issues we had suffered from in the old property.

I commuted without any significant problems initially. A friend of mine in British Airways could check on the loads, as all my tickets were on a standby basis. I also used British Midland from Heathrow to Teesside, and the Midland ticket desk people were always very helpful. There was also CityFlyer, a subsidiary of British Airways, who flew between Gatwick and Newcastle and, for a short time, Gill Air also flew the same route. They used small, slow, unpressurised aircraft that flew at much lower cruising altitudes, so a flight in winter with bad weather and storm force winds could be interesting. There were always passengers on board in bad weather that left the contents of their stomach behind before they disembarked.

On one particular trip to Boston, the morning after our arrival, I went with the first officer and flight engineer for breakfast. By this time, we had moved hotels to one about thirty minutes or so to the north of the city. It was slightly remote but was in a beautiful area with a couple of very expensive golf courses surrounding it. As usual, the crews had found the best place for a "value for money" breakfast and their speciality was Boston baked beans. They came in a large bowl and were made with a thick, very tasty sauce. The unfortunate side effect usually occurred about twelve hours later and some said a minute or two could be knocked off the flight time as a result!

After breakfast, we decided to go to Sears, a large shopping chain in the US, which we found provided a good source of "boys' toys" such as tools. We parked the car and, as we walked into the shop, I noticed that they were giving a large discount on artificial Christmas trees. We went to the specific department, and there I found a tree that was approximately 8-feet high and just what Jan was looking for.

"Does this tree come apart?" I enquired.

"Oh yes, of course," the shop assistant replied.

"How big is the box that it goes into?"

"Not very big," he said, indicating very small dimensions with his hands.

"I'll have it," I said, all the while thinking about getting it home. It shouldn't be any trouble from what he'd told me.

"OK. I'll get it taken apart and placed in the box. Give us thirty minutes, and you can pick it up from the collection point."

I duly parted with my $80 for this magnificent specimen and off we went to the tool department to part with some more money.

Imagine my surprise when we arrived at the collection point to find a box almost the size of a Mini Cooper waiting for me. This was going to be a problem but, undeterred, we managed to lower the back seat of the estate car we were in and get the box on board. The flight engineer sat on the floor, behind the front seat somewhere, cursing me quietly for having taken on this large parcel.

When we were picked up by the crew bus that afternoon, we managed, to the amusement of virtually all eighteen of the cabin crew, to get the box on the bus. I slipped the bus driver a few dollars and thanked him profusely for taking it with us. I had to get an extra large trolley at the airport and, having dumped my suitcase, had to proceed to security with my purchase. This was before the tragedy of 9/11, and they were amused but also very helpful. I very much doubt that the same parcel would be accepted on to an aircraft today. It had to go through the X-ray machine and only just managed to fit in the hole. When we finally got it out to the aircraft, we had then to manhandle the parcel up the spiral stairs, to the upper deck, where it went on to the bed in the crew rest area.

"Unfortunately, crew rest is off the menu tonight," I told the other two occupants of the flight deck. "It's a very short flight, so we don't need it." I'm not sure I was very popular.

On arrival at Gatwick, we then carried out the whole procedure in reverse.

My two colleagues from the flight deck were glad to see the back of me when we parted company to make our way home. I still had my flight to catch to get back to Newcastle.

On arrival at the CityFlyer desk, they took one look at my parcel and said, "You can't take that. That will have to travel by air freight and you will have to pay for it."

"I spoke to your operations department, and they agreed that they would carry it for me as a favour."

The two guys looked at me and obviously were thinking that they could ask me to return the favour one day if they needed to travel on the flight deck for whatever reason.

"OK, we'll make an exception."

I hadn't spoken to anybody in their ops department but was trying to bullshit my way through this issue. Fortunately, it worked.

Eventually, I got back to Newcastle where Jan met me at the airport, horrified at the size of the box that was accompanying me. We managed to get it in the car and, with the tailgate left open, eventually got it home. The tree was, and still is, magnificent. It is approximately twenty-five years old now and has been passed on to our daughter, Kay, for her and her family to enjoy. It is still stored in the original box and is far too heavy for Jan and I to get into the loft. We have something much more modest. If anyone were to try and get a parcel like that home from the other side of the Atlantic these days it would not be allowed and it would be foolish to even attempt it.

I had another interesting trip to Boston that winter. There was a snowstorm forecast to hit the eastern seaboard the day we were due to leave Boston. It was what they call a "nor'easter" which was a small area of low pressure that travelled up the eastern coastline gaining strength over the sea. We arrived in Boston in beautiful weather but, the following day, I had watched the snow falling from my hotel window and the forecasts were such that the main strength of the storm would hit at just about the time we were due to leave. We left the hotel in the crew bus, which took forever, as the driver had to carefully make his way to the airport. Cars and lorries were already becoming stuck at the edge of the freeway, but eventually we arrived having taken much longer than usual. The paperwork that awaited us showed that we were going to have problems departing Boston. Not only was the weather forecast abysmal, but already the airport authorities were having trouble keeping the snow off the runway and the braking action (which shows a coefficient of friction) on the runway surface to an acceptable figure. We got all the passengers on board and the doors closed, and we commenced our de-icing process on the aircraft. This is done to ensure, amongst other things, that the flying surfaces are clean and will do the job that they are designed to do i.e. make the aircraft fly. A wing that has the smallest amount of contaminating snow or ice will not provide the lift required. Many accidents have resulted in an aircraft not being properly de-iced. The de-icing procedure on a 747 takes some time, due to the sheer size of the aircraft, and therefore the ground authorities may use more than one de-icing rig. When the de-icing is started, the stopwatch then begins, as the procedure is only valid for a certain amount of time. If it is still snowing then the wing becomes slowly more contaminated and if the allowed time expires, and one has not become airborne, then the aircraft has to go back to the gate and the procedure must be repeated.

In this case, we had two de-icing trucks undertaking the task. The trucks usually have "cherry pickers" as part of the rig. The "cherry picker" is a platform with a hydraulic lift that enables the operator to get up to the higher points on the airframe. Just as one of the operators reached the area around the flight deck window, one of the girls came up to see what was going on.

"What's he doing?" she asked looking out of the window.

There was the operator, standing on his platform, up at our level. The weather outside was a blizzard, and the poor bloke had a balaclava covering everything except his eyes with the large de-icing "gun" in his hand ready to squirt the liquid on to the aircraft. We explained what he was doing.

"My God, he looks frozen," she said. "I'll make his day for him." At this point, she lifted her blouse and gave him an eyeful. "That'll warm him up!" she laughed and left the flight deck. Not only was the poor guy so taken aback by what he'd seen, he must have almost fallen off the rig. The three of us, on the flight deck, roared with laughter.

With the de-ice complete, we asked ATC for pushback clearance. Time was now of the essence. Unfortunately, after the massive amount of snowfall, the tug could not get enough grip to push us back. We went backwards and forwards, just a few yards, several times whilst he tried to adjust his position to get a grip on the large wheels of the tug and get us moved. It was all in vain. The inevitable happened, and we ran out of time for the de-icing that we had completed and had to start the procedure all over again. The second time around the young lady did not join us again on the flight deck but, after another hour of going through the de-icing procedure for the second time, the airport authorities closed the airfield for the night. We stayed overnight in a hotel in the city, as the journey back to our normal hotel was now out of the question.

The nor'easter had dumped 2 feet of snow on Boston in twenty-four hours.

CHAPTER 17

In just over a year, since gaining my command on the 747, I was asked if I would like to start training other pilots. I thought carefully about this, as I didn't want to be away from home any more than usual. However, line training would involve me flying the routes as usual except I would now be training new captains and first officers. I decided to accept the offer and go back into the training world with Virgin Atlantic. As had happened previously in Dan-Air, the line training aspect started with me observing a few line training flights and then conducting a few flights whilst being observed. Should all go well (which it did), I would then be certified as a company line training captain.

A diversion from Boston to New York (JFK) with a brand-new first officer was quite a busy day. This was due to snow. Another nor'easter was drifting up the east coast of the States dumping several feet of snow on the airfields near the east coast. The snowploughs at Boston were doing their best to clear the runways, but the snow banks at the edge of the runway were slowly building up as they continued to clear the main runway surface. This can be critical for a 747, as the outer engines are very near to the runway edges, and if the snow banks get too high they can cause damage. There is a limit to the height versus the distance from the runway centre line. On this occasion, the snow banks were outside the limits we could accept, and they could not clear them before we were going to be down to our diversion fuel. So off we went to JFK.

Having arrived at JFK, a frantic dispatcher came on to the flight deck and announced that we would be refuelled and then sent off immediately back to Boston. I told him that we would set off to Boston when we received word that the snow banks would be cleared and not before. Eventually, word came through that work was underway, and we duly set about returning to our original destination. We landed without any further problems.

About a week later, I was in our head office at Gatwick and met George, who was our fleet manager.

"Ah... Pete, I've just had a fax through from someone who calls himself director of North American operations saying that, after you diverted to JFK the other day, you refused to turn around and go straight back to Boston. What exactly happened?"

I told him the story and said that I had refused to set off again for Boston until the snow banks were being dealt with. It would be a complete waste of time and cost the company God knows how much in fuel if we had to come back to JFK for a second time.

"OK, so if I write bollocks across the fax and return it, would that be about right?"

"Absolutely it would!"

George was a superb manager and very highly regarded amongst the crews.

The line training continued apace and, at times, I was crossing the North Atlantic up to ten times per month. The commuting from the North East was still workable, albeit difficult at times. Although I carried plenty of tickets, there were times when Jan had to take me down to Teesside or pick me up from Teesside at the last minute as flights from Newcastle were full. At times, there was a funny side to commuting. I had just boarded a British Airways flight from Newcastle, one morning, when the cabin crew put out an announcement.

"Ladies and gentlemen, we have just found a tie on the floor. It's a clip-on tie. Oh dear… it's a Virgin Atlantic tie!"

There was a loud cheer from the rest of the passengers, as I claimed my tie back which I had dropped. This was a time of great rivalry between British Airways and Virgin Atlantic.

The end of 1996 finished with me undergoing my annual line check. The route was a quick Boston and back, and the training captain undertaking the check was on the jump seat. When we arrived at Boston, the traffic pattern was extremely busy and the aircraft landing ahead of us was slow to clear the runway. ATC asked us to go around, as there was not enough space between ourselves and the aircraft making slow progress to clear the runway ahead of us. As I increased the power, the number three engine ran down completely. We carried out the checklist and landed without any further problems, but the training captain claimed that he had organised the failure just to make life interesting. Such is the type of humour in the aviation industry.

As time went on, I was offered the opportunity to become a type and instrument rating examiner. This was a qualification that was partly to represent the company and be able to carry out proficiency checks on the pilots' six-monthly simulator checks, but it was also used to renew the instrument rating qualification which we all had which enabled us to be proficient flying in all weathers and all types of approaches throughout the world. The instrument rating examiner (IRE) qualification started with a two-week course with the Civil Aviation Authority. Many years ago, pilots who were sent to undergo this course were "invited" to renew their own instrument rating qualification with a CAA examiner on a twin-engined piston aircraft which they had probably never flown or seen before. This, in most cases, ended with their qualification being awarded a "fail", and it was more or less from that point where the course started and they could be shown the error of their ways. Towards the end of the course, they would be given another test resulting in the restating of the privileges of their licence.

The more up-to-date way of undergoing this course was much more realistic. I was teamed up with a fellow training captain, Jim, who had joined the company just after me. I had seen the name of the CAA trainer who was to conduct the course, and his name rang a bell. It was the same man who had put me through the training standards department at Oxford with the Oxford Air Training School. Almost twenty years later, we renewed our acquaintance. We spent several days studying many parts of aviation law and the differences and definitions of all types of airspace. It wasn't the most enthralling of subjects but had to be done. The more interesting time came when we had to brief and debrief our student on his or her "attempts" to renew their instrument rating. This was done using an HS125 simulator. An HS125 is a small executive jet seating somewhere in the region of eight to ten passengers. Jim and I did not need to know how to fly the aircraft, as we hadn't completed the required conversion course. What we needed to know were the speeds and altitudes at which the pilot was going to fly so that we could watch him fly the requisite approaches and then make a judgement on whether or not he had flown the patterns to within the required limits. This proved to be great fun for Dave, who was conducting our course, as he was proficient on the HS125 and could take the aircraft right up to the limit of where he could pass the requirement without actually going beyond and being awarded a full or partial fail. It was up to us, as potential examiners, to make the decision as to whether or not he deserved to pass. In the meantime, we also had another CAA man who was acting as air traffic control. He had a wonderful gift for creating his own world of all the "ghost" aircraft around us using all the various accents of nationalities from around the world. At times, he could be so funny that concentrating on the job in hand proved to be somewhat difficult.

Jim and I would take turns at being the primary examiner. We would fully brief our candidate, go into the simulator and conduct the full detail. At the end of the activity, we would give judgement on the exercise and decide whether it was a full, or partial, pass or even a fail. We then took turns at going into detail, whilst Dave would take the part of a possibly very aggrieved candidate. At times, his performance could be worthy of an Oscar. One particular lady CAA examiner was so good at conducting this course that it was hard to tell if she was actually crying if one had decided to fail her. I had several colleagues who went through her hands on this course. She was exceptionally good at acting the part. The CAA examiners could push you into a corner if you were not careful, but it was all detail that we had to learn to cope with when released to become examiners within our own company.

The course came to an end, and we then had to conduct several renewals with our own pilots at Virgin with a fully experienced examiner observing. As we had not yet received our authorisation, the qualified examiner was the one who signed the licences. He was perfectly entitled, of course, to make his own judgement and disagree with our decisions.

The day came for another CAA examiner to observe me conducting an instrument rating renewal on one of our own crews. The examiner was the head of standards within the CAA. I had not met him before but was told he was a very pleasant chap. The time of his scheduled arrival at our office in the simulator block came and went, and he had not appeared. I gave him another ten minutes and then asked our secretary in the office to try and find out what had happened. He had forgotten his appointment! He sent a message asking that I go ahead and brief the crew, and he would be along as soon as possible. In some ways, this was rather good, as he had to start with an explanation as to why he had been delayed. I felt, rightly or wrongly, that I was starting the procedure one step ahead.

A nicer gentleman one could not wish to meet. All went according to plan, and I was really lucky, as I knew my candidate well and he was a really sharp guy and a way above-average pilot. He gave me no cause for concern during the sim detail, and I was able to pass him with only a few minor points to talk about. The CAA examiner was happy with everything that he had seen. He wanted to chat about various aspects of examining, and he went on his way having left me with a written, temporary authorisation. My fully typed up one would be in the post.

I now had another qualification which I was pleased with. The only drawback was it would mean more time in the simulator which meant more time away from home.

It had been a busy start to the following year. Another amusing incident involved a line check which I carried out on one of the very experienced ex-British Airways captains.

We parked at JFK on a very difficult stand to manoeuvre on to. When we looked ahead at the guidance system, it gave the command to stop just as one thought the nose of the aircraft was going into the windows of the office ahead. The office was said to be that of the chief pilot of Delta Air Lines, so one would hope that kind of accident would not happen. One of the ground staff for Virgin Atlantic, at New York, was an ex-Miss Venezuela. She was absolutely stunning. As we approached the gate, this particular lady was standing in full view of us. She was there to move the pier up to the aircraft door when we had parked. Unfortunately, the captain involved was mesmerised by the sight of the lady concerned, and I could see that he was not fully concentrating on the left/right/stop guidance ahead. At the critical point, I shouted "stop" and, as he braked sharply, the nose nodded up and down and we received a curt phone call from the cabin crew who had nearly fallen flat on their faces.

"Oh my goodness," he said, totally embarrassed. "I'm dreadfully sorry about that. How embarrassing... Have I passed?"

"I think you've just scraped through," I said, laughing.

"The view was tremendous. I lost my concentration."

Soon after this flight, I broke my ankle and leg.

I had been tasked by my good lady to help with some decorating at home. Not my favourite pastime, but it had to be done. I had left a round curtain pole lying on the floor. (There is a slight disagreement over the facts here, as I am fairly convinced it was my wife who left it lying there.) However, the result was the same; I stood down from a stool I was on to reach the ceiling light and stood on the curtain pole lengthways. I was wearing trainers, and my foot slid down the pole and there was a mighty crack and feeling of numbness from my ankle. I was fairly convinced that my ankle was broken, and Jan rushed around asking me if there was anything she could do.

"I suppose a sympathy shag is out of the question?" I said trying to be humorous.

"You'll have to walk out to the car, and I'll take you to A & E," she said.

"But my ankle's broken," I said. I was sitting upright and, when I tried to move my foot one way or the other, it just flopped over.

"No, it'll be strained. You'll be fine."

And so I was made to hobble out to the car. We went to the local A & E, where it was confirmed that not only had I broken my ankle but the shock had travelled up my leg and broken that as well.

Following forty-eight hours in hospital and several pieces of titanium being bolted through my various bones, I was discharged. The company was not exactly thrilled to hear that I was signed off work for thirteen weeks. Well, at least it was summer. I sat quite happily in the garden whilst reading and pottering away with making a model aeroplane to help pass the time. After a week or so, I managed to hobble into the field adjoining our garden with our faithful golden retriever, Fudge, who was always happy to go for a wander and a sniff. After a couple of months, I had to go back into hospital to have some of the metalwork removed before undergoing some physiotherapy.

Eventually, I was given my medical back and it was back to work. I spent a few sessions in the sim and then had to fly with a trainer on a line trip. Tony Foote had volunteered his services, and we went off to Newark together. I was now back on the line!

As always, things were not straightforward, and I found myself coming back from San Francisco one night just a few weeks later. We were way up in northern Canada, somewhere in the area of Baffin Island. All was very peaceful, and then in-flight supervisor rang me to tell me she had a passenger who she suspected was suffering from a possible heart attack. We were out in the wilds of nowhere, and my first thought was of a possible diversion to Iqaluit where there were full hospital facilities.

"How about you put out a PA asking if there are any doctors on board?" I suggested.

(Virgin Atlantic always had their aircraft extremely well equipped with medical gear including defibrillators, and the cabin crew were, and still are, very well trained to deal with all kinds of eventualities.)

She came back to me within ten minutes to say we had 67 doctors on board and most of them were cardiologists. Apparently, they had been to a large seminar in the United States and were making their way home together. What luck! This was excellent news, as I now had the best possible information to act upon. A couple of them took charge. I got them to let me know if the passenger concerned needed to be on the ground immediately for more medical help or if we could we proceed with caution. Virgin Atlantic also had a satphone which gave satellite communication to anyone we needed to speak to.

We continued through the night and, as the distance between Iqaluit and ourselves increased, we looked ahead to where we could divert should the passenger's condition suddenly deteriorate. We needed somewhere not too far away to land at and were using airfields as "stepping stones" along the route. The cardiologists kept us closely informed, and the journey continued, passing just to the south of Iceland, before we contacted the UK air traffic control authorities. They were aware of our plight and, as soon as we had made the initial call to them, they cleared us direct to left base on the easterly landing runway at Heathrow. It was superb service, and we had made up a considerable amount of time with the help of the authorities along the route.

Our operations department had an ambulance waiting for our passenger who was in a stable condition thanks to our on-board experts. We thanked them profusely and passed on their details to our management who, in the weeks ahead, got in touch with them and offered some "goodies" to make up for their disturbed night's sleep.

I spoke to my mentor, Bill Moore, one day and asked him if he knew of any flying groups that were in existence at Carlisle. I was keen to renew my acquaintance with light aircraft, and I had not flown one for several years.

"Yes, lad," he replied in his broad Cumbrian accent. "I run a small group. You can join if you want. I would look forward to checking you out on our aeroplane and giving you hell again!" He was giggling, as he was obviously relishing the thought of us flying together after all those years.

I had to go over to Carlisle, which held all those memories from when my career started, and fly with a local examiner to get my light aircraft rating revalidated. I then had some fun flying with Bill whilst he enjoyed "giving me hell" and checking me out on the light aircraft. There is a darker side to the story of this particular light aeroplane which was to occur in another year or so. In the meantime, it gave me a lot of pleasure to be able to fly it and take not only Jan and the kids flying but also several good friends.

The darker side of the story came about a year or so later when the light aircraft had been in for maintenance due to a regular major check. Unfortunately, the aeroplane need a flight test following the check, and the gentleman who normally had the qualifications to carry out this flight was indisposed. We couldn't get anybody to do this flight within the next month or so unless we agreed to pay a small fortune to get somebody to travel quite a long distance to Carlisle.

Bill was not happy about this, as the group members were unable to do any flying and were going to have to undertake another flight check with him as their recencies were about to expire.

"Bill, why don't you approach the CAA and ask them if I can do the flight test as a one-off?" I suggested. I had the necessary licence and it was worth a go.

Bill rang the CAA, and they begrudgingly agreed to let me carry out the flight. They would send me the paperwork and then, after a long briefing over the phone about what they required, I could go ahead.

As this flight test involved writing down lots of figures, I enlisted the help of my old mate Cliff. We were both living in the North East, working for Virgin and still saw a lot of each other. There were things to note on the flight test such as the time required to climb from one altitude to another. It needed another bloke with a pen and paper, and it was a good excuse to go flying with each other.

The day arrived and off we went to Carlisle. The weather was superb, and we got in the aircraft and started to make copious notes on all the various parameters that the CAA required. After about forty minutes of covering the requirements, the only thing left was a dive to VNE. The VNE speed of an aircraft is the "never exceed" speed. The definition speaks for itself. From memory, the VNE speed on this particular aircraft was somewhere in the region of 165 knots. We had to achieve this speed in a dive and then recover. We climbed up to 5000 feet somewhere to the west of the Lake District hills and started our dive. As the speed increased, so did the noise and, as we were both experienced, "wide-bodied" captains, it was obvious that we were both slightly uncomfortable with carrying out this exercise in this little tin can that didn't seem anywhere near strong enough at the best of times.

As we passed 130 knots, we looked at each other and said, "That's fast enough!"

Looking back, I'm so pleased that we finished the dive at that point.

Just a few months later, the aircraft was involved in an incident where the airframe was damaged. It was one of those unfortunate incidents that occur occasionally with one of the group who lacked a little bit of experience. The aeroplane was taken out of service, and the engineers started to carry out a detailed inspection to decide how much work was required to rectify the damage. After several of the panels were removed and various tests carried out, they reported that they had found a crack in the main spar of the wing. This crack was not as a result of the incident but apparently had been there for some time and had possibly been missed at the last major check. This was part of the main structure of the wing and, unfortunately, was going to prove so expensive to fix that it was beyond the finances of the group. Sadly, the aircraft was sold to someone who was willing to spend the money and our small flying group was disbanded. The question as to whether the wing would have parted company with the rest of the aircraft had Cliff and I carried out the VNE dive to the full VNE speed has always remained with me. We shall never know, but the thought of it still sends shivers down my spine.

Part of my job in the sim was to assess new applicants to the company and to decide whether or not they had a good flying aptitude. If they were successful at interview stage, they were then put forward for a sim assessment similar to what I underwent when I joined the company. Most of these people were very good. We didn't expect them to be able to fly a 747 at this stage but, before they arrived at the sim, they were sent a briefing which gave them power settings, attitudes and speeds to fly along with the required flap settings. Part of the assessment was whether or not they could take on board the information and put forward a reasonable demonstration of their ability to fly the aircraft from the briefing. All the information they needed at this stage was there.

The assessments were quite fun from our point of view. We were teamed up with a training flight engineer, and it was something different from the usual licence requirement renewals every six months. It also gave us the opportunity to have an input at the recruitment stage. A lot of the flight engineers also had strong views about whether they could work with these particular candidates. Were they the kind of people that they could spend a long time with on the flight deck? Were they “team players”? On one particular day, I had met up with the training flight engineer in the office before we met the candidates. The flight engineer in question was a great character who didn’t suffer fools gladly. We went to introduce ourselves to the candidates and one, in particular, was a fast jet pilot who, before we even started the sim work, informed us that we had his permission to call him by his nickname.

Needless to say after the sim exercise (and it didn’t matter how well he had done), the training engineer said to me, “We’re not having that cocky bastard are we?”

On another occasion, we had a senior ranking ex-military officer for assessment. It really didn’t matter where they came from or how high ranking they were, it all depended on their ability to fly the sim with the information they were given and how they seemed as a person. For several reasons, I decided that this particular chap was not the sort of person who would get on with our company philosophy, and I recommended that, because of his character, we did not recruit him. The company accepted this and did not offer him a position.

A few weeks later, I was chatting to a mate of mine who was senior captain with us and also an ex-military man.

“Pete, did I hear correctly that you ‘chopped’ such-and-such on his sim assessment?”

“Yes,” I replied. “We didn’t think he would fit in.”

"Well, I owe you a beer. In fact, I owe you several beers. I knew him in the air force, and he was a complete arsehole. He was the kind of man who had no empathy with other people and just enjoyed failing pilots on their checks. He and his missus were part of a group of the same kind of people."

I was fascinated by this description.

"Yes," he went on. He was on a roll now, and I could see that he had really developed a disliking for this man in his past. "Their group of wives would plan out their careers for them. It was automatically assumed that they would be recruited by companies like ours to fly the 747. They would spend the minimum time as a first officer because they should really be in the left-hand seat. They would become captains very quickly and then, of course, would automatically be promoted to training captains. It was all planned out!"

"Well you needn't worry," I assured him, "he hasn't been offered a job."

"Fucking marvellous, the system works! What a relief!" He was a happy man.

Another few months passed, and I was called into the office in Crawley, as the chief training captain had got a message to me saying that he would like a word with me the next time I was in the area. I was still commuting from the North East but now spending a lot of time in the simulator which was just around the corner. Although I was using a lot of the local "cheap" hotels, I also spent quite a few nights staying with friends such as Julian and Alison or Tony and his wife, Claire. I had acquired a rather old Ford Fiesta from my old mate Terry, and we used it for our daughters, as they reached seventeen, to learn to drive. The insurance was cheap and, when the girls passed their test, we could let them use it whilst starting to build up a no-claims bonus. It was a good little car, and I spent a few bob "fettling" it up. I eventually took it down to Gatwick to use it around the local area, and it was quite handy to get me home without having to wait hours following a sim detail for the next flight.

The chief trainer and I met up, and he suggested we go to the staff restaurant for lunch.

"You've mentioned in the past that you would be interested in doing some base training."

"Yes," I replied whist chomping away on my curry. "I'm down here anyway doing loads of sim work, so base training would be a pleasant change."

At that time, part of the requirement to achieve the "type rating" (which was to get the aircraft qualification on one's licence) was to go and actually fly the aircraft for approximately five or six take-offs and landings. This was done with an empty aircraft. As the years progressed and the quality of simulators improved, this could be completed in a simulator. It is known as "zero flight time", and the first time a new pilot to the type gets to actually perform the take-off and landing is with passengers on board. Although we could train the basics of take-offs and landings, including scenarios with engines failed, our old simulator was not approved for this hence the requirement for base training.

"There are just two of us qualified to base train, at the moment, and it would take the load off us if you join us."

I didn't need to be asked twice. Base training was quite an honour in my mind. It involved disappearing with a group of trainees, for most of the day, with an empty aeroplane, and was fun. It was just as well, as the extra money involved for a day's work only just covered my standby ticket to fly down and home again.

I therefore had to start jumping through the same hoops as I had done with the sim; observe a group of pilots on base training, conduct base training with a group of pilots, whilst under supervision, and then another check out with the CAA.

We went down to Châteauroux, in central France, where I observed a few guys being trained. Fortunately, I was able to conduct a session under supervision on the same day. We did the usual and sent a crew to the supermarket once they had completed their six take-offs and landings. This gave us a few bottles and some cheese to take home.

A month later, my check out with the CAA was booked, and we went off to the old RAF airfield at Manston in Kent. The airfield had a nice long runway with very little other traffic, apart from a few light aeroplanes, and was ideal. The only issue with Manston was that the runway was much wider than a normal runway and the visual aspect or "look" of the runway could be off-putting to new pilots flying large aircraft. It could give new pilots problems in the last 100 feet before landing. For this reason, we eventually stopped using Manston and concentrated on a handful of other airfields. I note, when looking back in my logbook, that one of my first candidates on base training was an exceptionally nice chap undergoing his command training. He went on to become well known with Sir Richard Branson's space flight company, Virgin Galactic, and I still see him being interviewed on television occasionally.

Part of the base training with captains gave us the option of simulating an engine failure at the critical point during take-off. This was done by reducing power back to idle on one of the outboard engines (to give the largest "swing"). One had to be careful here, as should your candidate apply rudder in the wrong direction, in order to oppose the swing, then you had problems. You always had your foot well up against the rudder pedals to stop any mistakes.

The CAA check out was passed, and I was now fully qualified as an instructor/examiner on both the simulator and the aircraft.

As the other two base trainers were management pilots most of their time was spent in the office. This meant that I was used regularly for base training and could be called in at short notice. It regularly occurred over the months that I was rung up at home and asked to base train the following day. This I was happy to do, but it could be very frustrating to get a flight down to London, where they had decided they could spare an aircraft, stay the night at my own expense in a hotel, only to report the next day to find the aircraft had been sent off to the other side of the world, as the scheduled aircraft was grounded with a technical problem. It was all very frustrating but that was part of the job.

Shannon was another popular destination for base training with a nice long runway and very accommodating air traffic control. It was also available most of the time and not too expensive with landing fees.

This was a really enjoyable time for me. Although it could be disruptive if one "lost" an aircraft having travelled all the way to London, I really enjoyed the training aspect. One was given an empty aircraft, trusted to get the training completed and bring it home at the end of the day.

I got a call from the chief training captain one day.

"You're taking an aircraft to Dublin for maintenance tomorrow."

"Yes, that's right."

"I want you to take this particular young first officer with you and go via Shannon. He's failed base training once, and I'm not sure that he'll make it. Give him five circuits and landings at Shannon and, if he doesn't come up to standard, I'm afraid you'll have to stop his training permanently."

This was a great shame for the young man concerned, but there are times during training that a different training captain can see a different problem that the initial trainer can't. It's no reflection on anybody it's just the human element.

Runway 24 at Shannon

Note the lights (PAPIs) either side of the runway threshold are switched off. This was done on several of the approaches to make sure the trainee could judge correctly whether they were too high/low or about right

Off we went to Shannon. The guy was incredibly nervous, as he could see his career was on the line. Round and round the circuit we went and, slowly, his confidence improved. I could see where I thought he was going wrong and the five circuits came and went. In the end, I gave him thirteen circuits and he was up to standard. I signed him up! Some people just take a little bit longer than others. Some people just take longer to learn certain aspects of flying but, when they have grasped them, they have them for life. This particular young man went on to become a 747 captain and is still enjoying a good career. What a waste of time and money it would have been if we had got rid of him. A similar problem arose with another candidate on base training. He was given to me to try and sort him out and, with a little extra help, he got there. I met him approximately fifteen years later at one of the training centres we used. He had progressed well, achieved his command and was undergoing a course to become a training captain himself. Excellent!

The base training took up a lot of my time now, and we were regularly pounding the circuit at Prestwick, Shannon or Châteauroux. I look back on that time as one of the highlights of my career and enjoyed the flying and training thoroughly.

Organising the "goodies" run at Châteauroux

Photo with kind permission of A.R. Foote

Take-off from Châteauroux

Photos with kind permission of A. R. Foote

Round the circuit at Châteauroux
Photo with kind permission of A. R. Foote

More base training at Châteauroux
Photo with kind permission of A. R. Foote

Chicago and the Caribbean had now been added to the route structure which made a pleasant change and was somewhere different to go. Chicago was exceptionally busy, and the Caribbean was very pleasant but some flights involved a transit flight to one of the other Caribbean islands following our arrival. This transit was as a passenger, in a small aircraft, which could be rather nerve-wracking for us if the weather was thundery. The time on the various islands was spent mostly on the beach. If I was lucky, I was given a suite which was right on the beach, and I could open the large glass doors and more or less walk straight into the sea. It was pleasant to be able to go for a swim in the early hours of the morning if I couldn't sleep and there was nobody else about.

I took Jan with me on a trip to Barbados. We managed to get to into Bridgetown for a look around. There was a bus service from outside the hotel, and we joined some of the local community for the journey in. There were large, old ladies with fresh vegetables and live chickens on their laps on their way to market and a Rastafarian gentleman with his radio blaring away. The whole of the bus was bouncing up and down to the beat, as we made our way along the dusty roads into town. As we explored the small but lively capital, we turned down one particular road and were immediately advised by one of the locals not to go down there.

"Too dangerous down there!" We heeded his advice.

That afternoon we sat on the hotel beach. There were quite a few of the cabin crew also enjoying the sunshine. A local guy was wandering about and offering a quick shoulder massage to the girls.

One of them eventually agreed to this massage and, when he had finished and relieved the lady in question of some of her cash, the first officer, who had been watching the proceedings, piped up and said, "Annie, if you only wanted your tits rubbed, you should have asked me. I would have done it for nothing!"

There was much hilarity all round!

It was another seventy-two hours, in a different country, enjoying the sunshine and away for a short break from the bleak British winter.

I also managed to take our middle daughter, Louise, on a quick trip to New York. She sat on the jump seat both ways and, as always, the cabin crew were really kind and looked after her well. It was still winter, and the few hours we had in New York were spent battling icy cold winds to try and take her to the likes of Macy's to spend some of Dad's money. On the way home (we were actually flying to and from Newark on this trip), we had a stunning view of Manhattan on the departure. Depending on the runway in use at Newark, and how high the cloud base was, the city lay straight down on the right-hand side of the aircraft. All was there to see, lit up like a Christmas tree. We climbed up to our initial cruising altitude passing Massachusetts and New Hampshire and on towards Maine.

All of a sudden, as we cruised along quietly, there was a massive flash. My heart missed a beat, and the first officer and flight engineer looked around to see what disaster had befallen us. Unbeknown to me, Louise had spotted a rather stunning sunset, way off to the west, and had decided to take a photograph. Her camera, due to the failing light had activated the flash. I had to have a quiet word and suggest that if she was going to try and take a picture she should warn us. This was not long after the TWA 800 disaster where a 747 had exploded mid-air, off the coast, in the vicinity of New York. After an in-depth investigation, it was found to be an explosion of fuel vapours in the centre fuel tank caused by arcing of wires in the fuel quantity indication system. Nerves were still a little fraught!

I had my own annual line check due and noted, from my roster, that it had been scheduled on a Washington trip from Heathrow. Another training colleague was to act as first officer, and he would conduct the line check. The flight engineer was a highly experienced guy and good company. As we met up at Heathrow, we decided that a visit to the Smithsonian National Air and Space Museum in Washington was in order. The forecast was good and, hopefully, it was going to be a pleasant trip.

Due to extremely strong headwinds along the route, our Atlantic track had been planned quite far north. This meant that, although the distance was slightly longer than usual, our flight time was as short as possible as the planners had kept us out of those strong headwinds. We got airborne from Heathrow a few minutes early and made our way north towards Manchester. My colleague in the right-hand seat got our Oceanic clearance which took us well to the north of the usual tracks but was expected. All went well, and without incident, until we were about halfway across the Atlantic.

We were now so far north that we could see the snow and ice-covered southern tip of Greenland off to the right. As usual, this was the point at which one would hope for no problems occurring. Although we always had a "bolthole" in the back of our minds, this was a region well away from any largely populated areas with airfields which had good facilities. Sondrestrom was to the north-west of us, or there was always the possibility of turning back towards Iceland. Other than that, the next "stepping stones" were Goose Bay in northern Canada or Gander which was further south. The weather was the biggest factor for using any of these fields in an emergency.

It was therefore unsurprising that a problem would now confront us. The in-flight supervisor called me up.

"Pete, I have something that one of the girls has just handed to me, and you need to see it."

"OK. Come on up to the flight deck."

A couple of minutes later, she arrived on the flight deck. She handed a paper towel to the flight engineer whose face dropped slightly. He then passed it on to me. Written on it, in what looked like black ink, was the word "bomb".

The IFS now had my full attention.

"One of the girls was doing her regular inspection of one of the rear loos. This was lying next to the sink adjacent to the toilet itself."

"So, did anybody happen to notice who the last person to go into that toilet was?" I asked.

"No. There are a group of young people sitting not too far away from that particular loo, but they are well behaved and haven't been any problem. There are no packages or anything untoward in the loo itself or in any of the other loos adjacent."

We had a think about matters. It was going to take some time to get to the nearest airfield and we, of course, had procedures that we could follow but only if we could actually see a device. We got the cabin crew to have another quiet look around the toilets without drawing any attention to anything possibly unusual happening. In the meantime, we made the decision to contact the company through our HF radio. This could be done by getting in touch with particular stations around the world that would help get through to one's operations departments by using a "phone patch". This is exactly what it sounds like. We used high-frequency radio to call the station, and they could "patch" us through to whoever we wanted on the phone. The usual stations we used were generally Stockholm Radio or "Speedbird" which was British Airways headquarters.

Having got in touch with our operations department, we told them of our predicament and asked them to consult our security department to see if any threat had been made against either the company or our particular flight.

After ten minutes or so had passed, we got the call back from the company to see what they had to say. They had spoken to the security people who informed us that no threat had been made against either the company itself or our particular flight. There was no one on board of any particular significance; no politicians or any other people who may have had some form of issue against them and were a target. The final decision lay with me, but they recommended that we should continue to destination.

I was slightly uneasy about the situation but, after a bit of thought and discussion with my colleagues, I decided to follow the company advice. They were probably in possession of more information than I was and it did seem unlikely that there was any evidence that we had been targeted at all. We were not the national flag carrier and were not carrying anybody of significance. Should we decide to divert immediately, it would take us some time before we reached the nearest suitable airfield and, having reached it, the passengers would probably have to go through a rapid disembarkation using the emergency slides into bitterly cold conditions with possible injuries on their way out.

It was a difficult decision but, hopefully, there was nobody on board who wanted to blow themselves up as well as the aircraft.

The company had told us that they would speak to Washington and advise them of the situation. We continued on as planned, eventually passing Goose Bay where we had considered diverting. We were now back into an area with more options for diversions should the need occur.

This, of course, had to happen on an annual line check! The other trainer, who was conducting my line check, was extremely helpful and, between the three of us on the flight deck and a very able cabin crew who monitored the passengers very carefully, we planned our arrival into Washington.

We decided to make a long, slow descent. Should there have been an explosive device on board, it might have been linked to a particular cabin altitude. The cabin altitude was around 9000 feet in the cruise and came down slowly, towards the elevation of the airfield, during the descent so that the aircraft was unpressurised just before landing. Should anything happen, we didn't want any structural issues with the airframe occurring at high speed so we slowed it all down somewhat.

Needless to say, the descent, approach and landing all went without any problems, and we eventually landed at Washington. Air traffic control told us which gate to park the aircraft and, as soon as we shut down the engines, the ground engineer contacted me through my headset.

"There are a load of FBI people here and the senior man wants to talk to you."

"OK, put him on," I said. This was a first for me.

"Good afternoon, Captain. My name is such-and-such. This is what happens now. We are going to bring the 'people-eaters' up to the individual doors on the aircraft. [The 'people-eaters' are the extremely large buses that carry people to and from aircraft. The bodies of the vehicles can be lifted up and down by large hydraulic jacks in order that they can reach the doors of the 747.] We have our own people on the 'people-eaters', and they will mix and observe all the passengers as they disembark. They will be taken to the terminal where they will be quickly spoken to by our people, and any person who we consider worth interviewing further will be taken to one side. All luggage will be inspected closely and the contents of all the toilets will be inspected as well. Lastly, we would ask that all the crew meet on the upper deck of the aircraft when they have finished their individual duties so that I can have a word with you all."

The FBI took complete control of the situation, and we all waited upstairs on the upper deck until they appeared. I have never seen so many heavily armed people in one group before. The head man introduced himself again.

"Now, who has touched this paper towel that you found?" he asked.

We explained that it had been touched by the junior cabin crew member who found it, the IFS whom she gave it to, the flight engineer who then passed it forward to me and, of course, myself.

"Can you get fingerprints off that?" I asked.

"You would be surprised what we can get off this," he said. "Assuming we can find a suspect, we should be able to find something to link this towel to them."

Having had a chat with some of the crew who were on duty near the loo where it was found, our FBI friend told us that they would be in touch if they needed any more information. In the meantime, he would meet us in twenty-four hours' time when we reported back at the airport for the flight home.

"Do you want a list of the crew's contact details in case you want to talk to us in the future?" I asked.

He looked at me and said... "We're the FBI. If we want you, we'll find you."

Enough said.

We had a quiet evening in a local hostelry and, after the day's events, we had a couple of small beers. The next day, I met the first officer and flight engineer for breakfast, and we made our way to the Smithsonian Museum. I always enjoyed a visit to this museum, as the amount of original air and space exhibits are wonderful to see. There is everything from the Spirit of St. Louis (which Lindbergh used to fly across the Atlantic solo) to the Enola Gay (which was the aircraft from which the atomic bomb was dropped on Hiroshima) and some of the space capsules from the original Mercury, Gemini and Apollo projects.

We were picked up that evening and taken back to the airport. As soon as we walked into the terminal, I was met by another FBI representative.

"Did you discover anything about yesterday's incident?" I asked.

"Nothing for certain, but we did have a suspect who we thought was probably the guilty party." The FBI lady was smiling as she relayed the story.

"Enlighten me please," I said.

"Well, this particular guy was obnoxious, and the cabin staff had given us one or two pointers which made us more suspicious. Unfortunately, we couldn't prove absolutely that he did this and any results from the paper towel will take time to get back, but we are pretty sure that if he did it he won't do it again. We think he did it as a prank."

"What makes you so sure that he won't do it again?"

She responded, still smiling, "Well, for a start, we kept him for ten hours before releasing him. By the time he left us, we knew every detail about him. Plus the fact we searched him thoroughly."

As she mentioned the search, she showed me the actions of putting a rubber glove on.

Nothing more was heard of the incident but, if we assume that the suspect had been guilty of this "prank", he had put a lot of people to a lot of trouble and the expense to the various organisations would have been extreme. As the aircraft had been thoroughly searched after we arrived in Washington, the outbound flight to London had also been delayed by several hours. He deserved everything he got!

I passed my line check!

By now, we had increased the size of the fleet and had several ex-Air New Zealand aircraft added. There was a slight "bone of contention" within the fleet, as management pilots went to pick these aircraft up and any delays resulted in a nice, long stay in New Zealand itself. The same few people were getting these nice trips, whereas we had asked for names to be put in a hat so that some of the other training pilots and engineers could get one of these delivery trips but it never happened. It left a slight sour taste amongst the troops who were not only working hard but filling the slots of those who were away having fun. Always the same the world over!

These aeroplanes were in beautiful condition and had different engines to what we were used to. The older aircraft had Pratt and Whitney JT9D engines, but the ex-Air New Zealand aircraft had Rolls-Royce RB211 engines. We therefore had to undergo a day's course on the engine details and parameters. These engines were exceptionally good, but one had to be careful particularly when base training. They did not like rough handling and whereas the P&W engines were a bit like an old Perkins diesel on a tractor, the Rolls-Royce RB211 was an absolute thoroughbred and a delightful piece of engineering.

Towards the end of 2000, the Hatfield rail crash took place. Sadly, due to the derailment, a few people were killed and there were many repercussions due to what had happened. There was a phenomenal amount of work required to put the damage to the railway itself right, and the delays on the railway system increased the journey time between London and Newcastle even when the east coast line was opened weeks later. Many business people could not get to Newcastle, Edinburgh and beyond quickly, and the flights between London and Newcastle were always full. This made my commute to work and back home again a nightmare.

The company now had a fleet of Airbus A340s. I thought it might be interesting to consider a change to a more modern aircraft. This would also give me the opportunity to have a look at other destinations and other parts of the world. The older "Classic" 747 was slowly due to be replaced with more modern aircraft which were also much more fuel-efficient. The A340 also covered some longer range routes, and this would make my commuting slightly more palatable as I would, in theory, operate longer flights but fewer times during the month. I went to see Steve, who was my best man all those years ago and now held the post of training manager. I wanted to know how long I would have to wait for a course. How many people were above me on the list? This would be quicker than I thought, and I therefore asked to be informed when my turn came. I would miss the old 747 greatly, but I felt it was time to move on to newer equipment.

A few weeks later, I heard through the grapevine that the company was due to increase the size of the 747-400 fleet. The 747-400 was the next stage on from the old 747 "Classic" that I was flying and would be a welcome opportunity for me to stay on the Boeing fleet but with a much more up-to-date aircraft. The 400 was a two-man crew (except on the longer sectors where we carried an extra pilot to cover the flight time limitation requirements) and, sadly, the days of the flight engineers were numbered.

I went back to see Steve to ask him about the 747-400 crew requirements.

"You didn't tell me we had more 400s coming," I said.

He smiled and said, "I thought you wanted to go on the Airbus?"

"Not if there's a possibility of me staying with a Boeing."

"Well, you can have a 400 course. Your seniority is right, and there's a course early in the new year. I can pencil you in on that if it's what you really want."

"Yes, please. Much better idea than an Airbus," I smirked. He was an Airbus pilot.

So I was lucky. Staying on a Boeing was ideal for me.

I continued with my training duties on the old Classic for my final few months. On one particular flight, I was sitting at Gatwick waiting to depart for one of the Caribbean islands. We had Sir Richard Branson on board, and he asked if he could quickly come up on to the flight deck to say hello before departure.

"Hi guys," he said. "I just wanted to come and wish you all a very merry Christmas and a happy New Year. Have you heard the news about the new 747-400s?" he added. "What do they mean for you all?"

I told him that I had a course early in the New Year but, as he looked at the flight engineer, the reply was, "Redundancy."

The boss had purely asked without thinking too deeply about his question, but it was certainly a sad time for the flight engineers.

As the old "Classic" fleet was being replaced by the 400s and A340s, so the base training became less and less. The line training was also being reduced, as newer pilots were not required on the fleet. Towards the end of 2000, I finished my last flight on the old 747 and prepared for my course on the new aeroplane.

There were only two of us on the course. I was commuting from the North East, and my colleague was commuting from Scotland. As we were based in London, the company would not pay for accommodation, as they assumed we lived locally. This was fair but created a burden of finding somewhere to stay in the area during the week. It was a matter of finding somewhere that didn't break the bank but was comfortable and quiet enough to be able to study in the evenings.

Fortunately for me, my old friend Tony Foote offered me the opportunity to stay with him and his family in East Sussex. This was an extremely kind gesture and was much appreciated. It was, therefore, my responsibility to keep the bar at their home topped up for the duration of the course!

The ground school part of the course took place in Crawley. This was only a short drive in the mornings and evenings and, as the ground school instructor was kind enough to finish at lunchtime on Fridays, it gave me the opportunity to drive home to spend most of the weekend with the family. Sunday evenings were always a wrench, as I climbed back in the car to go back south to be ready for Monday morning.

The next few weeks were always bound to be tedious, as all ground school conversion is, but it was a great relief to go back to stay with Tony and Claire in the evenings. Claire was kind enough to cook a hot meal to enjoy around my timings. I would then study, for a couple of hours, before joining them for a nightcap before bed.

Following the ground school, we passed the required CAA technical exam and completed the various requirements before going on to the simulator. That was done at Cranebank, the British Airways simulator training headquarters at Heathrow but using Virgin Atlantic training captains. There was no requirement to undergo base training on the actual aircraft, as it could be completed in the simulator for candidates such as us who had flown a "heavy" aircraft previously. The older simulator that we used on the original 747 did not have the clearance to cover what was called "zero flight time training". The first time a pilot actually handles the real aeroplane is on a commercial sector with passengers on board. The older sim also had a poorer quality visual, whereas the more modern equipment not only had a full colour visual but could be programmed for day or night-time. The newer simulators were a large step forward for pilot training.

My first trip on the 747-400 was to San Francisco. This was a familiar destination but a new aeroplane. Despite a flight time of over ten hours, the time went quite quickly. Due to the length of the flight, we carried an extra first officer, but he was also there as an extra pair of eyes, as I was under training. I was impressed with the 400 and found it quite different in some ways including the fact that the flight engineer was missing! I had to complete ten sectors under training. All of these sectors were flown with training captains who were colleagues on the old Classic. They had gone to the 400 much earlier than me and so it was great to meet up again. Apart from the serious side of the training, there was also a lot of friendly banter. Anything but a perfect landing from either pilot drew a lot of derision. My final line check eventually came, and I was to undergo it with our lady training captain who, again, I knew from the Classic. We were rostered for Los Angeles. The flight went without any problems, and I was signed up for the new aeroplane.

Final line check completed in this aircraft (747-400 G-VAST)
Photo by kind permission of Angelo Harmsworth

Having been checked out on the 400, a few weeks of consolidation began. This was an enjoyable time as, being the "new boy" on the fleet, I was rostered to fly with experienced first officers who could impart more information to me about the aeroplane at a nice, leisurely pace. My first flight by myself was to Newark. It was unfortunate that, as mentioned previously, the last 100 miles or so during the descent into Newark was very much "dubious" airspace in that there were many light aircraft and gliders entitled to be in the area, and air traffic control did not always have the time to give you proper warning. On this particular flight, the aircraft systems gave us warning of a light aircraft which was far too close. Fortunately, the aircraft system is so designed that it gives the pilot the exact instructions as to which flight path needs to be followed to remain safe and clear of the conflict. In this case, it was a rapid climb. We carried this out, informed air traffic control, who gave a rather poor apology, and later that evening I filed the necessary paperwork.

Nothing came of the matter, as the ridiculous situation was that the light aircraft was actually allowed to be there. In those days, the last part of the descent into Newark for us could be rather nail-biting.

Fortunately for me, the 400 had now taken over the San Francisco route completely. This had to be one of my favourite destinations. After a few weeks, I became an "experienced on type" captain and was allowed to fly with any first officer on the fleet. It just so happened that the first officer who I had gone through the 400 course with was rostered to fly with me on one of the San Francisco trips. I had two first officers because of the limitations of the flight time restrictions. The 747-400 had a superb "bedroom" for the flight deck rest just behind the flight deck itself and, as we would generally split the sector length into three more or less equal time segments, each of us knew when we would be taking our rest period. After checking in at Heathrow and saying hello to the cabin crew, we were bussed out to the aircraft and got on with our various flight deck preparations. It had been decided that I would fly the sector out to San Francisco. We left the gate at Heathrow a few minutes late, due to a passenger discrepancy, but that was soon resolved and we were on our way.

It was a beautiful day over the British Isles, and our route took us north towards Manchester and then over the Western Isles of Scotland. It was a welcome and fairly rare sight to see all of western Scotland covered in unbroken sunshine. All went well and, over lunch, we had the most stunning views of Iceland and Greenland before proceeding further towards the northern latitudes of Canada.

Greenland - always a stunning sight
Photo with kind permission of A. R. Foote

Company over Greenland for some of the time!
Photo with kind permission of A. R. Foote

I had been keeping an eye on the weather as we went, and one of the favourites to watch when in the vicinity of Hudson Bay was Churchill. Unfortunately, although the weather was just acceptable in the case of an emergency, it certainly wasn't good. They were showing reduced visibility in blowing snow, which was not very friendly should we need to divert quickly, and I made a mental note that the runway braking action would probably preclude us from using that airfield.

We were now just on the northern edge of Hudson Bay in the vicinity of Baker Lake and Repulse Bay. Both of these airfields couldn't be used by a 747, except in a dire emergency, as they were gravel runways and very short in length.

As always, with matters of concern, these things happen at the wrong time, and it was about to happen now. Out of the blue, we got a notification on one of the screens that one of the engines had a low oil quantity. I put my newspaper down to concentrate on the unusual situation of seeing such an unwelcome warning. We went through the checklists and discussed the problem only to find, a couple of minutes later, we received the same warning but for another engine. This was incredibly unusual, but one thing that was going through my mind was an incident almost two years previously.

A Queen's Flight BAe146 had been on maintenance somewhere in the UK. An aircraft engine is fitted with magnetic chip detectors. Should any of the engine bearings (or other parts) start to disintegrate, the magnetic chip detectors will pick up these small pieces of metal which can be seen easily by an engineer during a regular inspection. They are also taken out to enable the engineers to take oil samples from the engines.

The 146 in question had the magnetic chip detectors removed during the maintenance check it was undergoing and, unfortunately, when they were replaced the seals were not fitted. During the subsequent flight test, the crew started to lose oil quantity on all the engines. They managed to declare an emergency and get the aircraft on the ground fairly smartly at Stansted. Before the landing roll was finished, they had shut down three of the four engines.

I contacted engineering in London, on the satellite phone, and told them of our problem and asked them for an opinion. As I was talking to them, a third engine now indicated low oil quantity. This was getting serious.

"We'll get back to you in thirty minutes," they said.

"You'll get back to me in five minutes, maximum," I said, "or I'll have to put the aircraft on the ground somewhere fairly quickly."

Three engines now showing low oil quantity, but oil temperatures and pressures were all rock steady.

Whilst we made preparations for a diversion, we discussed the various options. Churchill was the closest airfield, but the conditions were not as I would have liked.

After what seemed like a long time, but in reality were only a few minutes, the engineers got back to us.

"We are virtually certain this is some kind of software issue with the oil quantity indication system. Assuming there is no problem with pressures and temperatures then you will be safe to continue. We'll let the engineers at San Francisco know what is going on."

Another crisis averted.

We continued on to destination whilst keeping a very close eye on the other indications.

After a pleasant forty-eight hours in San Francisco, we had an event-free flight back to the UK. I was met by the base engineer who gave me a rather complex explanation as to what had happened on the outbound flight. It was something to do with a master oil quantity transmitter and comparison with the other engines. Enough said. It all worked out well in the end!

The only matter of significance on the return flight was a stunning view of the Northern Lights which was a relatively common occurrence at these northern latitudes. This display was always very impressive and this trip was no exception. The lights were clearly visible for over an hour and a half, and we called the cabin crew to come on to the flight deck in turns to see this incredible display. The only person to miss it on this occasion was one of the first officers who was fast asleep on his rest period in the bunk.

Northern Lights over northern Canada
Photo with kind permission of A. R. Foote

The Selby rail crash had, sadly, occurred not that long after the Hatfield rail crash and, due to significant disruption on the East Coast Main Line, my commuting had become difficult. Yet again, due to the increased times on the rail journey, the business fraternity were tending to fly more to and from the North East and they were accepting the increase in costs compared to the train. I could land in London around breakfast time and, by trying to get home on the train, due to the fact the flights were fully booked, it could be late afternoon by the time I walked into the house. I was usually completely and utterly exhausted.

It was, therefore, quite a good opportunity when I was asked if I felt ready to go on an instructors/examiners course for the

747-400. This meant ground school and simulator work with a partner (another old mate from the Classic 747) over a period of about a month. We went through the course at Heathrow using the British Airways facilities and simulator. Monday to Friday was spent at Heathrow and, as I had my car and was acclimatised to the UK, it was no great issue to travel home for the weekends. The course was hard work and, at the end, we went through an assessment with the 747-400 fleet standards captain.

Again, all went to plan, and we both passed through the course and, after a quick observation by the CAA inspector, we became examiners on our new fleet.

The simulator work was mainly at the British Airways centre at Cranebank but, for a while, we also used the Lufthansa simulator at Frankfurt.

Sunrise approaching somewhere in the region of 30 west

Sunrise... at last

Photos with kind permission of A. R. Foote

I quite enjoyed the simulator sessions in Frankfurt. We stayed at one of the airport hotels, and the simulator was somewhere below ground level. Unfortunately, most of the sessions that I was rostered for were either late at night or in the middle of the night. As the simulator belonged to Lufthansa, they got all the prime daytime slots.

Following a late simulator session, we could adjourn to one of several staff restaurants, which were also below ground level, where we could find something to eat and a beer. On one particular occasion, I was booked on a flight home very early the following morning. We enjoyed a meal and one beer followed another. After a few hours, I decided, along with my companions, that it wasn't worth going to bed and so we had another beer... or two. As check-in time for my flight approached, I managed to find my way back to the hotel room to pick up my bag and went to book in. I don't remember too much about it but, fortunately, despite the strong German beer taking effect, I ended up on the correct flight for Heathrow. I slept through the whole thing and had to be woken by the Lufthansa cabin crew to get off the aircraft upon our arrival at Heathrow. Feeling dreadful, I managed to catch my flight up to Newcastle where Jan met me. She took one look at me, knowing that I was the worse for wear, and took me home where I went to bed for the rest of the day. Bloody pilots who get close to a pub!

With all the extra problems of commuting on a staff standby ticket between the North East and London, plus the disruption of the east coast train services, the job was becoming more difficult. I was also away from home more and more, plus there was the fact I had been crossing the north Atlantic up to ten times per month. A lot of the line training flights were put on the New York, Washington or Boston flights, as they were the shortest routes, and the company wanted to get as much out of the trainers as possible to get through the training commitment.

I had toyed with the idea of going back to short-haul work for health reasons as much as anything. I have always been a "home bird" and have always done anything possible to maximise my time at home. I didn't have much time for hobbies and pastimes, as my days off always seemed to be spent recovering before picking up my bag and going south again.

Jan was a keen golfer, and I tried to take up the sport, as it would give us more time together. On the days I arrived back in the

UK, I spent virtually all day trying to get home. Having got back to the house, I would go to bed for a couple of hours, get up and have my supper before enjoying a couple of hours watching the TV. Very quickly, I would find I couldn't keep my eyes open any longer and would disappear off to bed again only to sleep for up to twelve hours. I called this "the sleep of death", as I was so knackered nothing seemed to exist any more. The following morning, I would enjoy my breakfast and think I was back to normal. Jan and I would go to play golf and usually, after about three holes, my legs became like lead and I would have to tell her that I needed to go home and have some more rest. Something had to change.

747-400 G-VGAL Gatwick
Photo with kind permission of Chris Wood

At that time, EasyJet were recruiting pilots and it seemed to me that there was a great future in the idea of low-cost flights. The nearest bases that they had to home were Edinburgh and

Glasgow. I decided to go for an interview and see what was on offer. I have always been of the opinion that an interview is a two-way thing and it pays to see what they have to say.

I went up to the EasyJet head office in Luton for an interview. Their philosophy was completely different to anything I had been used to and, when I turned up in a suit and tie, one of the first things they said to me was "You can get that off" with regards to the tie! It was all very relaxed and, after a chat with one of their senior training captains and a "team exercise", I was told that I would be offered a position at either Glasgow or Edinburgh. I had the choice. I told them Edinburgh, as it was only 100 miles from home. It was not close enough to commute for every trip, but Jan and I had decided that if I were to accept the job then we would buy a flat in Edinburgh which would act as an investment.

This was now a rather difficult position to be in. Should I remain flying the 747 but put up with the difficult commute and the never-ending fatigue? Or should I go back to short haul, which I always thoroughly enjoyed in the Dan-Air days, with a company that, as yet, did not have much of a track record? Jan and I talked about it at length and, fortunately, I had a very old friend, who had been with not only Dan-Air but also Virgin Atlantic, who I talked to about the pros and cons of a move.

After much soul-searching, I decided to make the move to EasyJet. I wrote my letter of resignation and posted it knowing that I had to work three months' notice. I received a very pleasant acknowledgement from George, my fleet manager, who said he fully understood my reasons for the move and wished me all the best on my chosen path.

Photo with kind permission of Chris Wood

During the three months' notice, I managed to get a trip to Johannesburg which was a new destination for me. This was a route which had its own problems, and I can't say that it was one of my favourites. The flight left Heathrow late in the evening, and we routed south through France and over the island of Majorca. From there, the route crossed the North African coast and onwards over the Sahara Desert into deepest Africa. Air traffic control could be an issue in the African continent. Some of it was VHF, which was ordinary line of sight communication, but some of it was HF, long-distance communication. It was not unusual for the HF communication to be ignored by the ground station which could mean that, in parts of Africa, one had to carry out a "DIY" air traffic control. We always listened out on a separate frequency and, more often than not, called up other aircraft which we could hear to ask them exactly where they were and what their estimate was for their next reporting point. That way, we could build up a mental picture of who was where. One instrument that we had on the flight deck (TCAS, traffic collision avoidance system) would show aircraft in our vicinity so, fortunately, we could see aircraft quite close to us. Unfortunately, occasionally we saw traffic appear on the TCAS who were not talking to anybody, and we were left wondering "Where the hell did he come from?". We would fly an offset of 2-3 miles left of track on the main north/south route through Africa. The southbound flights were parallel to the route by 2-3 miles to the left of track southbound, and the northbound flights were also offsetting 2-3 miles to the left ensuring that, if ATC (should we be able to get hold of them) were not on the ball, we had a distance of 4-6 miles between aircraft at the same levels. The offset and talking to each other on the "watch" frequency worked quite well.

We did have a list of en route diversions we could use in case of dire emergency, but some of these I considered rather dubious. Regarding such-and-such a place, how the hell could we ensure the safety of not only the passengers but also the very attractive cabin crew, in those lovely uniforms, should we have to divert? I found the matter of concern and just hoped that the problem never occurred.

One of the other problems on this route could be the ITCZ (intertropical convergence zone). This zone encircles the Earth near the equator but moves north and south depending upon the time of year. This is an area where the trade winds meet and can result in the formation of very big thunderstorms. These storms can not only produce problems with icing but also turbulence. The turbulence can be enough to cause damage to aircraft and, in certain cases, fatal damage. They should be avoided at all costs which can mean a deviation off track to get round them. This is a typical example of speaking to ATC to ask permission to deviate due to the weather but, as can happen in Africa, they do not respond then one has to deviate anyway! In this case, the crew would inform other aircraft on the "watch" frequency which, again, allows everybody to build up a mental picture of where everybody else is.

In June 2009, an Air France aircraft crashed whilst making their way through the ITCZ. This was not solely due to the weather in the ITCZ alone, but the aircraft airspeed sensors had iced up which lead to other issues with the aircraft and crew.

Although we carried an extra pilot on these long trips, I always made it a rule that I was "in the seat", and not in the bunk, for the transit through the ITCZ. I also was not shy about routing around these heavy storms if they were present. On the return journey, on this particular trip, I ended up 300 miles off track to avoid some of the worst of the weather.

There is only a very small time difference between Johannesburg and London which is one of the bonuses of this destination. As the sun came up, we eventually passed the equator which was a first for me. I looked down and saw nothing really; an area which, in the haze, looked sandy and with very few geographical features. It was a bit of an anticlimax.

The further south we got the ATC improved to normal levels and, eventually, we landed at Johannesburg around breakfast time.

I was quite shocked at the drive into the city centre. Many of the areas of good-quality housing were surrounded by barbed wire with guards on the entry gates. Other areas of poorer housing were ramshackle with what seemed to be a large amount of abject poverty. This was 2001 and a different world. Things are vastly different now. The hotel was in the centre of the city, and we were warned to be very careful where we went. Many areas were just not safe. The two first officers with me had been to Johannesburg before, and so I stuck with them, as they knew the places to go. A good meal was to be had at "The Butcher Shop" which specialised in well-aged, high-quality beef and, of course, South Africa is a high-quality source of red wine.

The return flight left Johannesburg in the evening. This was summer in this part of the world, and the temperatures were fairly high. Johannesburg is almost 6000 feet above sea level where the air is less dense. This, and the temperature, can give a reduced performance for the take-off with an associated long take-off run. The take-off roll seemed to have gone on forever but, eventually, we were airborne and on our way.

The same problems northbound, with poor communications in certain areas and large thunderstorms to circumnavigate, existed once again. Eventually, the north coast of Africa appeared and we were back into Europe and familiar territory with first-class ATC. It's not a destination I would bid to fly to regularly.

My last trip with Virgin was to Orlando, and my old friend Julian had managed to wangle himself to come along with me. We took turns for the left seat. I flew the aircraft there, and he did the return sector. A good time was had by all, and the cabin crew gave me a card which they had all signed. I still have it!

Last flight with Virgin 30th December 2001

CHAPTER 18

EasyJet had booked me on a Boeing 737-300 course, in the south of England, with a company who provided the ground school for the type rating. They also provided accommodation, and I spent several of the weekends staying with our old friends, Julian and Alison in West Sussex. Jan also managed to fly down for the weekend to join us. The course consisted of a few new pilots but also some very experienced ones. Unfortunately, the company who provided the course were used to dealing with cadets. These young people were brand new to aviation and were very young. Some of the older instructors still felt they were dealing with cadets when they spoke to the more experienced amongst us and sparks flew! We had frank discussions with the management and told them that we were not prepared to be treated like children or we would take our concerns to EasyJet themselves. Things changed rapidly.

One of the other pilots on the course was a chap by the name of Chris Kingswood. He had been with Virgin Atlantic but on the Airbus fleet and ours paths had never crossed. Chris and I became good friends during the course and are still in regular contact. He is one of those chaps who is a natural trainer and has a whole host of training qualifications to his name.

Following the ground course, it was back to Luton for the other requirements and the simulator course. Having flown the 737-200 with Dan-Air, I found the 300 series very similar and the conversion was therefore very straightforward. There were several EasyJet "consultants" who acted as instructors on the simulator course. Most of these people were either retired or had lost licences due to medical problems. One particularly nice chap, who myself and my simulator partner were programmed with in the sim, was an ex-Concorde captain with British Airways. He was an extremely pleasant and quiet character who had a lot of very interesting stories to tell us about his experiences of flying Concorde. Some of the briefings had to be completed in a short time, as we had spent so much time talking about his career flying this unique aircraft. I have to confess to asking him so many questions about that aircraft that it was probably my fault.

Unfortunately, at the other end of the spectrum, we also ended up on one particular exercise with another instructor who lacked patience. My partner in the sim was a slightly immature chap who was struggling at times with the conversion. This particular instructor was not a good advert for his trade and actually reduced the young man in question to tears at one point. After a pep talk in the evening, he managed to sort himself out and we continued with the course.

The simulator completed, we went on to base training in the actual aeroplane. Here, I caught up with an old friend who I knew in both Dan-Air and Virgin Atlantic and so, as we flew around the circuit at Shannon for the requisite number of landings, there was much leg-pulling from him.

Jan and I had decided to buy property in Edinburgh. Due to the family (and ourselves) being settled in the North East, we decided that I would stay in the flat in Edinburgh during my working week and Jan would come up for occasional weekends so that we could enjoy the delights of Edinburgh. After much searching, we found a new-build property on the top floor of an apartment block on the south side of the city. The paperwork went through quite quickly, and I only had to find accommodation in Edinburgh for a couple of weeks before we could get the keys. In the meantime, my line training had started out of Edinburgh. I flew with the base captain who was a jovial character and well liked. We did a few days flying together before I went down to Luton to complete my line check. This involved a trip to Inverness on a glorious winter's day. I hadn't been there for years, and it was a crisp, cold day with never-ending blue sky. The ground was covered in snow, and I had forgotten how stunning the view could be in this part of the world with this kind of weather. Of course, when the weather is bad it can be hard work!

Life eventually settled into quite a pleasant pattern. The days were quite long flying from this base. It was either very early starts or very late finishes. The good thing was that, after a late finish, the roads were empty and, if I had a couple of days off, I could get back to Northumberland very quickly. The crews were exceptionally friendly with a large amount of Belgian pilots. All these folks had come from Sabena, the Belgian national airline, which had gone bust in 2001. For whatever reasons, a lot of the pilots decided to come to Edinburgh when they were offered positions with EasyJet. They were a pleasant bunch, very able and highly experienced. It was a good day out flying with them.

Our new flat worked well and was only a thirty-minute drive from the airport. It was good not to have to live in digs somewhere or to be confined to a hotel room. Time off, when Jan wasn't with me, was spent drifting around the city of Edinburgh or having a round of golf at one of the municipal courses. We had extremely large pine trees surrounding the apartment block, and the squirrels enjoyed getting fed from our small balcony. I had another old friend living east of the city who was still working for Virgin Atlantic, and Jan and I socialised with Bill and his wife quite a lot. Bill was also an accomplished golfer, and we played, or should I say, were beaten by him quite a few times on some of the top-class golf courses in that area. I could now get round a golf course without fatigue stopping me after the first three holes!

One or two other mates from Virgin Atlantic had also seen the advantages of changing paths and moving away from long haul to EasyJet. The company offered bases near to home for many, and the change to short haul played less havoc on the body. I had several calls to discuss the pros and cons of the move that I had made and, in the end, several people followed me and went to bases near home such as Edinburgh, Glasgow, Liverpool and those in southern England. It was all a matter of whether one wanted to go home at night instead of spending time away in another time zone.

After a few months, rumours began to circulate about a new base in the north-east of England. Could this possibly be true?

I rang all contacts I had around head office only to be told, "No, I don't think so, Pete," or "Yes, I've heard it may be a possibility."

I spoke to the base captain in Edinburgh. "No, it'll never happen," he said with confidence. But it did.

The company had started to buy 737-700s. This was another jump forward with the 737 family, and we started to see them appear in Edinburgh on flights out of Luton and Gatwick. They were due to be based in Edinburgh imminently. My turn came with the conversion course which was a day in the classroom and a couple of sessions in the simulator. I then had to undergo a couple of sectors with a training captain and a line check on the new aircraft. I enjoyed the 700 immensely, and my line check involved another trip into Inverness on an equally pleasant day. The 700 has always been one of my favourites of the 737 family, and the years I spent flying it were always a pleasure. It was hoped that the new base that had now been "firmed up" at Newcastle would have these new aircraft from the beginning of operations there. Unfortunately, it was not to be, and we operated the older 300 series for the first few months.

As soon as Newcastle was confirmed as a base, I had been told that I would get based there and this was yet another improvement in lifestyle for me. I now really could go home at night.

So, on the 29th March 2003, I flew an empty aircraft from Edinburgh to Newcastle for the new routes at the new base. Another old friend of mine, Derek Wright, joined me at Newcastle, and we made up the first crew to be based there. For years, Derek had worked in the briefing office at Newcastle and regularly handed us all the necessary paperwork when I was based there with Dan-Air. He went on to join the low-cost airline "GO" which was quite successful but eventually bought by EasyJet. We had been in touch about the possibility of the base at Newcastle, but now it was a reality. It was a real gift to both of us, after years of commuting we could now stay in the North East every night.

We started the base with Belfast, Barcelona, Alicante and Stansted (which had been a "GO" route). Local cabin crew had been recruited, and I caught up with a few familiar faces including one girl from Virgin Atlantic. She had had enough of commuting as well. The routes were popular with people from the North East and southern Scotland, and the base began to thrive.

Myself landing at Newcastle from Barcelona, 14th April 2003 - Boeing 737-300 G-OHAJ

Eventually, there was news about the new 737-700s coming to Newcastle. It had been a while since I had flown a 700 and was sent down to Liverpool to be checked out again. I flew with the base captain down there who had also flown long haul in the past. We got on well and spent the trip across to Belfast and back chatting about days gone by flying long haul.

New routes were announced for Newcastle. These included a few places which I knew well and some where I hadn't flown to previously. It was always a pleasure to go back to Berlin. It brought back good memories from the days spent over there with Dan-Air. Prague was new to me. Just over a couple of hours away and always a good view of the city and its 18 bridges spanning the river Vltava. Budapest was also a new destination. The airport there had an extremely long runway which we needed one particular evening. The authorities were giving information for the braking action on the runway which was well within the requirement that we needed to land. When we landed, the runway in places was extremely slippery. We eventually came to a halt and taxied to the terminal. There was already an EasyJet aircraft parked there and, after the passengers were off, the captain of the other aircraft came up to see us.

"How did you find the braking action?" he asked.

"Maybe not as good as advertised," I replied with a grin.

"Blimey," he said. "I had to go into the terminal and have a fag. We had real problems with the braking."

They closed the runway, following our reports to ATC, and spent more time treating the surface. Whilst we sat there, I could see it was raining. I went outside to do the "walk round" to check the outside before our departure.

When I got back on to the flight deck, I said to the first officer, "Go and have a look at the airframe. You won't actually see what's happening there many times during your career."

He went outside to have a look. At first it was difficult to see, but eventually he came back and said, "I've never seen that before."

It had been so cold during the descent into Budapest that the airframe had stayed well below freezing after we'd arrived. The rain was falling from warm, moist air above the cold air in the area. As the rain fell on to the cold airframe, the raindrops became supercooled and froze on impact. It was actually quite difficult to see in the darkness with all the bright lights reflecting off everything around the aircraft, but if one took one's hand to the airframe it was very noticeable.

We were delayed quite a long time that particular night. By the time the rain had stopped, we then had to get the whole of the airframe de-iced which seemed to take forever. Flying in Europe in the winter can be challenging.

Nice also appeared on our schedule which was always a popular destination for me. Nice can be challenging. It's usually very busy, but interesting, with stunning views of the South of France both on the way in and on departure. The arrivals are fed towards the north-easterly runways after being vectored by radar past St-Tropez, Fréjus and Cannes. From there, the radar controllers position one to make an approach around Cap d'Antibes where "the other half" live. It's then a sharp right turn to line up with the runway. The sea is normally a beautiful shade of blue (Côte d'Azur), and one is immediately inspired to go home and book a holiday at this destination. It's usually the north-easterly runways in use at Nice, but if the wind is favouring one of the reciprocal runways then the radar controllers drop us down to a fairly low altitude having passed to the south of Cannes on an easterly track. This is always slightly annoying, as more fuel is burnt on a jet engine at lower levels, so if one suspects that the south-westerly runways are in use, then it's always a good idea to have just a bit more fuel. After what seems like an eternity on the easterly track, admiring the luxury yachts, then we are given a turn towards the coast on, more or less, a northerly heading. Ahead of us lies Monaco and Monte Carlo. All that money in such a small area! We are told to pick up the procedure inbound to the field which then drops us down to an even lower altitude for the final approach. We are now abeam Saint-Jean-Cap-Ferrat with the "Baie des Anges" or "Bay of Angels" ahead and Nice sitting on the edge of the bay. The airfield is off to our left. The rest of the approach is now by "eyeball" or visual. The aeroplane is configured fully for landing, and we take the autopilot out to hand fly the aircraft around the coastline whilst reassessing our altitude as we go using the "PAPIs" either side of the runway threshold which will tell us if we are too high or too low. Once lined up, we are cleared to land. In the last few hundred feet, we pass the Hotel Negresco on the promenade. Featured in many films, it has been a destination for the rich and famous for many, many years. We also pass the old apartment of an aged aunt of mine who used to live in Nice on the "Rue de France", one street behind the seafront. As a child, when we visited, I spent hours watching the aircraft take off and land at Nice from her balcony. Who would have thought? It's an interesting and quite exciting approach.

Having arrived at Nice, we taxi to one of our usual gates for parking. The doors are opened, and the lucky passengers make their way out. The first officer will fly the aircraft back home, and part of my duties is to do the walk around. It's always a pleasure to have ten minutes outside in the warmth of the South of France. The refueller has seen the card in the window next to the first officer, and he knows how much fuel we require. I exchange pleasantries in my schoolboy French, and he smiles politely, but I am fairly certain he hasn't a clue as to what I've said. The agapanthus flowers are enjoying the full sun around the edge of the terminal and, when I look to the east, there is another stunning view of that side of the city. I would really enjoy a night stop here, in the unlikely event that we end up stuck overnight, but it just won't happen.

The departure from Nice takes us out to sea initially. There is significant high ground to the north, and we have safety altitudes to achieve before crossing the mountains. Whichever runway has been used for departure, we are taken out over the sea whilst "clawing" for the required altitudes before getting a turn back to the north. We then cross the coast, usually at least above 7000 feet, having accelerated and climbed rapidly. The view is stunning with the airfield now way below us on our right. We are handed over to the ATC centre at Marseille, and we are on our way home. In a few minutes, we are passing Mont Blanc off to the right with Geneva just beyond. Lyon is to our left. We eventually pass to the east of Paris and, shortly after, we have the latest weather for Newcastle. Not quite the same as Nice. I always look forward to the next trip to Nice on my roster.

By now, I had been approached by training management at EasyJet to ask if I would be interested in joining the training team. I had enjoyed my time out of training circles, just flying the routes with a normal crew, and I initially thanked them for asking me but the answer was "no". However, there were an awful lot of very young first officers joining the company straight from training school and most of us spent our time passing on knowledge to them. They were very highly qualified academically, and incredible bright, but very much at the start of their flying careers.

A training captain said to me one day, "Pete, you may as well join the training department and get paid for what you are already doing with these new first officers."

In the end, I decided he was right. I therefore agreed to join the training department.

I had to have an interview by a member of the training standards team. I was sent up to Edinburgh for a chat with my old friend who had completed my base training when I'd joined the company. Having completed this, they also asked me to undergo a training standards flight with one of the team. This was completed on a flight out of Newcastle to Nice which was thoroughly enjoyable, as usual.

One of the issues being based at Newcastle was how to get to our headquarters in Luton. This was where everything was based including the simulator that we used at the time. Getting there was a pain. Although we had a scheduled service from Newcastle to Stansted, we then had to stand in all weathers waiting for a taxi. The journey across country could take forever with different taxi drivers using their preferential routes. Having to go to Luton for a six-monthly simulator check was bad enough but now going down for training meetings was something that I didn't relish. The inevitable happened and, having been a line trainer for a fairly short period of time, I was asked if I would start simulator training and examining. This I definitely did not want to do and, despite regular requests from the company, I managed to keep it at bay. I had spent enough time in my life away from home. I decided not to get involved in simulator work. Being away from my home base would mean hours spent sitting in a hotel room between simulator details.

The line training continued apace. Apart from new crews coming to Newcastle, new crews for all the bases were sent to wherever a line trainer was available. It ended up with most days being line training days but, as we were so busy, the company tried to accommodate us by giving us a quieter day during the working week with a day free from training. By this, I mean flying with fully qualified crews thereby not having to line train at least once per week. That was a pleasant change. Although there were a large proportion of British cadets to train, there were also many from other European countries who were to be offered employment by EasyJet at the end of their training. By now, the company was opening bases all over Europe. It was always pleasant to fly with these folks and chat about their backgrounds and their different countries and culture.

By now, we had added other destinations to the Newcastle routes. Alicante was always a very popular destination. A certain proportion of the people going to Alicante were going on package deals, but there were others who had their own properties and, of course, many of them, particularly the young, were off to Benidorm.

I set off to go to Alicante, one day, with a brand-new cadet on a line training flight. The routing was different to the normal route. We normally went down the centre of France, across the Pyrenees and from there more or less a straight line to a point about 20 miles due west of Alicante. This took us west of Barcelona and Reus, passing Valencia on the left-hand side. We would normally join a procedure which took us around a 20-mile arc from Alicante to join the centre line for the easterly runway. This was fairly straightforward and a route which we all got to know very well, as there were so many flights scheduled to this popular destination. On this particular day, we were routing a slightly different way. We flew south through central France but then routed over Toulouse, on towards Barcelona and, from there, we were sent to cross a beacon on the north-west corner of the island of Majorca. From there, we passed over Ibiza and then towards Alicante itself where we were landing on the westerly runway. Not a common routing for us, as more often than not we were landing on the easterly runway.

I had given the first officer the sector into Alicante to fly. I thought he would not only enjoy landing somewhere different rather than Newcastle, which was a very straightforward arrival, but it would also make him think about something new. As we approached Toulouse, I suggested he gave a PA to the passengers. This was always dreaded by some of the new, young first officers, but it's part of the job and they had to get used to it. I told him that all he needed to say, at this point, was to introduce himself, tell them where we were, how high and how fast we were going and what time we would be landing. He should also let them know what the weather was like. There were never any thunderstorms, only heavy showers. There was never any fog, only mist. Any mention of thunderstorms or fog would induce immediate terror.

The advice I was given, when I first started flying, by a very old, cynical training captain was, "They're only interested in what time we're going to get there and what the temperature is. They want a fag, a drink and a shag. Not necessarily in that order."

I preferred to be slightly more couth.

As part of the weather pack that we were given before flight, there was a sheet with significant weather shown on our route. Generally, it showed the part of Europe over which we were flying and covered things such as areas of turbulence or wind shear and also jet streams (very strong winds aloft). Just before the young man was about to give his PA, he pointed to the Mediterranean on the weather sheet and asked which sea it was. I was quite taken aback, but I could not believe he didn't know which sea it was.

I said, "It's the Pacific," just to see what his response was.

"Oh, thanks," he said, about to start his speech to the cabin.

"Nooo, it's the Mediterranean," I said with some concern. "You don't know which sea that is?"

"Well, I wasn't sure. Geography was not my strong point at school."

As we continued south towards Barcelona, I asked him which city was on the screen in front of him about 100 miles ahead.

"I haven't got a clue."

"Which mountains are these that we are about to cross?" (The Pyrenees.)

"Well I think they must be the south-west corner of the Alps."

I was quite astonished. I also asked him where Nice sat in relation to us. He had no idea whatsoever.

Westerly runway at Alicante. My colleague did manage to find it!

The problem with the lack of situational awareness geographically in an aircraft is that, should the captain become incapacitated, the first officer takes over command and is in charge. In aviation, one must always be aware (believe it or not!) of where we are. The reasons are many, including the fact that we always need to know where the nearest suitable airfield is for diversion. This could be for a short notice diversion due to a medical emergency on board, a technical problem, such as an engine failure which would require putting the aircraft on the ground quickly, or maybe the fact that due to reasons such as having to fly at a lower level, or strong headwinds, it means we need to uplift fuel to continue safely to destination. The list could go on and on.

Really enjoyed the Boeing 737-700 series
Photo with kind permission of Chris Wood

When we got back to base, I had to make a note of the concerns regarding my colleague, and I heard, a few weeks later, that he unfortunately had failed the conversion course. The reasons were other than his geographical awareness, but there was a high standard to be achieved and if it wasn't met then maybe this wasn't the correct career for him.

I had tried to keep my light aircraft experience going, and I joined a small group of enthusiasts flying a light aircraft locally. My old friend, Derek, had introduced me to the guys who ran the group and, after a quick check out ride with Derek, I was ready to go. It can be slightly boring flying by oneself, and we did quite a few trips together. It was about an hour's drive from where we lived, and by the time we had got down to the airstrip, opened the hangars, refuelled etc., etc. several hours had passed. Following an hour or so in the air, and after putting the aircraft back in the hangar and driving home, the best part of the day had gone. I decided that we should plan a more interesting trip rather than just "buggering about" in the local area. We did this a few weeks later.

I've always had an interest in classic cars. Back in the days of Dan-Air, I bought a Triumph Stag that was in need of restoration. The work took place at home in our garage, and Sid, who was a panel beater by trade, had given me a lot of help. The car eventually went to his garage for the paint job which gave him the work in return for all the help he had given me. When I lost my job with Dan-Air and didn't know what the future held, I felt that it would be sensible to get rid of the Stag. It was advertised at a price well below what I had spent on the restoration and duly went to its new home somewhere in the West Country.

Having found my new job with Virgin Atlantic and settled in to the new routine, the urge came back to have a new project in the form of another classic car. I eventually settled on a Triumph TR4 and found one in reasonable condition near Heathrow. A price was agreed, and I drove my new acquisition proudly back to our home at the time in West Chiltington.

I pottered with the car for a while and eventually decided that, although it was in reasonable condition, it could do with some serious work on the inner front wings. I contacted a Triumph TR specialist, TR Bitz, and this was the start of a long friendship with the owner John Sykes and his team. John eventually retired from TR Bitz, and the company continues to this day under the ownership of Craig and John who I still deal with.

It was always a pleasure to be around John and his team at Warrington. There was always good "banter" and, with their help, I eventually got the car to a superb standard. This was just the start of my relationship with this company and, over the years, they sold me several cars for restoration which kept me occupied on my days off and which I went on to sell through them. I enjoyed the work with what was, in effect, a giant Meccano set, and I was always, much to Jan's consternation, ready to sell them and move on to the next project when they were finished.

I went on to sell that first TR4 through TR Bitz, and it was eventually bought by a dentist. With the new owner, it went on to win "best car in show" at various classic car gatherings. Another, which I took our middle daughter to her wedding in, was sold to a farmer in Derbyshire. I regretted selling this particular car because it really did go like the wind but, hey ho, that's life! When the farmer bought the car, he asked John to weld a metal ring in the back of it. The car was a two-seater but had a small squab seat behind the two main ones. The farmer wanted this ring so that he could attach the lead of his Labrador to the car so that the dog could squeeze in behind him and couldn't jump out. Less than twelve months later, I was down at TR Bitz getting some spares for my next project when I saw the car back in the showroom for sale.

"What's that doing back here?" I asked.

"The dog didn't like it," John replied with a grin on his face.

The car was sold again and went to Rome where it still lives. The owner is still in touch with John and emails him regularly to say how much he enjoys the car. Bugger, I should have kept that one.

This one lives in Rome. It went like the wind.

Shouldn't have got rid of it... Damn!

I had several friends of a similar age who also went through the "classic car phase", and we used to meet up at several classic car shows throughout the summer. A favourite of these was one on my home patch near Ullswater in the Lake District. We would set off early in the morning and roar across the Pennines, with me as a potential Stirling Moss enjoying open-top motoring from the sixties, whilst Jan would be shouting "That's fast enough!" from the passenger seat. We would scream across to Alston, taking some of the tight corners at breakneck speed, and stop at the Hartside Cafe on the top of the world (or so it seemed) and enjoy a large breakfast whilst admiring a panoramic view of the Lake District. From here, it was another fast run down the other side of Hartside to Penrith and on to the show near Ullswater. Here, we would meet up with other friends including Terry and Alison in their old MGB. Jan always baked and took all her produce with her to the show, where we always got together for a picnic lunch. In latter years, we restored an old VW camper van. When we took this to the show, we always had a large crowd around us. Some people were there to admire the camper van, but others were there to admire the cake.

Towards the end of the show, it was another race home, stopping at the same cafe for more tea and cake. As usual, everything centred around food.

John's business (TR Bitz) sits next to an old airfield. He owns about 400 yards of one of the old runways. I had my eye on this strip of concrete every time I was down at Warrington and had it in the back of my mind that, one day, I would like to take a light aircraft into that strip.

The camper van became the centre of attention at car shows. Mainly because of the home baking!

It was this idea of flying into John's strip that came to fruition one day in early spring. Derek and I decided to take the light aircraft, which we both had a share in, down to John's strip at Stretton. The length of the runway was a little "tight" on the performance, but we decided we could get down there in one flight but would have to stop somewhere on the way home for fuel. I wanted to fly the aircraft into Stretton, as it was to visit my mate, and Derek was going to fly it home. It was a frosty, crisp but beautiful morning, and we set off across the Pennines passing abeam Settle. We could see the Settle viaduct in the distance. We had chosen a good day! The little Airtourer bobbed up and down slightly in the light turbulence caused by the wind blowing across the hills. Eventually, we had a good view of the west coast down to Blackpool, and we turned south near the gliding site at Chipping. There was nobody there at this time of the morning... great! As we flew towards the more built-up area to the north of Manchester, we called Warton. We were passing very close to the airfield. They didn't have any traffic to tell us about and so, as we crossed the M61, we called air traffic control at Manchester.

There is a low-level corridor to the west of Manchester Airport for light aircraft. This makes it easy for them to keep an eye on light aircraft in the vicinity of Manchester to avoid any form of conflict with the "big stuff" flying in and out of the main airport. We had to keep inside this corridor, as the strip at Stretton was right underneath. They were very helpful and, having given us the surface wind at Manchester, we had a good idea which direction we would be landing at Stretton. It was going to be towards the east. In the bright sunshine, we could see the industrial estate next to the strip a few miles ahead, and I positioned the little aeroplane for a landing towards the east. There was not much spare runway here, and so the aim was to touch down as near to the beginning of the runway as possible without hitting any trees and bushes on the way in! Touchdown achieved, John was waiting on the edge of the strip. We came to a halt, shut down the engine and climbed out.

"Typical bloody airline pilot," John said with a twinkle in his eye, "too high, too fast and too much money!" He roared with laughter. "I love taking the piss out of you airline pilots."

John has a private pilot licence and has done a lot of flying in his time. He has owned some very interesting vintage aircraft which were quite rare. He not only had a vast knowledge of classic cars but was also an experienced light aircraft pilot.

Having taken my old car bits out of the aeroplane, we went across to TR Bitz and I picked up the bits I needed for my new project at home. John got us to sign the visitors' book in which I included the date, time of arrival and details of the aeroplane. I also added "Much more fun than a Boeing 737" in the comments column.

When we came to leave John, we took the Airtourer right up to the end of the runway and virtually had the tail sitting in the bushes. Derek pushed the throttle wide open and when we felt there was no more power in the engine to give, he released the brakes and off we went. We were about to see if our performance calculations were correct. Sure enough, we were airborne and turning left without any problems and talking to Manchester again with all our details. We had decided to route back home through Sherburn in Elmet to pick up some fuel. Located in North Yorkshire, Sherburn has quite a history. The author Nevil Shute was a member of the Yorkshire Aeroplane Club which was based there, and the military used the airfield during the Second World War. From 1940, the Fairey Swordfish torpedo aeroplane, which was used to help sink the German battleship, Bismarck, was built there. I had also arranged to meet up with Chris Kingswood, who did a bit of part-time instructing there, and give him a fly round in our aeroplane.

We made our way north out of the Manchester low-level corridor and turned east towards Sherburn. This route was nowhere near as pretty as the southbound journey. We were passing over Bolton and Rochdale and on towards Huddersfield; all a big, built-up metropolis. Soon we were passing to the south-east of Leeds and, having spoken to them about any conflicting traffic, we were getting very close to Sherburn.

Sherburn had an advisory radio service and, having contacted them, they gave us the runway in use. Derek positioned the plane accordingly, and we landed on one of the grass runways. It was still a beautiful afternoon, and Derek disappeared to the "greasy spoon" whilst I went to look for Chris. After we met, he came over to have a look at our aeroplane.

"I haven't flown one of these before," he declared.

"Well, let's go and have a whizz around."

And that's what we did; a twenty-minute fly around with Chris having a go with this new toy.

We eventually said our farewells, and Derek and I set off on the forty-minute flight back to Peterlee. The sun was starting to sink in the west and, having routed west of York, we talked to the various military controllers in the Vale of York. They gave us a direct routing towards Teesside, who then cleared us through their zone, and we landed back "home" well before sunset. The aircraft refuelled, we pushed her back into the hangar and made our way home up the A19. It was rush hour and the busiest traffic of any kind that we had seen all day. It was a great day out and another box ticked!

Life was incredibly busy on the 737-700, and there was no let-up with the training. We had a superb chief training captain, based at Luton, who was extremely approachable for any problems that occurred regarding the training programme. The training captains were fortunate in that a training meeting had been arranged at an extremely posh hotel near Luton where our new company CEO joined us for dinner one particular summer's evening. This was an extremely pleasant affair, as the bill was paid by the company!

We were all asked individually if we had come across anything significant recently with the latest batch of cadets. I enjoyed relating one particular story which will remain with me for the rest of my days.

As I have previously mentioned, the majority of the cadets were very young but highly intelligent young men and women who had completed a course to achieve their flying licences in New Zealand. This was where most of their flying training took place, and they then came back to the United Kingdom to complete a "type rating" which qualified them on the Boeing 737-700 before starting their line training with people such as me. One particular young man was sent to Newcastle to fly with me for a few days. He was a very pleasant young chap and, as I found out, was a pleasure to fly with. Our first flight together was from Newcastle to Paris. After we had introduced ourselves, I had a look through his training file which all the cadets had to carry with them whilst under training. The write-ups from previous training captains indicated that he was doing well.

"I see that you haven't been to Paris yet. You fly the aircraft down to Paris, and I'll talk you through all the ins and outs of Paris as we go. It'll be a nice change and give you some serious problems to think about."

"That will be great," he replied.

The weather in Paris was good and, as I looked at the wind direction down there on the weather reports, I knew that we would be landing on one of the easterly runways. Paris Charles de Gaulle has four parallel east/west runways, and I knew that only one of two of the runways would be the landing runway we would use. French air traffic control would decide which one.

All planning complete, we walked down through security to find our aeroplane. I left him on the flight deck to complete the necessary preflight checks, whilst I went outside to do the walk around.

All was as expected, and we left Newcastle on time. The route down towards Paris took us down the centre of the country, to pass just to the west of the capital, and across the south coast near Worthing. Whilst we were level in the cruise, I showed him the arrival we could expect into Paris.

"Looking at the wind on the ground at Paris, we'll be landing on one of the easterly runways," I explained. "I think it will most likely be 09R (right) but you can also think about 08R (right). They will let us know as we get a little closer.

"As we are landing on one of the easterlies, you can expect a DPE 5E arrival."

I pointed out which chart he needed to refer to.

"OK, I suggest you start your briefing now, as we will be given descent fairly early. Somewhere just after crossing the boundary just south of the south coast."

He started his briefing. "OK Pete, from what you say, we can expect the Deepee 5 echo arrival."

I interrupted by mentioning that it was not called the Deepee 5 echo, it was the Dieppe 5 echo arrival.

I went on to say, "It's named after Dieppe. Dieppe is a town on the north coast of France which we'll cross as part of the initial arrival." I added, in jest, "When the Germans were occupying France during the war, we used to bomb the shit out of the place occasionally."

He looked at me and replied, "Did you fly Lancasters?"

I shall never forget those words.

"How old do you think I am?" I asked. "No, I didn't fly fucking Lancasters."

I smiled to myself, as he carried on with his briefing.

We carried on towards Paris, eventually lining up with a different runway 09 Left which gave us an impressive view of the city off to our right. Paris ATC kept giving us speeds to fly and, although it was a busy flight deck, I managed to quickly point out some of the landmarks including the Eiffel Tower. We landed, cleared the runway and, having called the ground controller, we were given taxi instructions towards one of our regular parking places.

He had done really well, apart from suggesting his training captain was possibly thirty years older than he actually was!

Having told this story over dinner at our training meeting that night, word inevitably got back to Newcastle where I was subjected to a load of verbal abuse from colleagues.

It was all friendly banter, of course, but included comments such as: "Berlin tonight, Pete?" or "Are you joining the Pathfinders?"

People still mention the story to me, all these years later, and the young man in question went on to make a good career for himself and is now an experienced captain, which is marvellous!

Life with EasyJet continued at a busy pace with new routes again being added to our network from Newcastle. We started a route to Rome. I had quite a lot of experience of this airfield from my Dan-Air days. We used the airfield at Ciampino from Newcastle. This was an old airfield which had been used by the military in days gone by. It was then considered an airfield for charter operators. The main airfield at Rome was Fiumicino, which was situated on the coast, a few miles to the west of Fiumicino.

Flying into Ciampino could give all kinds of problems. When we were given our weather briefing, crews were also given notams (notices to airmen). These notams contained information concerning such things as serviceability of navigation beacons en route, at destination and at diversion airfields. They also warned of any military exercises that might affect the specific flight. They had a mass of information and, in a lot of cases, one had to go through them carefully and pick out the relevant information that one needed. In some cases, they were not quite up to date with what was actually the case and this seemed to apply regularly with Ciampino. This was due to them not being updated by the relevant authorities. The notams would give us information regarding the landing aids that we would be expecting to use, and we would arrive in the area expecting to use a particular landing aid only to find that the aid was not available or possibly on maintenance. This could also be the other way round in that an aid was notamed as unserviceable but would unexpectedly be in use. This made life difficult at times. We would conduct a landing briefing before the descent only to find a lot of information that had been discussed was irrelevant, and we had to brief again whilst flying an arrival into Ciampino. This was far from ideal.

There was high ground to the east of Ciampino, and air traffic control would take us off the standard arrival to vector us all over the place whilst giving us different speeds to fly. Bear in mind that not only was there a lot of traffic into an out of Ciampino, but Fiumicino was only a few miles away. When we were eventually cleared to make an approach, the instrument landing system (ILS) might not be available on the usual south-easterly runway, and we would have to use another less accurate aid which involved check altitudes being called at regular intervals during the final descent. When the north-westerly runway was in use, it involved long, drawn-out radar vectors to an approach aid which was not as accurate as an ILS. Add to this the possibility of poor weather, or even thunderstorms, and one was very busy. It was therefore decided that we would not take brand-new cadets on line training into Ciampino for their first few sectors. They would be way behind what was happening and the training captain would have too much pressure on him. This was a sound decision.

Of course there were bonuses to flying in and out of Ciampino, and one of those was the scenery. If all went according to plan, and we got straightforward vectoring to the ILS for the south-easterly runway without any conflicting traffic or great dramas, one could enjoy a superb view of parts of the country.

Having started what was always an early descent and passed just to the west of Florence, we would pass Perugia in the Umbria region of Italy. This was on the border with Tuscany. To the west of Perugia lay Lake Trasimeno. As we got nearer to the city, the radar vectors would come thick and fast and, eventually, one was left on the centre line to fly down the approach. The Vatican City passed down the right-hand side just to the west of the River Tiber. Next was usually a good view of the Colosseum. As we got closer to the airfield, we were now into "airport territory" where the surroundings became rather drab. To the east of the airfield were masses of old apartment-style buildings. They were old and depressing. The runway was not generously long, but we would touch down in the correct place and, by the time the aircraft was approaching taxi speed, we'd clear the runway to the right. A quick change of frequency, and we would tell the ground controller which stand we were parking on, as we would have contacted our handling agents before landing; a somewhat different approach to normal, as the ground controller would normally give us that information. That was the way it was in Ciampino.

In the middle of winter there could be snow in Ciampino, but in the middle of the summer it could be stifling hot. Our programme normally gave us an arrival in the late afternoon. It could still be in the high thirties and, due to not only the rather short runway but also the extinct volcano at the end, we had to make a very careful check of the maximum weight we could take off at. In the old days, on the 1-11 with Dan-Air, we were very limited, and there were times where we had to sit and wait for the temperature to go down to be able to take off with all the passengers and their baggage. Modern aircraft, with more powerful engines, had improved things considerably but care was still needed.

Eventually, the passengers would make their way out and, if we were lucky, we would get start-up clearance straight away. However, there were times when we were given an air traffic control "slot" and we would have to sit and wait until the allocated time came. The small auxiliary power unit, in the tail of the aircraft, was not only giving us electrical power until the engines were started, but it was also providing cold air through the air conditioning to try and keep us all from melting.

Eventually, air traffic control would clear us to start and the process got underway. It would quite often happen that start clearance was given and we would have to get airborne quickly. Such was the sequence of events, having waited for indeterminate periods of time, they wanted it all to happen quickly! Start-up and pushback complete, we would taxi out for the south-easterly runway. As always happened, we would have to wait a few minutes for another aircraft to land. We were now watching the clock carefully. Would we get airborne before the slot expired? The landing aircraft would finally touch down and we would be given clearance to line up on the runway and, finally, get underway.

The departure out of Ciampino all happened very quickly. As we'd line up on the runway, there was an extinct volcano straight ahead of us. There is a beautiful lake now in what was the crater, Lake Albano, and on the edge of the lake lies Castel Gandolfo, the summer residence of the Pope. The departure involved a noise abatement procedure and a very early right turn towards the coast. We didn't want to disturb His Holiness! We'd pass over Fiumicino and shortly after that we were cleared to turn to the north-west direct to Elba, Italy's third largest island. Here, Napoleon was first exiled in the 1800s. There was always something of interest to gaze down upon. After Elba, we would route along the coast towards Nice before turning north and, from there, the routing was the same as what we would follow on our way home from the South of France. Another trip to Rome completed.

There was one last incident of interest which I had before leaving the Boeing fleet. This involved a cracked window on the flight deck.

We were on our way home from Nice, and I was busy programming something into the flight management system, when the first officer, who had been eating his meal, remarked, "Look at that. My window has cracked."

Sure enough, when I looked across, his window had a crack in it from one side to the other. Aircraft windows consist of several layers, and there is usually no immediate problem. We had time to run through the checklist together and that gave instructions to descend to a much lower level. We notified air traffic control and made the decision to divert to our main base at Luton. We were descending to a lower level, which would use significantly more fuel, but we also had a large engineering backup at Luton. We crossed the French coast northbound at

11000 feet. It was the closest view I'd had of this part of the world since my days in light aircraft when flying across the Channel from Lydd to Le Touquet. I had explained in detail to the passengers what the technical problem was and, as always, they accepted the truth. We landed at Luton without further problems, and the company had arranged a replacement aircraft which was parked and ready to go next to us. The only further delay was continuous requests from our passengers to have a look at the cracked window as they disembarked! We duly complied, and they filed in and out of the flight deck with their curiosity having been satisfied. We eventually landed back at Newcastle only an hour and a half late.

Farewell to a good friend

Photo with kind permission of Chris Wood

By now, the new Airbus aircraft were arriving thick and fast at the various company bases and, eventually, the turn of Newcastle came for the pilots to undergo their conversion course. I was sad to be leaving the Boeing fleet but, as the Airbus provided a new challenge, it was time to look forward to the future.

Late in 2009, I made my way, along with one of the first officers who I had been teamed up with for the duration of the course, to Burgess Hill. This was the beginning of another conversion course.

We stayed in one of the hotels near Gatwick, and there were quite a few of us from Newcastle on this particular ground school. This phase of conversion is never particularly enjoyed by pilots and this case was no exception. The Airbus is a different concept to the Boeing aircraft, but I must admit that it is a technically impressive aircraft. A friend of mine, who I was with at Virgin Atlantic, had also joined EasyJet and told me there were three things that he particularly liked about the Airbus. He liked the electric seat that he could move backwards and forwards with ease. He liked the tray that folded down in front of him so that he could eat his meal in comfort. Lastly, he particularly liked the large windows so that he could get a really good view of the good-looking birds as they boarded! I think he probably had his priorities wrong!

Sure enough, the concept was very different to what I was used to but, after much burning of the midnight oil, I passed the required ground school exams and we went on to the next phase which was the simulator.

Eventually, my line training started out of Gatwick, and on my second day I flew with yet another old colleague from Virgin Atlantic. We went off for the day to Milan and Berlin, and he spent all the time giving me the benefit of his vast knowledge of the Airbus. As always, after weeks in the classroom and the simulator, it was a delight to get into the air again. We left Gatwick and made our way through France before starting our descent over the Alps towards Milan. I hadn't been to Milan Linate before, so this was a pleasant change. The weather was beautiful and the view of the mountains, as always, made the job a delight. Despite having flown to various parts of the globe and over various mountain ranges, there is always something new and interesting to be seen over the Alps regardless of how many thousands of times I have flown over them in years gone by. Many of the Italian airfields have that old, Second World War look about them and Linate was no exception. Air traffic control was friendly and, as we were passed on to other frequencies, there was always the farewell "ciao" as we left one sector for the next one. We were sequenced for landing and eventually cleared the runway and taxied to the terminal. The buildings were like old warehouses and there was a sad, neglected look about them. However, it was just another airfield and very few airfields hold architecture of interest. It was another gateway to a beautiful country and, as usual, I envied the passengers getting off. A few days in the Italian sunshine would have been most welcome.

The turnaround was completed in a businesslike manner, and we were soon off on our way back to Gatwick. Linate is surrounded by high ground, and the departure procedures kept us safely clear of the mountains whilst we gained altitude. There was also the mandatory noise abatement procedure to be followed. More technical questions were asked on the way back to the UK and, after another quick turnaround, we were ready for a visit to Berlin. Unfortunately, we were now running twenty minutes or so behind schedule, as we had been given an air traffic control slot time. Nothing could be done about that except to make sure we were absolutely ready to go with the doors shut and to ask ATC if there was a possibility of any improvement. It didn't happen for us that day. Berlin was old, familiar territory for me but, instead of landing at Berlin-Tegel as I did in the Dan-Air days, EasyJet used Berlin Schönefeld. This airfield was to the south side of the city. The new part of the flight was the aeroplane, there was a lot still to learn but, nevertheless, it was a pleasant environment to work in.

I had a few days off after the first couple of days, so it was back home to catch up with the usual household bits and pieces whilst also keeping my head in the books. It was then back to Stansted for my final three days of line training.

Following the completion of the course, it was back to the usual rules of me being only allowed to fly with experienced Airbus first officers until I had gathered the required time on type. I have to admit that flying with these young first officers was a great pleasure as always, but most of them were so adept with the computer side of the aircraft that they taught me a lot. With any conversion course, the real learning continues well past the course itself when one is flying in a relaxed atmosphere without a training captain breathing down one's neck.

After two or three weeks of flying the route with experienced first officers, I started to feel more at home on this new aeroplane. I also received a phone call from our chief training captain asking me if I was ready to start line training new first officers.

"We're desperately short of trainers, Pete. How would you feel about starting to train again? I know you've just been on line a short time, but we need you to help."

I made the mistake of saying yes to this request but, after an uneasy night's sleep, I rang the chief trainer back the next morning.

"Look, I'm flattered that you are asking me to start training again so quickly but, having thought about things overnight, I really don't feel comfortable starting training new pilots just yet. Give me a few more weeks of consolidation."

"It's not a problem, Pete. Give me a ring when you feel ready."

And that's how it went. After a few more weeks, I felt ready to plunge back into the training world. The management at EasyJet were always exceptionally good, particularly in the training department. Another flight with one of the training standards captains followed to check me out in the right-hand seat of the Airbus. My old friend, Chris Kingswood, was the man in question, and this trip was out of Paris, Charles de Gaulle where he was based. We were rostered to go to Marrakesh, Morocco, another first for me, and I took the opportunity to get all the tips for this new destination from him. The flight time from Paris is in the region of three hours. Plenty of fuel was advised, and we used Casablanca as a diversion. There certainly were a few idiosyncrasies with Marrakesh particularly with the approach. It was an instrument approach to one runway with a circle to the reciprocal runway should the wind dictate.

After the flight together, he took me back to the village, to the north of the airport, where he lived, and we enjoyed a couple of good steaks together outside one of the restaurants in the main square whilst sampling the delights of the local wine.

I was to return to Paris to fly with Chris again in a few weeks' time. This time he was observing me train a new first officer; all part of the sequence of events to start training on a new type.

The majority of the rest of my professional flying career was still heavily involved with training. I still resisted the pressure to return to training in the simulator, as I was quite happy to continue flying the routes with new guys and enjoyed going home at night. Despite the fact that the routes from the North East could become rather repetitive, there was always something different to deal with. This could vary with anything from assessing first officers for their suitability for command, to issues such as weather diversions or medical emergencies. Unfortunately, the medical issues could happen without warning and, a couple of times with EasyJet, I had to divert due to suspected heart attacks. I am pleased to say that, in my forty-odd years of professional flying, I never lost a life! One of these medical diversions took place on a command assessment. I had briefed the first officer that, although I was still technically the aircraft commander, I wanted him to deal with any issues that should occur during the course of the day. We had departed Bristol, on our way to Malaga, when we got a message from the cabin saying that there was a suspected heart attack down the back. I looked at the first officer and asked him what we should do. Although the power to veto remained with me, he rapidly made the correct decisions and we were on the ground in Bristol very quickly. An ambulance was waiting, and the passenger was blue-lighted off to hospital. I then left him to deal with everything from more fuel to a new load sheet and liaising with air traffic control for a new slot to get airborne again for Malaga. We were now into an extra sector for the day. Did we have enough duty hours to be able to complete the new duty?

How would he approach the crew to discuss any extension of duty hours that may be required? All these matters have to be considered by a commander. Although, in this case, I knew the first officer well, as we had flown together many times, we still had to go through the necessary process on the day. He didn't disappoint me and was very suited to undergo a command course. It was always a pleasure to put people like him forward for promotion. On the downside, it could be difficult, but very necessary, to not recommend people who were not suitable. In training circles there is a saying which is so true: "Where there is doubt, there is no doubt."

Malta had now been added to our destinations from Newcastle. It was a relatively long old flog from the North East, but at least it was something new. The flight was a little short of four hours, both ways, depending upon the winds. It was initially an early afternoon departure getting back around midnight. As the light faded, as the trip progressed, there wasn't much to see but, depending upon the time of year and when the sun was due to set, we could still get good views of different parts of Europe. Although the route generally took us over the western edge of Sicily, we sometimes could see smoke coming from Mount Etna over on the east coast. At almost 11000 feet above sea level, it still makes its presence known and, should it be grumbling away with unfavourable winds, we would receive warnings in our paperwork with possible changes of routing to keep us well clear of any volcanic ash. Malta was always efficient in my experience and the people very friendly. It was the usual quick turnaround and then back, this time routing over Sardinia and Corsica, before passing over Nice and then the same routing as if we were returning from Nice. Sicily, Sardinia and Corsica are three islands I have not visited. They are "on the list".

I was due to operate a double Newcastle to Bristol one particular evening. There was an extremely active area of low pressure over the British Isles, and the winds at Bristol were way over the crosswind limits for the Airbus. I rang our operations department and asked them if they had any preference as to where I diverted should an approach at Bristol be out of the question. Although the forecast was for the winds to remain at an incredibly high strength, sometimes the forecast is not quite as accurate as one could hope for and there is always the possibility of the wind diminishing in force which could put the crosswinds back within limits. On occasions such as this, it is quite often prudent, with the backing of the operations department, to carry sufficient fuel to divert back to Newcastle. A large proportion of the business passengers would rather stay in Newcastle rather than be left at the other side of the country following a diversion. However, in this particular case, having suggested coming back to Newcastle, the company decided that, if necessary, we should divert back to Birmingham. From there, if necessary, the passengers would be put on a coach to Bristol. This was going to be quite a long day for them, but at least it meant that they would eventually get to where they wanted to be.

This was yet another training flight. I was training a delightful young man with whom I had already spent quite a few days. He was exceptionally young, but very keen, and was progressing well. He made me laugh, because his mum used to come to the airport every day that he was flying and watched him as he took off for another training flight. She was exceptionally proud of her boy! I had a feeling that tonight was going to test his mettle. I was honest with the passengers and explained the situation before we departed. There was a good chance that we were not going to be able to land at Bristol and Birmingham was the more likely option. A few decided to get off and delay their journey until another day. Once we had unloaded their luggage, we got underway. As we approached the north of Manchester, we picked up the latest weather for Bristol which showed us that the wind had absolutely no intention of dying down. It was still above our crosswind limit and aircraft were diverting from as far afield as one of the London airports. The decision was made, and we informed air traffic control that we wished to divert to Birmingham. The winds were exceptionally strong all over the UK and that included our choice of diversion. The good news was that, although the winds were very strong, they were within our maximum crosswind limit. I briefed my colleague for the approach and put a lot of emphasis on the fact that the wind was from the south-west and it would be extremely turbulent during the final stages, as several other aircraft were also diverting from airfields around the country and we would have to hold before being allowed to start our approach. It was extremely rough in the lower levels, and I wondered what it would be like for my colleague during the final stages. Could I rely on him for all the necessary requirements and assistance on this particularly rough night? We eventually were vectored by the radar controller on to the ILS. As I had briefed my friend, the runway eventually appeared way over to the left of the windscreen. (The wind was blowing strongly from our right, and we had to point the nose of the aircraft towards the wind direction in order to keep the aeroplane on the runway centre line. Should we just point the nose at the runway, the aircraft would be blown over to the left.) This is standard technique for flying an approach with a crosswind. The issue comes when we are just above the runway with the aircraft still pointing towards the direction of the wind. If we touch down and the aircraft is not properly aligned with the runway then enormous stresses can be put on the undercarriage. At this point, therefore, we use the rudder to align the aircraft with the runway centre line. This can take a considerable amount of experience to get just right and can be quite a challenge when the wind is at the crosswind limit for the aircraft. I need not have worried, as the young man in question was absolutely superb. He was a great help in every aspect and, when we arrived on stand, I told him so.

With the passengers disembarked for their coach ride to Bristol, we flew back to Newcastle. I fully expected the second rotation to Bristol to be cancelled but it wasn't. Ops wanted us to have another go, so we boarded the few passengers who wanted to try to get to Bristol, having explained yet again what our intentions were. As we approached the north of Manchester for the second time that night, we were told that Bristol had closed due to the winds and ops suggested we go back to Newcastle! So ended an eventful evening, but my young colleague went home with a glowing write-up in his training file.

My final approach in an Airbus A319 on my last day

By now, I had just passed my sixtieth birthday. I felt as if I had almost had enough of early mornings and late nights. Maybe it was time to retire a few years early. I could still continue in the job until I reached sixty-five, but I was also starting to feel that I would like to step down so that Jan and I could enjoy some travelling and taking a back seat (literally) in the aeroplane. I was flying the same routes and I knew them well. I even knew at which geographical point along the route the air traffic controller would call us with a frequency change. Hell, I even knew what the next frequency was!

After some careful thought and much deliberation, I decided to keep going that summer and give it another twelve months. Anybody who has flown aeroplanes for a living knows how difficult it is to make the final break. For the final six months of flying, I also decided to step back from the training aspect of the job. I felt that it would be nice to just fly the line with my young colleagues without the stresses of training brand-new cadets. Eventually, on 14th May 2015, the day came for my last flight. I was rostered for a Malaga and back, and my old mate Chris Kingswood arranged to come up to Newcastle to fly as my first officer for my last ever flight as a commercial pilot. When we arrived at the aircraft, I found that one of my colleagues at Newcastle had got to the aircraft before us. He'd left a pair of slippers resting on the rudder pedals along with a dressing gown hanging on my seat. My tray had been pulled out and on it sat a pipe, a tube of vitamin tablets and a packet of Viagra!

A dressing gown for the old bloke

Slippers on the rudder pedals, a pipe, vitamins and Viagra!

We had a great day out together, and my last landing back at Newcastle was of a good enough standard to be proud of. Back in the crew room, I was presented with a picture of an Airbus suitably signed by the management.

Last commercial landing after more than forty years of flying – May 14th 2015

A group of colleagues and friends then adjourned with me to the local pub where we spent the afternoon together. It was a sad time, in many ways, but I felt that I had "done my bit" and hopefully other adventures still lay ahead. Other old mates in aviation were also either retired or seriously considering retirement. Taking early retirement depends very much on the individual's circumstances. Coming from an industry with a very high divorce rate, it also very much depends on how many ex-wives one has! Fortunately, I am still with wife number one after well over forty years of marriage!

My picture still hangs on the wall of my study

It just so happened that, like many retired pilots, I couldn't just walk away from it. My dad had died five days after I retired, and I spent many weeks trying to tidy up his affairs. Like many old-fashioned marriages, my mum did not have a clue about his affairs, and I spent a lot of time following a paper trail. This was to prove a very interesting exercise.

After about twelve months of retirement, I decided to renew my acquaintance with light aircraft flying. I went over to my old stomping ground at Carlisle and, with the help of one of the local clubs over there, I renewed my private pilot licence. I did quite a bit of flying around the local area and the Lake District which I had enjoyed over the years. As always with me, another idea started to form in my mind, and I thought it would be fun to try and find a Beagle Pup to buy. I had flown and instructed on these little aeroplanes all those years ago at Lydd and, with hindsight, I suppose I was trying to relive those fun, early years. Unfortunately, Beagle Pups only come up for sale very rarely. The smaller engine 100 series are quite limiting with less power, and the 150-horsepower engine aircraft are very much sought after. After a search lasting over a year, I found an aircraft which was coming up for sale in the Isle of Wight. I had been in touch with a maintenance organisation, which had looked after this particular aircraft, and I happened to make one of my regular calls to them to see if they knew of any aircraft coming up for sale on the right day. I contacted the owner, and a date was set to meet and have a look at this prospective purchase.

I caught an early morning flight to Southampton where I met up with my old friend Tony Foote. I had been discussing this project with him for some time, and he decided he would join me for the day out to the Isle of Wight. It was a pleasant, sunny day, and we sat outside on the ferry for the short crossing to Cowes where we met with the owner of the Pup. After a quick cuppa at his home, we were driven across to Sandown Airport where the aircraft was hangared. I have to admit to not being overenthusiastic with the aeroplane when I first saw it. It looked rather tired and had not flown for some time. All the aircraft maintenance checks were out of date and it needed some money spent on it. The engine was started and run up without any issues and, eventually, I left the owner with an "I'll sleep on it and give you a ring tomorrow".

Tony and I chatted about the Pup on the ferry back to the mainland. Neither of us was that impressed, but Tony dropped me off at the airport for my flight home and I chatted to Jan about it that evening. The next day, I rang the owner with several questions, and in the end I made him an offer well below the asking price. He accepted. The little aeroplane needed a lot of work and my offer reflected this requirement.

The next problem was to get the aeroplane across to the mainland to have the work done. We needed some brave soul to fly it across the water from the Isle of Wight. The maintenance company had somebody approved by the CAA to undertake this brave deed and, after a week or so, this was done. It took another few weeks to get the engineering work completed, and eventually the day came when it was pronounced ready for collection.

Although I was perfectly legal to fly light aircraft, it was over forty years since I last flew a Pup. Fortunately, I had a friend who I knew from my Virgin Atlantic days who had a part share in one of these aeroplanes and, having made contact with him, he volunteered to help me get it back up to the north of England. The day in question arrived, and we met at the little airfield in the south of England where the Pup had been "brought back to life". We planned to make the first half of the flight to Gamston where Robert and I would part company. He would catch the train home, and I would take the Pup on to Eshott where I had arranged hangarage. The forecast wasn't too bad. It was showing showers over the south of the country but hopefully brightening up the further north we got. We filled the tanks with fuel which would give us about three hours' endurance; plenty for the flight to Gamston. Paperwork complete, we climbed aboard and, having started the engine, made our way out to the active runway.

Having got airborne, I turned right on track to make our way north towards the old airfield at Greenham Common. Almost immediately, the cloud base started to lower and the rain started. We fortunately had a handheld GPS with us to help with navigation, but the further north we got the worse the visibility became.

Safely back at home

Robert was busy talking to Farnborough Radar, whilst I did my best to stay below cloud and see where we were going. Maybe we should turn back? We got the weather reports for further north, and they were no worse than where we already were so the decision was made to continue. We crossed the M4 at 500 feet and decided to stay slightly to the right of track, as the ground was rising ahead of us. We needed to keep clear of this and also keep well clear of not only some obstacles at Didcot but also the built-up area around Oxford. I felt like an absolute beginner again with a light aeroplane. What on earth were we doing? This was not pleasant. With regular applications of carburettor heat to ensure there was no ice forming in the carburettor intake, we continued through the murky conditions. Here we were, two retired 747 captains who would be quite at home in a fully loaded 747 in any weather conditions but struggling through the murk in a little aeroplane. We must be mad. As we approached the Bicester area, we could see from the charts that it was an area of intense glider activity. No chance of that today. They would be safely tucked up in the clubhouse telling each other stories of impossible things they had done in their gliders. They should be with us! We eventually passed just to the west of Silverstone and decided we could safely make our way towards the aviation beacon at Daventry. We had both passed over this beacon thousands of times in our airline careers at several thousands of feet above the ground. Today we felt as if we could touch the ground.

We eventually crossed the M1. It looked brighter ahead. It turned out to be what pilots call a "suckers' gap". For a short while, things seemed to be looking better and then they got worse. We had not yet got above 1000 feet. Most of the little airfields we had passed had no traffic. We had tuned into the various frequencies but, sensibly, most light aircraft were transmitting to say the weather wasn't good and they were returning to their various airfields. Maybe we should divert into Sywell which was now off to our right?

"Let's keep going," was the usual comment. "We can always turn back."

We spoke to Wittering. Nothing much going on there but, as usual, the service from this military field was superb. They could see exactly where we were and would keep an eye on us.

We zoomed over Rutland Water. There were quite a lot of fishermen around the water. I would have been quite happy to be down there with them.

As we approached Syerston, the weather brightened considerably. Typically, we had flown the vast majority of the trip in crap weather and, as we neared our first destination, the weather brightened up for the last 30 miles. No more issues with high ground and obstacles, the weather was getting better!

We landed at Gamston. It had not been a pleasant flight, but we were there!

After a cuppa, Robert left me for the railway station and, having refuelled, I set off for home. I flew west out of Gamston to avoid getting involved with the Doncaster area and eventually turned north towards Wetherby. The weather was bright and breezy now with virtually unlimited visibility. I spoke to the military in the Vale of York, and they kept a close eye on me as I made my way towards the Teesside area where I hoped they would let me fly straight through their zone. It was quite bumpy with the wind blowing across the North York Moors, and eventually I spoke to Newcastle who told me the wind at the airfield was from the west at 15-20 knots; it might be bumpy going into Eshott. There was nobody answering the radio at Eshott, so I joined the pattern over the airfield and landed on the westerly runway. I had phoned Jan from Gamston, and she was waiting for me.

We pushed the Pup into the hangar, where its new home was to be, and drove home. I was totally knackered! Give me the warm, air-conditioned flight deck of an airliner any day. That day was too much like hard work, but I knew that it was a one-off, difficult day. There would be fun times ahead.

Tony Foote was keen to join me for a flight in the Pup, and he came to stay with us for a few days shortly after I had brought the aeroplane north. We made our way up to the airfield and, after pulling the beast out of the hangar, we refuelled and had a good look at the aircraft before climbing on board. I thought we had locked the doors correctly but, as we got airborne, Tony's door became unlatched. Without thinking, I leant behind him and unlatched the door fully; a big mistake. The airflow caused the door to open further and made the problem worse. Whilst Tony hung on to the door to try and stop the problem getting even worse, I turned back into the circuit and landed without any further delay. Tony's fingers were numb. Trying to keep the door from opening any further used a lot of effort. The small piece of metal, which was normally used to close the door whilst on the ground, had only a couple of centimetres to hang on to. I got a lot of stick from him as we drove home.

This incident was entirely my fault.

The next few months gave the opportunity for quite a lot of aircraft flying. I had to take the aircraft back south for maintenance. I needed a more up-to-date radio fitted and one or two issues had been found which needed to be put right. Robert was more than happy to meet me at Gamston, and I set off one spring morning to fly south and meet up with him. As I passed the Teesside area, I found myself not holding my heading accurately. I thought I was not concentrating properly but then saw that I needed to keep aligning my direction indicator very regularly with the aircraft compass; very odd. After a few more minutes, the penny finally dropped. I looked at the vacuum gauge and saw it had fallen to zero. The vacuum pump drives the gyro which drives the direction indicator. The artificial horizon was also starting to topple which was another clue. It was also a gyro-driven instrument. Not a problem. I would continue, but I just needed to keep a close eye on the compass and decide which way I needed to turn to increase or decrease the headings. On a good day like this one, I could choose a reference point on the horizon and just keep pointing towards that. I found my way to Gamston without any problems and pointed the issue out to Robert. He was happy to continue the flight south, and so I got a taxi to the railway station at Gamston and made my way home.

Occasionally, I had to go across to Carlisle and fly with an instructor to ensure I had three landings in my logbook. Whilst the Pup was away having maintenance done, I had to maintain my recency of having carried out three landings every 90 days to allow me to carry passengers. This was more expense. Owning a light aircraft is not a cheap pursuit. Eventually, I got the aircraft back and enjoyed some really good flying. Cliff and I positioned the aircraft back down south for a fifty-hour maintenance check one particular day. We landed at Gamston for fuel and a cuppa and then set off for the last leg. On our flight south, we came very close to a Spitfire. It was a two-seat Spitfire used to give paying passengers an experience of this iconic aircraft. It was wonderful to see from the air.

Tony and I had a very enjoyable day flying over the hills and lakes of the Lake District. We set off to land initially at Kirkbride in Cumbria. Kirkbride is an ex-RAF airfield still used by light aircraft and autogyros. I had set up an account over there, as the fuel was slightly cheaper than other local airfields. The guy running the airfield was a most interesting gentleman with a good historical knowledge of RAF Kirkbride. Amongst other interesting facts, Kirkbride was used after the war to gather wartime aircraft to be dismantled and destroyed. At the time, there were brand-new Tiger Moths in crates awaiting their turn for destruction, but they could be bought for £65 each. If only they were that cheap now. The control tower had been completely restored, and the airfield had a pleasant atmosphere of times gone by. The local people were friendly, and it was a great place to stop for fuel and a cup of tea.

Tony wanted to do a few circuits at Kirkbride so that he felt completely at home in the Pup, and we eventually headed east towards the hills on this perfect day. The visibility was unlimited and the winds were very light. No turbulence was expected over the mountains of the Lake District.

After a quick visit to Workington on the coast, we headed east to cross Loweswater and on over Crummock Water and

Buttermere. It was slightly hazy over the Lakes but, eventually, after a good look at Windermere, Thirlmere and Keswick, we made our way back east to Eshott.

Leaving Kirkbride – The restored control tower bottom right

Buttermere, Crummock Water and Loweswater (looking west)

Photos with kind permission of A. R. Foote

I took Jan for a trip north of the border to Perth. It was just over an hour's flying time and the weather was good. Just after we passed Kelso, I noticed a slight flicker on the charging light. The ammeter was also showing a slight discharge. This was of concern to me, but Jan was enjoying the view and was not aware of the issue. The Beagle Pup has electrically operated flaps, and I was now thinking in terms of losing the alternator and ending up on battery power. If that was to happen then we would probably end up with a flat battery, no radio and no flaps. The radio wasn't a particular problem, as Perth knew we were coming and would see us join the circuit and realise what was going on. The flaps concerned me slightly more, because if we were to turn around, go back to Eshott and land without flaps then we would use up a little more runway than usual. The runway in use at Eshott was always slightly "tight" for landing in a Pup. I decided to continue towards Perth. The only issue was that we would get stuck there.

We continued with the discharge light flickering. As soon as I increased the power the light went out, but it was fairly obvious that the alternator was on its way out. We crossed the Firth of Forth and, still having some electrical power, we spoke to Edinburgh, but they weren't worried about us as it was a quiet Sunday morning. Eventually, Perth came into view and we landed without further issues. By now, I had told Jan what was happening and left her at the "greasy spoon" cafe whilst I went to look for some help. Unfortunately, there was no engineering help on duty, but there was a local engineering company who I was able to speak to on the phone. They promised they would take care of things first thing on Monday morning. The day out in the aircraft was now at an end, and a young chap in the airfield office, who had been doing some local flying, offered to give us a lift back to Edinburgh, as he was about to drive down there. We took up his kind offer and, having dropped us off at the local railway station, we caught a train to the main station and, after a couple of hours wait, got on a train home. Our very kind neighbour picked us up, took us back to the airfield at Eshott, where we got into our car, twelve hours after leaving it, and finally drove home.

The reader might wonder why I am constantly writing about tales of woe with my aeroplane. The writing was on the wall. Ten days after the incident at Perth, I got a phone call to go and pick up the Pup, as all had been rectified. Of course, I now had to make the journey back to Perth in reverse. Included was a night in a cheap hotel in Perth in order to get away first thing in the morning, as the forecast in the north-east of England later in the day showed a marked deterioration. There was also a bill of almost £1000 to pay. There is a saying in aviation, particularly amongst those who have had several wives... "If it flies, floats or fucks don't buy it... rent it"!

I had obviously tried to recreate my early days in aviation with the purchase of this aircraft and it just wasn't working. In the early seventies, I had started my flying career at a time when light aviation was exciting and was blossoming in this country. Flights could be taken to all kinds of small airfields throughout the country. At these small airfields, there were thriving aero clubs with large social followings. One was always assured of a warm welcome and lots of local bullshit stories with large exaggerations to listen to whilst having a cup of tea before flying back home. Today, lots of these small airfields have disappeared, along with the flying clubs, to make way for housing or industrial estates. West Malling, where I flew into all those years ago for my flying instructor upgrade, is long gone. A fascinating airfield with lots of wartime history, it has been bulldozed as modernisation creeps in. Even Carlisle, where I learnt to fly and went on to become a commercial flying instructor, has become a quiet airfield with the sound of skylarks dominant. There is, of course, the odd light aeroplane but not what it was back in the seventies when it was a large commercial flying school. In those days, there could be six or seven aircraft in the circuit at one time with air traffic control working hard to keep them all separated. Millions have been spent on Carlisle airport in recent years, as the airline industry attempted yet again to make it a commercially viable airfield with new routes for one of the smaller airlines. It was not to be, as the pandemic has taken its toll. Airlines have come and gone at Carlisle, and the skylarks have always been the winners in the longer term.

I decided to put the Pup up for sale. I shuddered when I worked out what it was costing me for an hour's flying. Enough said that it was over twice as much per flying hour as it would be if I was renting an aircraft from the local flying club. One of the last flights I did was with Jan to a wartime airfield in Yorkshire.

We got airborne and I said to her, "Are you bored?"

"No, I'm enjoying the view."

"I'm bored," I replied. What I really needed in the Pup was a 400-knot button. Complete the take-off, climb up to our cruising altitude and then press the 400-knot button to get us where we wanted to go quickly and then I could enjoy the approach and landing. Never try to go back in time.

Despite what my mother said to me all those years ago, it just wasn't fast enough. I think my time of cruising around at 90 knots was over.

Eventually, a buyer was found for the Pup and, on a blustery day, he came to Eshott to pick it up and fly it to its new home. As I watched him disappear to the south, I had no feelings of regret.

I have had a fantastic career in aviation. I have been extremely lucky and enjoyed every minute of it. People ask me which aircraft I enjoyed flying the most. I usually reply "all of them". They were all a wonderful part of my life, and I thoroughly enjoyed them all for different reasons. The 747 was a superb pinnacle, especially the base training where I was given a multimillion-pound aircraft to go away to a quiet airfield and teach people the practical issues of take-offs and landings for the first time.

We are now eighteen months into this dreadful pandemic. Many people have lost jobs including thousands in the profession I enjoyed so much. Terms and conditions have been drastically eroded to try and keep airlines solvent until the flying public can return. Despite two Gulf wars and several other skirmishes around the world, I never saw anything like this during my career.

So what now? Do I really want to put myself through the stresses of another medical?

I have decided to only fly in a light aircraft to do something new. Maybe go to do a seaplane rating. I haven't done that. Maybe go to fly a Harvard with my old mate Chris Kingswood. A Harvard is a Second World War trainer with a big radial engine. That would be something new.

But what next in my life? Well, as it happens, something very interesting has just happened.

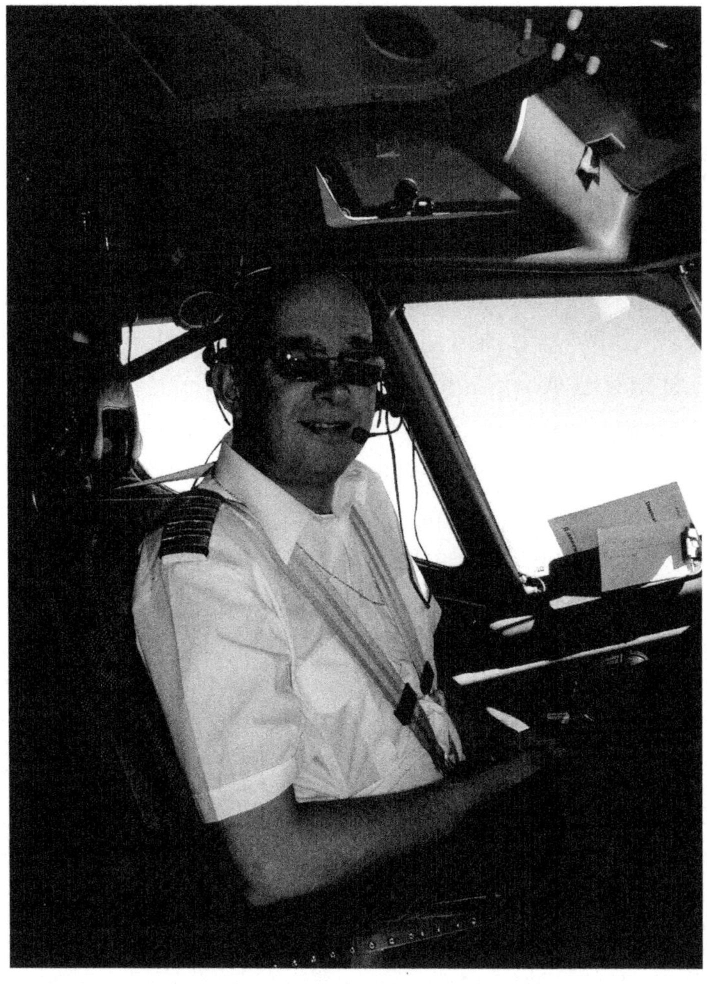

CHAPTER 19

My father died May 15th 2015. As has already been mentioned, my mother was an old-fashioned housewife who did not leave the home to work in the traditional sense. She brought my sister and me up, ensuring that we were warm, clean, well fed and generally well provided for. My grandfather had come to live with us in Workington in 1960, and he was also well cared for. By that time, he was in his mid seventies but still travelled and enjoyed a regular day's fishing on the River Derwent. We had Mary, a live-in help, who really came on board to look after Grandfather but ended up as a greatly loved addition to the family. Her greatest bond was with my sister, Helen. When Helen was learning to talk, as a young child, she couldn't say Mary. Mary became known as Meena which was the closest Helen got to Mary's name as a young child.

As the weeks went by following Dad's death, I had the task of sorting out mother's affairs ensuring that she had enough money to keep her little house, be kept warm, be taken shopping by Jan and myself along with any other needs that she had. This was organised fairly quickly, and she was very happy. Sundays were spent with Jan and I. Jan would organise usually a roast, and Mum would have enough to take home for a good meal the following day. For the rest of the week, she managed quite happily to cater for herself with us popping over midweek to take her shopping. The dust settled following Dad's demise, and I managed to get her affairs in order. We made a few changes, ensured that her finances were in good order, and she eventually got used to using a bank card herself and understanding the various bills which would appear through the letter box. She didn't have a computer, let alone know how to use one. Dad had always done everything for her. He had kept her wrapped in cotton wool but, slowly, her knowledge of the practicalities of running a home started to improve. It was a few years later, as she advanced into her nineties, that her health started to deteriorate and life started to become very difficult for her as dementia took over.

As I made my way through the mountain of paperwork which Dad had left, I found a letter amongst the rest of his papers. It appeared to be from a firm of German solicitors. Initially, I looked at it and put it to one side, as there were more important issues to deal with on Mum's behalf. A few days later, as the rain was bouncing off the window where I sat at my laptop, I decided to have another look at this letter. It was from a firm of solicitors in Berlin saying that they represented clients who might have claims for restitution of property or other assets. It stated that they had been doing this since 1993 and they had been successful on behalf of, amongst others, Jewish heirs of property that had to be sold or were stolen because of Nazi persecution.

Something inside pushed me to look a little further into this matter. I had vaguely remembered my father telling me that a company had tried to make contact regarding restitution of family belongings, but he'd said it was a scam. Throughout most of my adult life, my father had vaguely mentioned property that was lost due to the Nazi regime, and I had constantly made a joke of it all to friends and family. I was the one who would say, "And whatever happened to the family valuables?"

I "googled" the name of the solicitors in Berlin. There were three names on the letterhead but only two partners seemed to be listed. There was also a general email address and thinking "what the hell..." to myself, I sent off an email which was to be the start of another big adventure. The date was 3rd February 2019. The next day, I received a reply from one of the partners named on the letterhead, Mr Lothar Fremy. Mr Fremy told me that he was on holiday at that time but would get in touch again as soon as he was back in the office. He had also forwarded my email to another gentleman in Tel Aviv.

After a few days, I received another email from Mr Fremy saying that he had contacted my Uncle Charlie in 2006 and he had assumed that Uncle Charlie, in turn, would speak to my father regarding this matter. They did indeed discuss the letter and Uncle Charlie contacted his solicitor who, in turn, wrote to Mr Fremy in early 2007 saying that he did not wish to pursue the matter. In February 2012, Mr Fremy again contacted Uncle Charlie's solicitor to tell him that he had come to a settlement with the current holder of one of the objects of the Oppenheimer porcelain collection which had been sold by Sotheby's in London. Mr Fremy suggested that it would be beneficial for my uncle and his brother to reconsider their position and cooperate in order to benefit from the financial outcome of this settlement. Thinking this was all a scam, the solicitor wrote back on February 23rd informing Mr Fremy that his client did not wish to be involved in the matter or benefit from the proceeds.

Mr Fremy did not contact the lawyer again.

Just to remind the reader, Dr Franz Oppenheimer was a successful businessman who was a shareholder in a large coal business, Emanuel Friedländer. He was also on the board of other coal businesses. Born in 1871 in Hamburg, he had married Margarethe Knapp who was born in 1878. They had two children, Franz Karl (who I first met in 1963 in Malmö) who was known as Uncle Bobby and a daughter, Marie Louise (known as "Moupy") who was my grandmother. Marie Louise had two children, Uncle Charlie and my father, John (Hans) Peter.

My father and Uncle Charlie would visit their grandparents in Berlin during the holidays. Great-grandfather would walk along the Unter den Linden (one of the main avenues in Berlin where his offices were situated at that time) with them, explaining the names and histories of the various statues. The following days, he would ask them about the various statues, as they walked past again, to see if they had retained the knowledge he had tried to pass on. Afternoon tea was taken regularly with all the family in the Adlon Hotel next to the Brandenburg Gate.

There was one particular exciting trip for my dad and Uncle Charlie. This took place in Berlin, in August 1936, to watch the Olympic Games with my grandfather when Adolph Hitler was present. This was literally weeks before the great-grandparents left Germany. Little did they know then what an effect the man they were all watching would have on their lives over the next few months and years.

As the Nazis came to power in Germany, my great-grandparents could see the dangers of the anti-Semitic tone which was developing in the country and decided it was time to leave. Unfortunately, the Nazis demanded a "tax" from people of Jewish descent who were leaving the country. This was known as a flight tax ("Reichsfluchtsteuer"). The Nazis demanded a tax from Dr Oppenheimer of 1,060,000 Reichsmarks. (One Reichsmark was worth approximately two and a half dollars during the war.) The horrific alternative to not leaving the country would be written down in the pages of history. Dr Oppenheimer had, at the time, one of the best Meissen porcelain collections in the world. He was forced, under duress, to sell part of this collection in order to help pay the tax. They fled quickly to Vienna, where Marie Louise and her family were living, and rented an apartment at Reisnerstraße 48. A few pieces of their porcelain collection went with them along with various pictures. Most of these pieces were deposited in customs in Vienna and some of them were never seen again.

It is known that the porcelain collection was acquired by a Dr Fritz Mannheimer at a price which was to his advantage. Mannheimer was a German banker who was living in Amsterdam. He ran his own firm, the Amsterdam branch of the large bank Mendelssohn & Co. Over the years, he built up a large art collection which he kept at his home in Holland. He opposed the Nazis and provided aid to Jews who had fled Germany. As the persecution of the Jews escalated, following the "Night of the broken glass" (Reichskristallnacht), Mendelssohn & Co in Berlin were forced to close. The Amsterdam division of the business continued but, as they were heavily involved with the refinancing of the French national debt, the business eventually found itself in a severe liquidity crisis. Mannheimer, who did not suffer from the best of health, left Holland for his house in Vaucresson, in the western suburbs of Paris. Upon his arrival, he went for a walk in the garden, suffered a massive heart attack and died. Mendelssohn & Co immediately had to stop operating, and it was found that the debts of the business were huge. As Mannheimer's estate was liable for some of these debts, it was liquidated and experts from the Rijksmuseum were brought in to value the pieces of art in his collection. German art buyers had shown an interest in the collection along with a particular member of the SS who had been made responsible by the Nazis (Hermann Goering) to acquire art for the Third Reich. Although some of the collection had been left and stored in Austrian customs when the Oppenheimer family arrived in Austria, it eventually disappeared. It is thought highly likely that the Nazis had plundered these pieces. Most of the porcelain which was now in Mannheimer's collection was taken by him to the Netherlands.

CHAPTER 20

A simple "google" of Mr Lothar Fremy will show that he is a highly respected specialist in restitution law based in Berlin. He has acted for many anonymous heirs and also collections such as the Budge Collection.

As the Oppenheimer collection had to be sold under duress, Mr Fremy believed that it should be restituted to the Oppenheimer heirs after provenance was proven. The Oppenheimer estate is represented by an executor who was appointed by the responsible inheritance court in Berlin-Mitte who in turn appointed the firm of Rosbach & Fremy. Lothar Fremy was already in contact with the heirs of Franz Karl Oppenheimer (Uncle Bobby) but had been unable to convince my side of the family to pursue the matter.

I spoke to Mr Fremy by phone over the few days following our initial contact. He told me that he would like to meet with myself and other members of the family who were involved in the story. I, in turn, contacted all other family members concerned in the UK and relayed to them the story as it had developed. Intrigued by the issue, everybody agreed to meet with Mr Fremy at a hotel in Newcastle.

The day duly arrived, and we met with Lothar where he told us the whole story. Following their flight from Germany and Austria, the family arrived in Stockholm via Budapest. My great-grandparents initially stayed in the Grand Hotel, Stockholm. From there, they made their way to New York, where they lived quietly, becoming naturalised American citizens in 1947. They both died in 1950. My grandparents, father and his brother were a slightly different story which we shall come to later.

Returning to the story of the porcelain, Dr Fritz Mannheimer died in 1939, and a member of the SS then acquired the collection for Adolph Hitler in order to put it in the planned Führermuseum alongside other world-renowned pieces of (plundered) art. This museum was to be in Hitler's home town of Linz in Austria. As the war continued and the Nazis eventually realised that the tide was turning, the collection, along with other art and bullion, was hidden in various different locations in order that it did not fall into the hands of the Russians or the Allies. In the case of the porcelain collection, it was initially hidden in the Vyšší Brod Monastery in South Bohemia (Czechoslovakia) and later in the Bad Aussee salt mines in Austria.

A force comprising American and British museum directors and curators, alongside other specialists in art, had been formed to move into Germany, Austria and other European countries where the Nazis had plundered art, bullion and other cultural pieces. This group was known as the "Monuments Men" and were frantically racing against time not only to find hidden pieces but also trying to prevent destruction of irreplaceable art. The collection was eventually discovered by the Allied monuments officers and transferred to the central collecting point in Munich in 1946. (The film The Monuments Men with George Clooney relays the story of the Allied soldiers who found much of the plundered art and bullion.) Somewhere between 1946 and 1949, the collection was sent back to the Netherlands. Mannheimer's executors did not seek restitution, as they would have been obliged to refund the price paid by Hitler's curators. The collection went to the Dutch state holdings and some of it was sold with the rest going to the Rijksmuseum.

From here, we started a journey, guided by Mr Fremy, which was to last over two more years. The claim had been made with the Rijksmuseum for restitution, and the wheels were to turn very slowly. The Dutch government were really the people in control, as the Rijksmuseum is a state-owned and run organisation. Lothar and his researchers had done a remarkable job in researching the facts about what had happened to the family and liaising with the necessary authorities in order to list the restitution claim.

But turning the clock back over eighty years, what exactly had happened to the family when they were forced to flee Vienna? Part of this story is still being researched by me, along with one or two other people who have very kindly given time to help look into the matter. This part of the family history is mainly written for my grandchildren and future generations, because it is a story worth telling. Only the past generations could really understand the fear of the unknown as it happened to them, the fear of having to leave their homes in order to escape persecution, and the fear of where they would have to travel to in order to start life again in a new country, not being able to speak the language and not knowing how they would be received.

As has already been mentioned, Dr and Mrs Oppenheimer had already seen the Nazi menace growing in Germany and fled to Austria towards the end of 1936. He established his business interests in a smart office in Walfischgasse 11 to which he would enjoy the walk on most working days.

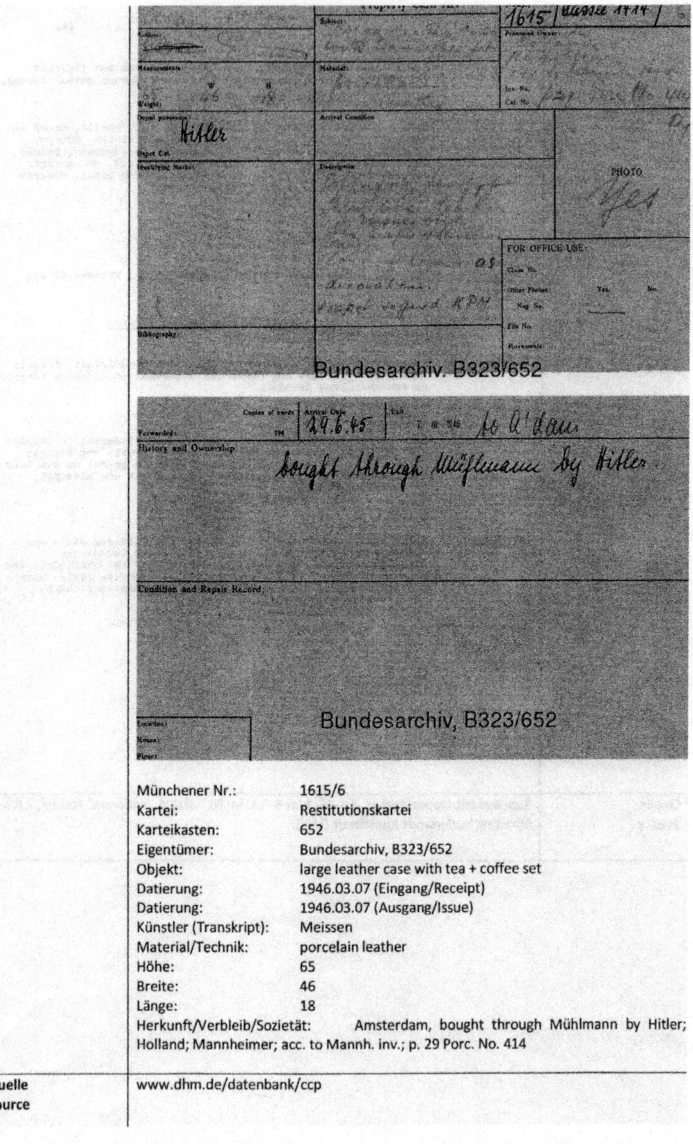
Subject:
Author:
Measurements:
Weight:
Depot possessor: Hitler
Depot Cat.
Identifying Marks:
Material:
Arrival Condition
Description
1615 Aussee 1414
Presumed Owner:
Inv. No.
Cat. No.
PHOTO
FOR OFFICE USE:
Claim No.
Other Photos: Yes. No.
Neg. No.
File No.
Bibliography:
Bundesarchiv. B323/652

Copies of cards: Arrival Date 29.6.45 Exit 7. III. 1946 to A'dam
Forwarded:
History and Ownership: bought through Mühlmann by Hitler.
Condition and Repair Record:
Location:
House:
Floor:
Bundesarchiv, B323/652

Münchener Nr.:	1615/6
Kartei:	Restitutionskartei
Karteikasten:	652
Eigentümer:	Bundesarchiv, B323/652
Objekt:	large leather case with tea + coffee set
Datierung:	1946.03.07 (Eingang/Receipt)
Datierung:	1946.03.07 (Ausgang/Issue)
Künstler (Transkript):	Meissen
Material/Technik:	porcelain leather
Höhe:	65
Breite:	46
Länge:	18
Herkunft/Verbleib/Sozietät:	Amsterdam, bought through Mühlmann by Hitler; Holland; Mannheimer; acc. to Mannh. inv.; p. 29 Porc. No. 414
Quelle Source	www.dhm.de/datenbank/ccp

The above is a photocopy of a document made by the "Monuments Men". It refers to a tea and coffee set in a leather case which was found by them in the salt mine at Bad Aussee near Salzburg, Austria. Note the name of the assumed previous owner – Hitler.

Walfischgasse 11 - Dr Oppenheimer's office as it is today

Reisnerstraße 48 as it is today

Being a shrewd man, he took Liechtenstein citizenship for both himself and his wife, as he felt this was probably a sensible route to take to not only avoid problems with the Nazis but also to make life easier should they have to flee Europe. It was probably wise to not be known for having German nationality. He could see the rise of Adolph Hitler and his ambitions would not be for Germany alone.

Both he and his wife enjoyed the company of their children and grandchildren in the vibrant city of Vienna. Both families lived within walking distance of each other, their daughter and son-in-law having created their home in an apartment at Taubstummengasse 2.

Taubstummengasse 2 as it is today

For a relatively short time, life was still good with regular visits to the opera, which they could see from their home, and the social life in Vienna was vibrant. My grandfather, Dr Oppenheimer's son-in-law, had bought a holiday home near Edlach an hour or so away from Vienna. Shooting and fishing was a big part of Grandfather's life, and he had several shoots and was assisted by up to three gamekeepers. In those times, there were still bandits in the countryside and Grandfather always kept a pistol in the house. All the family learnt how to use the various guns, and the best shot of them all was said to be my grandmother.

Holidays were passed there with my father and his brother spending hours in the woods exploring the local area. Although Dad and his brother grew up initially in Vienna, there were also regular visits to St. Gilgen for holidays in a large, wooden-built chalet which was owned by family friends and offered for use as a holiday home. This pretty, little village, in the Salzkammergut region, sits next to Lake Wolfgangsee, and it was here where the two young boys would learn to sail.

The holiday home at Edlach – The original was on the left, but my grandfather eventually bought the one on the right as well.

Hunting lessons in Edlach

However, the storm clouds of the Nazi regime were approaching from the north, and Hitler was to have his country of birth, Austria, as part of his empire. On the 12th March 1938, the annexation of Austria into Nazi Germany (Anschluss) took place. Dr Oppenheimer and his wife had fled the previous day. A car had taken them to Sopron on the Hungarian border and then on to Budapest. From there, they flew to Amsterdam and then to Stockholm in Sweden. Any pieces of art that they had left were immediately confiscated. The rest of the family had also left with the Oppenheimers, and they too travelled to Stockholm via Budapest where Dr Oppenheimer's son (Uncle Bobby) was living and working. The exception to this was my grandfather. Having ensured that his wife and children were safely over the border into Hungary, he decided to travel back to Frankfurt to ensure that his parents were safe. He had both an Austrian and German passport. Despite protests from friends and family who were concerned for his safety, he made his way back, deep into Nazi Germany, sheltered by friends as he travelled. The Gestapo were now looking for the family, but my grandfather insisted they would not be looking for someone travelling towards Frankfurt. He thought they would be looking for the family fleeing Austria and away from the country.

My grandfather eventually reached Frankfurt safely. His parents were still secure and insisted they would not leave. (Great-Grandmother was already in a wheelchair.) Sadly, Great-Grandfather died just after the outbreak of war on the 12th October 1939. Great-Grandmother died within a month on the 8th November 1939. The stress of war, alongside the provocation of the Nazis, was probably just too much.

After having checked on the well-being of his parents, my grandfather spent several days walking up and down the banks of the Main, the river flowing through Frankfurt. His idea was to swim across the river at night thus avoiding the various checkpoints. At the time, he thought this would be part of his escape route from Frankfurt to help him remain clear of German Army patrols and police. In the end, he decided that the current would be too strong for him, and he eventually managed to get a flight out of Frankfurt to Stockholm with the help of an official who turned a blind eye to his departure. The official was also a family friend.

Great-grandparents (Herzberg) – Karl and Amalie

Home for the family was now in Stockholm, with the young boys being sent to school in Uppsala, just outside the capital. My grandfather and grandmother eventually had to move to Paris to find work. This was before the Germans had invaded

France, and the boys were to visit their parents during the school holidays. We suspect the boys travelled initially to Malmö before catching a flight. This was quite a journey from Malmö to Paris, and it is thought that it was more than likely undertaken using a KLM flight through Amsterdam. I still have my father's "Kinderausweis" or child ID card which was issued in 1936.

In the meantime, my great-grandparents (Oppenheimer) had decided to move to the United States. Great-Grandfather knew that the Nazis would make advances to the west and was concerned that the British would not be able to hold out against a possible Nazi invasion. Their initial journey to the United States is still shrouded in mystery. It is very possible that their departure from Sweden was initially from Gothenburg via ship. It would have been another harrowing journey hoping that both the Allies and the Germans would respect the brightly painted neutral vessel. Following the German invasion of Denmark and Norway during 1940, Sweden persuaded Germany and the United Kingdom to let a few shipping vessels pass through to the Atlantic. This shipping was called lejdtrafiken or "safe conduct traffic". It was monitored by both Germany and the United Kingdom, and traffic was allowed to pass to the United States (until they entered the war) and neutral countries in Latin America. Ten of the vessels were sunk during the war.

We know that they left Barranquilla, Columbia, on the 14thDecember 1941 on board the SS Santa Rosa. This was one week after the Americans entered the war following the Japanese attack on Pearl Harbour. Four days after leaving Columbia, on the 18thDecember 1941, they arrived at Ellis Island, New York, to have their applications processed alongside the thousands of others. We also know that, having been accepted into the United States, they settled in a hotel, The Croydon, 12 East 86th Street, New York, NY 10028. The Oppenheimers were granted American citizenship in 1947.

After the war ended, Grandmother (their daughter) continued to visit her parents in New York. She flew from Bournemouth Airport (which was then the equivalent of Heathrow) regularly using piston engine aircraft which did not have the same reliability as jet-powered, weather-dodging, comfortable aircraft of today.

The Oppenheimers continued to live peacefully in the United States until their deaths in 1950.

Photo with grateful acknowledgement to Lockheed via the R. A. Scholefield collection

My grandmother travelled on this aircraft to visit my great-grandparents in New York. The aircraft registration on the tail fin matches that on the document below showing one of her entries into the United States.

Form I-466

UNITED STATES DEPARTMENT OF JUSTICE
IMMIGRATION AND NATURALIZATION SERVICE

INFORMATION SHEET (concerning passenger arriving on aircraft)
This sheet must be filled out in the English language, typewritten, or printed in ink
(Note further instructions on back of this sheet)

1. Aircraft NC 88838 (Registration marks) Departing from Hurn Date Mar 22 1946
2. Passenger: Arriving in area at New York Date 3/23 1946

NAME IN FULL		Age	Sex	Country of Which Citizen or Subject	Embarkation	
Family Name	Given Name				Place	Country
HERZBERG	Marie Louise	43	F.	STATELESS FORM. GERMAN	Hurn Mar. 22 1946	England

3. Destination in United States NEW YORK CITY 12 EAST 86th STREET THE CROYDON

Fill out spaces below in the cases of aliens only

4. Place of birth BERLIN GERMANY Race GERMAN RACE
5. Height: Ft. 5'4" in. ; complexion NORMAL PINK
6. Married or single M ; color of hair GREY mixed ; of eyes BLUE
7. Able to read YES ENGLISH – FRENCH – GERMAN Occupation Housewife
8. Immigration visa, passport visa, reentry permit, or other immigration document. (Prefix number with QIV, NQIV, PV, RP, or abbreviated designation of other immigration document, as case may be.) N.1.3(2) TEMP. VISITOR Number 3293 Issued at AMERICAN CONSULAR SER. LONDON Date of issue FEB. 11th 1946
9. Last permanent residence CONNAUGHT HOTEL CARLOS PLACE LONDON W.1
10. Final destination (intended future permanent residence) #9. Returning after 3 months stay
11. Going to join relative or friend in U.S. Father Name and address of such relative or friend: FRANZ OPPENHEIMER NEW YORK CITY 12 EAST 86th STREET THE CROYDON
12. Whether in U.S. before, and if so, where NO.
13. Purpose in coming to the U.S. VISITING ILL FATHER and when
14. Whether has ticket to destination Yes Length of intended stay 3 months
15. Whether ever in prison or in institution for the care and treatment of the insane No Amount of money shown $350
16. Whether ever excluded from admission to the United States or arrested and deported from the United States No.
17. Marks of identification:

(These spaces reserved for United States immigration officer)
Immigration list No. 1 Line No. 25
Name of person or transportation company operating aircraft: PAN AMERICAN AIRWAYS, INC.
Alien's passport will expire 12/3/46
Head tax status Paid
Held for BSI
Admitted under section N.1.3(2) B

Passenger inspected (and information hereon verified) by [signature] (Signature of immigrant inspector)

This form may be obtained upon prepayment from the Superintendent of Documents, Government Printing Office, Washington, D.C. It may be printed by private parties provided it conforms to official form in size, wording, arrangement, and quality and color of paper.

But what about the rest of the family? At the end of 1940, my grandfather decided to move to the United Kingdom. He thought the German offensive in the west was imminent, and he joined a company that had a factory based in West Cumberland making, amongst other things, plastic buttons for military uniforms. My grandmother moved to the north of England with him. Initially, they lived in the Armathwaite Hall Hotel on the edge of Bassenthwaite Lake near Keswick. They then moved to the "Red House" on the northern edge of Bassenthwaite. My grandfather moved to Hundith Hill which was the property owned by the company he worked for. Eventually, my grandmother moved to London where she could enjoy the life that she was used to with many social engagements which she enjoyed. She lived in the Connaught Hotel for quite some time before moving to a rented property in Curzon Street and, finally, a very smart apartment in Lowndes Square, Knightsbridge. The marriage was not to last and eventually, having moved to London to live, they divorced shortly after the war.

Hundith Hill November 1960

Grandmother married again, and her second husband, Albert, died in 1958. Up until that time, they continued to travel together including regular trips by both sea and air to New York to visit her parents. Following Albert's death, she continued to live in London, still visiting her family mainly in the UK but also spending time in France, with two elderly ladies who were also distant relatives, near the "Baie des Anges" in Nice. The three elderly ladies spent long evenings together playing canasta. As a small boy, I spent hours on the balcony in their apartment watching the aeroplanes landing at Nice.

Grandmother died in 1986.

My mother and Uncle Charlie are also, sadly, no longer with us.

Dad with my grandmother, Marie Louise, (the best shot in the family!) outside the Hornflowa factory, Maryport circa 1950s

The story regarding the porcelain collection rumbled on. We received regular updates from Lothar. He rang me, one morning, to tell me that the Restitutions Committee in Holland was asking for various members of families concerned to give a talk to the committee regarding their various family stories. I have never been that keen to stand up in front of large groups of people, but Lothar said it may well help our cause and so, reluctantly, I agreed. Having eventually received a date for the journey to Brussels, it was cancelled at the last minute due to lack of time available with the committee itself. I was saved from the ordeal.

Eventually, after much consideration, the Dutch decided to "do the right thing", and it was decided the porcelain collection would be handed back to the family. Whilst this was agreed in principle, there was still paperwork to complete and the Rijksmuseum contacted Lothar to suggest that they be given time to raise the funds to buy the collection themselves. Unfortunately, agreement could not be reached, after much correspondence, and the collection was to be auctioned on the open market. It was suggested by Lothar that we use Sotheby's in New York for the task. The collection of porcelain could not be split between the various family members who were entitled, and the only way to deal with the matter was to auction the whole collection. Various bills could then be paid and the remaining figure was to be shared proportionately. More months went by and, eventually, the collection was delivered to Cologne where it was inspected by several experts, including Lothar, to make sure nothing was damaged. It was then flown to New York to be stored by Sotheby's until the day of the auction.

The family story had been relayed by Sotheby's, in the period leading up to the auction, to the art world and the collection attracted a lot of attention. I was again asked by Lothar if I would accept an invitation to appear on Bloomberg to talk about the family and the collection, but I declined. I did not feel comfortable talking publically at this point in time.

Following the auction, it was all a bit of an anticlimax. It was slightly ironic that one of the biggest bidders was actually the Rijksmuseum, and over half of the collection went back to Holland to be displayed for public viewing. It is rather nice that the museum decided to put the pieces in a "Hall of Honour" along with some of the family's photographs and their story. This had not been the case when the collection was originally in the museum, but whole story of the Oppenheimers, their collection and their journey to safety had brought about more research and gathered a large amount of public interest.

For me, one of the big bonuses of the whole story was to meet up with family members (some still to be organised) who I had not met for many years. Much of the whole story was new to me and some of it is still to be revealed.

Jan and I went back to Berlin and then to Vienna in the same year. We walked up and down the Unter den Linden to see where Great-Grandfather's offices were and to see where he had walked with my father and his brother whilst explaining the history of all the beautiful statues. In Vienna, we went to find the homes and the office of the family. The last the family had seen of their homes had probably been a hurried glance whilst jumping into a car. Over eighty years later, we could enjoy the beautiful city with people going about their business, people enjoying coffee and cake in the street cafes and the friendly, welcoming faces of the local people. How times had changed!

Me and Uncle Charlie circa 1955

The following few pages were written by my Uncle Charlie and tell the tale of his time in Canada when he was considered "at risk". Having fled the Nazis, it follows his life after his "welcome" to the United Kingdom! It is an interesting story and one which I would very much like to include:

My family, both on my father's side as well as on my mother's side, were German. My father's family were smallholders in Hesse, from where my grandfather, as a 16-year-old, was taken to Frankfurt as an office boy in a German bank and ended up as its managing director.

On my mother's side, which came from Hamburg, my grandfather, like his father, started as an advocate in the German Marine corps but ended up as chief executive of one of Germany's largest coal mining and trading companies.

My father was a mining engineer with a doctorate degree in geology, specialising in iron ore. He was seconded by the German government to the Spanish government and worked finally in the Spanish Sahara as an explorer. He was retrained for petroleum, but with the First World War breaking out, he was called up as reserve officer in the artillery, served first on the Western Front, then in the logistics units on the Eastern Front and eventually as a junior officer in the German staff in Brussels. He did not know what the word "fear" meant and was popular with his men.

As the German state collapsed in 1918, there was chaos in Germany and the threat of Bolshevism. The landowners and businessmen set up a unit of 10,000 ex-regular NCOs, called the "Freikorps" to restore order, and my father was asked to act as go-between and paymaster to these troops.

He then decided he had to learn about finance and started as a junior in a small bank in Austria, where he met my mother who was there on holiday. They got married and started their married life in my father's bachelor flat opposite the stage door of the Vienna opera house. Perhaps my first memory was seeing the scenery moved out and pulled away by large tractors. My younger brother was born there too. My brother and I were always multilingual, as we had both a French and an English nanny.

After my primary school education, I was sent to the "Theresianische Akademie", a school founded by a seventeenth-century Austrian empress to train officers and diplomats for the Austrian Empire. The school was run on military lines.

When Hitler moved into Austria, the family moved for a few days to Hungary, near my father's shoot. My father then went "underground" back to Austria and, when tipped off by his friends in the authorities that the Gestapo was after him, he moved to Germany.

Meanwhile, my mother, brother and myself moved to Sweden, where we had a branch of my mother's family. My father meanwhile was again warned that the Gestapo was on his tracks, so he bought a return air trip to Amsterdam, went through immigration when he knew a friendly officer was on duty, but flew from Amsterdam to Stockholm where he joined us.

My brother and I, after a short Swedish language course, were sent to a Swedish boarding school.

My parents lived in Paris where my father worked, but his military staff training and the knowledge of the German Army caused him to assess the French Army as no match for the Germans. He was also sure that the Germans would move through Belgium and Scandinavia to attack Britain when they had overrun Poland and France. He was sure Britain would win in the end.

As a result of these deliberations, he looked for work in the UK and was eventually invited to join a company, originally set up by some Czechs in Cumberland.

My brother and myself had always visited our parents during our holidays, both in France and England. At the end of January 1940, my father decided that the German offensive in the west was imminent and ordered my brother and myself to come to the UK immediately. So on 26th January 1940, we landed in a, then neutral, Dutch plane in Bournemouth.

My father asked an old Scottish friend, retired from the Foreign Office, which school would be good for us boys and so we came to Fettes.

At first, we had some difficulty to understand some of the Scottish accents, as well as the schoolboy slang developed by all schools.

Fettes, during the early days of the war, was an interesting place. Most boys, after finishing at Fettes, were immediately sent to an officers' training unit and commissioned into HM Forces. When there was an air raid, the boys, or "men" as all boys at Fettes were called, went into the air-raid shelters which had been dug into the bank at the front of the school, but two senior boys were kept at the houses to "fire watch". Unlike the usual interpretation, that fire-watching was to guard the buildings against firebombs, our fire-watching was mainly concerned that the many open fireplaces in the houses and housemasters' houses did not get out of control!

Another feature of the old houses was that we actually had girls, called "skivvies", making our beds. To keep us apart, we were not allowed to go back to the dormitories until the girls had gone. We also had a houseman and a houseboy to help with the many menial tasks, such as carrying coal etc. I am sorry to say that the Fettes "men" did not always treat the houseboys well.

The school was, in fact, run by the prefects, like the army is run by the NCOs.

Boxing (army rules) was compulsory and stood me in good stead in my life, as was the tough regime and the potentially good food, badly cooked! Incidentally, bullying was not known in our time at Fettes. I think that boxing had something to do with this.

A few months after my sixteenth birthday, I was on a corps exercise in the Fettes grounds, when a runner came, who told me to report immediately to my housemaster's study where I found not only the housemaster, but also the headmaster, Dr Ashcroft, with two gentlemen in trench coats. I was told that, as I was over 16 and lived in a fortress area, which Edinburgh had become, I was to be interned as an enemy alien. The policemen thought that I would be out within a few days.

When I was interned, I was first taken to Donaldson's Hospital, which had been turned into a prison camp. From there, several of us prisoners were taken to the Old Scotland Yard in London, which was grim, and from there to Lingfield Racecourse in Surrey. There we met a lot of Germans, many of them Nazis, including Hitler's favourite pianist. I teamed up with three other young Germans. We were allocated a horsebox, with straw mattresses, boards and trestles. We called our home "Empire State Building". We joined the camp fire brigade.

After some time, Italy joined the war and Italian internees arrived. They were filthy especially regarding the lavatories, which the fire brigade had to clean, of course from a distance, with high-pressure hoses! But the Italians sang beautifully, especially during hot nights. The food was dreadful, mainly salt herrings and lettuce. When the wind was in the right direction one could hear the guns and bombs from the Channel ports. Dunkirk had begun.

One day, a number of prisoners, including myself, were told to pack. We went by bus and prison train to Liverpool where we arrived at night when a major air raid was going on. Troops brought a German aircrew into the train which had been shot down that night.

In the morning, about 2000 prisoners were loaded into the RMS Windsor Castle, and we sailed that night into the North Atlantic. Many were prisoners taken in Norway, soldiers, sailors from captured ships, and airmen. There were also quite a number of SS men who had been captured. At the same time, three other prison ships left the port, including the SS Arandora Star which was sunk by a U-boat with a loss of all crew and prisoners. The troops guarding us had just come back from Dunkirk and were probably rather tense. We sailed at high speed, without escort, through the Northern Atlantic. The weather was perfect and we saw icebergs and some whales.

The ship was not built for so many people, especially as prisoners were not allowed on the upper decks. We more or less organised into three watches, one on deck and two below. I remember sleeping under a small table with four German riflemen playing a German card game on top of me. I used my little suitcase containing my Fettes Sunday suit as a pillow!

The Germans were very cocky and convinced that they would be rescued near the American coast where they knew that merchant cruisers and U-boats operated. The situation got rather mutinous and the guards opened fire. One German sailor was shot through the head, within 2 or 3 feet of me, and several others wounded.

Discipline tightened up after this and the dead man was buried at sea.

We sailed into Quebec and were met by what must have been a brigade of Canadian soldiers. A batch of prisoners, including myself and three other young prisoners, were put on an old train. We steamed slowly westwards. We ended up at a place called Red Rock at the northernmost part of the Great Lakes, where there was a primitive railway station and an abandoned construction and timber camp. The work of making the camp into a prison had not been completed in time, and so we were locked up with virtually no space to lie down. There was also a particularly nasty Canadian sergeant major with a long rhino whip.

When everything had settled down, the Germans ran the camp on naval lines, with bugles for "reveille" and "lights out". Every day there was the roll call by the Canadian guards. We were guarded by the Fort Garry Horse, a Canadian cavalry regiment, waiting for their tanks. They were all prairie men, including Red Indians. The guards sometimes shot chipmunks inside the camp. If these animals crept under a hut to die, and could not be got out, the smell was terrible.

The German commander was an old Imperial German, Commodore Scharf. He was impressive and fair. The British commander we never saw. By the winter of 1940, most of us suffered from what we called "barbed wire psychosis". Whatever news we got was seemingly bad and we all thought of the best way to break out.

The huts were H-shaped with the ablutions in the centre. The walls were only planks of wood, covered in roofing felt. The nail heads holding the felt on to the timber protruded into the huts. At the very low temperatures (minus 40 degrees centigrade was usual), the humidity from the prisoner's breath froze on these nails and looked like rivets in a battleship. Heating in winter was by two coal and wood-burning stoves, manned all twenty-four hours. There was no hot water but a large hand basin with cold water only. I used to turn on all eight taps and slid under the taps for a cold shower. Once a week, we were taken out for a hot shower. We had double bunks and four blankets each to keep out the cold. Once or twice in summer, we were taken out to a bay in the lake for a swim. A heavy machine gun was placed at each end of the bay to stop us escaping.

Three prisoners tried to escape, at various times, but were all brought back dead, "shot whilst trying to escape". Several prisoners went mad. I had the duty, on one occasion, to knock out one prisoner, who thought he was a dog and started biting others. I first wound a towel round my hand to do as little damage as possible, but when I hit him he had his tongue between his teeth. Sadly, he ended up a horrible mess. Prisoners going mad were taken away, but we did not know where to.

I did some outside work lumbering. We cut down large fir trees, and eight men had to carry these out of the woods on our shoulders. If one or more dropped the tree without the others doing the same, the tree trunk would whip and smash the unfortunate person's shoulder. To protect our feet at those low temperatures, we wore first ladies silk stockings then army issue socks, then a layer of newspapers and then army issue felt boots. But after eight hours, the cold struck through. One had to wear a scarf or roll-neck sweater over one's mouth, as one's nose froze up and breathing cold air through the mouth hurt the front teeth! I also did some work as a steward in the Canadian officers' mess.

I met some interesting people. One made a violin from old boxes, using only a dinner knife and broken pieces of glass. One older prisoner was a von Richthofen, a cousin of the German World War I air ace, "the Red Baron". He had only one eye and one leg. He wrote his memoirs on rolls of lavatory paper, as there was at times no other paper available. I carried his typewriter when we were moving. I learnt how to make bottle ships and belts out of old cigarette carton wrappings and leather from old boots. One such belt is in the Fettes Museum.

Food in the camp was surprisingly good. We got Canadian soldiers' rations. Amongst the prisoners were the galley chefs from a passenger liner, who made the most of the materials.

The Germans were extremely clean and we had few health problems. We had a small sickbay staffed by a German Jewish doctor, who was, on one occasion, beaten up by some Nazi thugs who boasted that they were Gestapo men.

On one occasion, I was insulted by a Hungarian German prisoner. My fellow prisoners decided that a duel would have to be fought. It was to be fought by fist, no Queensbury rules, anything was permitted and it was to end with the disability of the loser. My seconds and friends had to advise me how to disable without damaging my opponent, as otherwise I would end up in the "cooler" which was a terrible hut, boiling hot in summer and freezing in winter. My team was headed up by an enormous German sailor who had sailed before the mast and was a real bruiser. He and my other friends decided that some psychological warfare was also indicated. So I was put, in full view of everyone, through a tough routine. On the day of the duel, a tight ring of prisoners was formed to avoid the guards seeing what was going on. At the start, my opponent, who was taller than me and had long arms, managed to hit the side of my head. But once he uncovered his side, I landed the intended liver hook. He collapsed immediately and I was declared the winner.

The news from home, which we got from an illegal radio and papers smuggled in as wrappers on food, was bad. The original troops which had guarded us had been moved to a tank training camp and were replaced by a home defence battalion.

Without warning, one day I was taken by two armed Canadian orderlies to the British commandant, a full colonel, whom we had never seen before.

He said to me: "144101, you do not look like a U-boat crew. Where were you taken?"

I said: "From the playing fields of Fettes!"

He jumped up, held out his hand and said, "I am Wellington!" I was then told that I was to go home.

The situation at my home, which I did not know, was grotesque. After I was interned, my papers got lost and the War Office told my parents that I did no longer exist, possibly drowned on the Arandora Star! Many friends and acquaintance who knew about me, including the Chief Justice of Scotland, who was then a governor of Fettes, tried to locate me without success. We did write Red Cross letters, but these did not arrive until long after my return home. My father told the story to an old friend, who knew the London director of the Canadian Pacific shipping line. The director did not believe this story and signalled all his agents my name and details with the instructions: "Find Charles Herzberg!".

By chance, one of his agents at Port Arthur, the northern most port of the Great Lakes, showed the signal to a soldier who was on guard at Red Rock. So I had been found, but no one told my parents. I found myself amongst a column of prisoners being moved at night. It was bitterly cold. We marched in columns of three with a Canadian rifleman or a soldier with a portable searchlight on the outside. The station was an old railway coach. We spent twenty minutes in the coach and forty outside in order not to freeze to death. After many hours, the prison train arrived and we were taken to a town in Quebec. The camp was a horrible, old railway roundhouse with hundreds of bunks covered with old blankets to keep out the drafts. I spent some time there laying pipes in the frozen ground. Pipes were laid 6 foot down to avoid freezing up in winter! It was more like mining than digging.

After some time, eight young prisoners, due for return home, were taken from the camp and sent under armed escort to Montreal. A very nice sergeant major took us in a crew van round Montreal to the Île de St Hélène, where we were supposed to be held. The camp was full of Italian prisoners who had been "troublesome", so we were lodged in the officers' mess. We were then taken to Halifax, Nova Scotia and put aboard the trooper, SS Empress of England. We were there joined by a huge convoy of other troopers and merchant ships. One day, queuing for rations, there was suddenly artillery fire, the boat shook, but the crew laughed. It was just an anti-aircraft practice! When we neared the UK coast a Sunderland flying boat flew over us and a few hours later, at dawn, our escort destroyers arrived. They turned at high speed and cut a terrific dash. The weather was beautiful and the sight of the convoy with escorts truly majestic.

We arrived at Gourock and were promptly rearrested because nobody told the British authorities that we were on board. We were guarded by men of a home defence battalion of the Argyll and Sutherland Highlanders. When we told a sentry who we were, he was so angry that he threw his rifle against the wall! Eventually we were freed, taken to a police station, and I was put on a night train to Penrith. I got a lift on a newspaper lorry and arrived at Keswick in the morning. I still had my Fettes best suit and stiff collar. As I walked towards my home, I suddenly saw my father driving our car, coming in the opposite direction. He went white, as he did not know that I was alive and he thought he saw my ghost! I was told to hide whilst he broke the news to my mother.

I then wrote to Dr Ashcroft, who sent a four-page, handwritten letter in reply. The gist was: "We want you back and come as soon as possible!" So I returned to Fettes, but to Glencorse because Kimmerghame had been taken over by the Admiralty. I then rejoined the corps.

I intended to read the mechanical sciences tripos at Cambridge. Jerry Lodge and Paw Edwards, who liked a wee dram during coaching, crammed me for the tripos qualifying exam, which during the war had to be taken before entry, not as pre-war after the first year. I was told to do a trial run and to mine, and everybody's surprise, I passed. After resitting the Cambridge entrance exam, because I had failed in divinity, I entered Sidney Sussex College. I then joined the Officers' Training Corps and obtained my cert "B" in the artillery.

As an enemy alien, I was under severe restrictions and caused some surprise when I asked for a permit to fire 25 pounders. After some consideration, the police decided that when I wore uniform I came under martial law. We had some interesting times in our battery. Our training NCOs were particularly nice. I remember one sergeant from the Royal Horse Artillery who made us take a 25 pounder to pieces and then could not put it back together again. A cadet volunteered to do it, which he did in a short time. When asked how he knew, he explained that his father was the director of the Royal Ordnance Factory, which had built the gun, and he had worked there! I learnt to drive everything from motorcycles to heavy gun tractors.

When on a Christmas holiday, I remember being woken up by the local police by phone in the middle of the night to go to a plane crash. As we lived near the scene, I was asked to go to the wreck of a bomber to see what I could do. I was told it was just behind our garden. I just slipped on my wellingtons and a roll-neck sweater over my pyjamas and went up the mountain. The weather was foul with driving rain and fog. The crash was much further up the mountain, and I had to climb rocks in my most unsuitable gear. I arrived at the scene, which was quite surreal. The wreck was on fire. Small arms ammunition still exploded and the charred bodies of the airmen were twisted into grotesque shapes illuminated by the fire. The rear gunner had part of his head blown off. The smell of burning rubber and bodies was most distressing. There was nothing I could do but wait. I hid behind a rock in case there were more explosions. After a long time, a policeman arrived and then my father and friends. They were sent back, but the policeman asked me to stay to help to identify the men by their identity discs, which had not been destroyed. It was a sad, but necessary, duty.

I took my finals for the tripos on or around D-Day. Rather than cap and gown, we wore our corps uniforms. All the regular troops had gone for embarkation and there was a possibility of a German diversionary parachute attack, which we were supposed to contain.

I was then told that no more officers were needed, but I was to go into the armaments industry. I was literally sent to Coventry where I lived in a government hostel for four years. I first became a toolmaker and worked on the bench. I then became a draughtsman and, eventually, I was made an assistant chief designer. I later joined my father in Cumberland as chief engineer. After the war, I became a British citizen.

Printed in Great Britain
by Amazon

47355527R00248